Footprints of the Montford Point Marines

Footprints of the Montford Point Marines

A Narrative of the Epic Strides in Overcoming the Racial Disparities of the United States Marine Corps

Eugene S. Mosley
with
Thomas Mosley

Published by Dagmar Miura
Los Angeles
www.dagmarmiura.com

Footprints of the Montford Point Marines: A Narrative of the Epic Strides in Overcoming the Racial Disparities of the United States Marine Corps

I have tried to recreate events, locales, and conversations from my memories of them. In order to maintain their anonymity in some instances I may have changed some identifying characteristics and details such as physical properties, occupations, and places of residence.

First published 2022

ISBN: 978-1-956744-07-1

This writing is dedicated to Mr. Thomas Mosley and in memory of Mrs. Rebecca Mosley, wife of Mr. Thomas Mosley and my loving mother.

Contents

Appendixes

Foreword

Master Gunnery Sergeant Joseph H. Geeter III

It is indeed my pleasure and honor to provide a foreword for Eugene S. Mosley's story about the Montford Point Marines, America's first African American Marines! I first met "Gene" soon after the Congressional Gold Medal was presented to the first African American Marines, the Montford Point Marines, for their pioneering service, in 2012. Gene's dad was an original Montford Point Marine and piqued the interest of his son about his exploits and experiences in the Marine Corps during World War II and beyond.

I know this work has been a labor of love for Gene the past eight years or so, and he has done extensive research to intertwine the Montford Point Marine story with the story of America and how our country was dealing with the overall civil rights questions of the day.

Since Gene lived relatively close to the Philadelphia Chapter of the National Montford Point Marine Association Inc., he joined this chapter as a valuable Associate Member and has participated in many chapter events and, sadly, funeral services of Montford Point Marines.

Gene is always on the lookout for other Montford Point Marines, like his dad, who served in the Marines from 1942 to 1949—the period that the segregated Montford Point Camp was opened in Jacksonville, North Carolina—to make sure they received the Congressional Gold Medal replica authorized by the U.S. Congress.

Gene has even spearheaded the awarding of the Congressional

Gold Medal replica to the family of one of his college classmates in a glorious ceremony at the home of the Montford Pointer in Lansdale, Pennsylvania.

Gene has often spoken with different media outlets to tell the story of the Montford Pointers, and I have been thoroughly impressed with his knowledge and motivation while putting together their incredible story.

I have been privileged to see this book project at different levels, and I'm sure the readers of this story will walk away with a much deeper appreciation of what the African American Servicemen and Women had to endure so that today's Marines and other servicemembers will have a more competitive and level playing field when it comes to assignments and promotions.

Semper Fidelis!

Joseph H. Geeter III
Master Gunnery Sergeant USMC retired
16th National President,
Montford Point Marine Association Inc.
2005–2009

Preface

Each day more and more information is surfacing and being revealed about the Montford Point Marines, who hailed from all parts of the United States but were brought together for a common cause in the town of Jacksonville, North Carolina, to begin boot camp for participation in World War II against the Japanese. Prior to being part of the Montford Point Marines, these men were involved in the everyday struggles of life as factory workers, teachers, skilled tradesmen, and other such tasks to earn a living for themselves and their families.

Corporal Thomas Mosley, 1943.

They were called the Montford Point Marines because they were either drafted or enlisted for the draft into the Marine Corps after Executive Order 8802 was signed into law by President Franklin D. Roosevelt. It stated, "There is to be no discrimination in the Federal workplace," so these enlistees were placed at a location called Montford Point Camp, adjacent to Camp Lejeune in North Carolina, one of the largest Marine bases on the East Coast.

Although Marines, they were not allowed to enter onto Camp Lejeune because of the color of their skin. These were

Black Marines, the very first Marines to enter the last segregated branches of the Armed Forces in the United States of America. Although obligated to accept these recruits, these were still segregated times in America. After all, this was 1942, in the South, and race-mixing was still a huge no-no, especially in one of the most esteemed and celebrated strongholds in this country.

From the outset, I want to declare that I am not a military historian, although I have found that military history is an extremely fascinating subject, and there is not a day that goes by that I don't find myself absorbed in something that I have read, heard, or watched by various means of visual or oral recording. That is compounded even more by the fact that I have witnessed my own father, and about four hundred other Montford Pointers, who traversed from all parts of the United States to receive the Congressional Gold Medal, in the highest ceremony possible, on June 26, 2012.

I am limited in the jargon that many military experts or military personnel may use and may even sound limited at times to those who have had a long-standing background, or who have used certain standard words or slogans. Please forgive me—I am not writing this book to exclaim how versed I am in military jargon, but to bring forth a portion of knowledge of some men who served our country in battle in the worst of times, in the worst of places, in the worst of conditions, and initially, with the worst of equipment (some weapons having been previously used in World War I), as well as I possibly can.

This documentation is designed to give an overall depiction of the Montford Point Camp and the harsh realities that existed there for these men, as well as to set the record straight about the fact that these men were involved in every major battle that took place in the Pacific Theater in the march that led to the victory against the Japanese Empire. Not completely historical in nature, but historical nonetheless and also a tribute to these men, who could not even purchase a sandwich in many of the stores in North Carolina and elsewhere, even though they were embarking on a journey to war, many of whom would never return, and many with scars and wounds both physical and mental in defense of those very ones who were refusing to let them purchase a cup of coffee or a snack to eat. So these men were in battle while on the home front and getting prepared to do battle thousands of miles away from home against another enemy, whom most had never laid eyes on.

Footprints of the Montford Point Marines is a must-read for every African American soldier—be they in the Army, Navy, Air Force, or Marine Corps. This is the beginning of the African American Marines' history. The foundation of the history of the African American Marines is contained here for the families of these servicemen to see and understand the sacrifices that were made while laying the groundwork for others to follow. It was hard and brutal, but the tarmac was laid down nonetheless for the other African American Marines to take flight from.

Footprints of the Montford Point Marines is not intentionally designed to put anyone or any entity down but is clearly designed to set the record straight regarding the noble Black soldiers who risked everything they had in a gamble that perhaps this war would be the one to finally give them, and their people, the freedom and justice they so longed for.

Having spoken with dozens of Montford Pointers both in person and by phone, I have inserted, to the best of my abilities at this time, those ideas that were expressed to me and also previously documented, about how some of these men felt about those early days. This book should grace the libraries of all African Americans. This is prominent history. The knowledge contained within will allow you to tell a large portion of the true story to your family, friends, and acquaintances. Not only should it grace the libraries of all African Americans, but at the same time should occupy a space in every person's library, no matter their ethnic background. The reason is quite clear. This country and its inhabitants should fully understand the sacrifices that were made for all of us by African Americans who went abroad to fight for, and participate in, what led to the freedoms that we have and enjoy to this very day.

Unfortunately, the United States Marine Corps took over sixty years to publicly acknowledge the story about these prominent men and to acknowledge the wrong for not bringing these soldiers into the forefront of Marine Corps history. The Montford Point Marines have received a Congressional Gold Medal and that, in and of itself, should tell anyone what type of soldiers these men were and still are. My hope and prayers are that we do not do the same by hiding this invaluable information regarding our heroes.

Acknowledgments

This writing is dedicated to the late Mr. Thomas Mosley and in memory of his wife—our sweet and dear mother, Mrs. Rebecca Mosley.

This journey began in order to document events during a brief period in the life of Thomas Mosley, from the Montford Point Marines to receiving the Congressional Gold Medal in Washington, D.C. The purpose of this undertaking was to inform my family and friends of the significance of such an award.

At first, I was only looking to produce a brochure of possibly ten to fifteen pages. One thing led to another, and at every end there seemed to be another beginning. There were some rough edges to get around with this undertaking.

I want to thank my beautiful wife, Soonai, for all of her help, encouragement, and support while I wrote what ended up being a book of substantial length. Soonai also understood the importance of my work and the benefit of my efforts and was incredibly patient with me.

Dad and Soonai artfully bantered regarding the words to be used. If Soonai said something was, for example, "beautiful," Dad replied with a fancier description. They went on until they had both exhausted themselves. I want to thank her for her enthusiasm, even as her mother lay gravely ill. Thank you, dear Dr. Pastor "Sergeant" Joseph Ginyard, also an original Montford Pointer and Congressional Gold Medal recipient, for giving such a fine and meaningful eulogy to my beautiful mother-in-law.[1] May her soul forever rest in peace.

The editorial process of this book was a daunting task. I want to thank Beverly Melasi-Haag, President of the South Florida Writers Association, who worked tirelessly to move this project along so that my dad's story could be told. The expertise she used in working through my original maze was profound. Beverly proofread, copy edited, and whatever seemed to be needed while this story was told. There is absolutely no way to thank her enough. Thank you so much, Beverly, for being a part of my team.

A wonderful thank-you goes to Christopher Church, my editor-publisher. His mastery of layout and all else that he does is unbelievable. From the moment Christopher was given the reins by my editor, Beverly Melasi-Haag, to do what he specializes in, he continued to move the project forward with amazing speed and thoroughness. I am extremely happy to work with someone such as Chris who made it easy for me.

A special thank you goes to Amanda Bailey of Macon, Georgia. Amanda was my father's caretaker for an extended period. It was through Amanda, in 2011, that our family received news that the Montford Point Marines might be receiving the tributes described herein.

I also wish to thank my wonderful sister Helen for all of her encouragement and just for being the wonderful person she is.

My sister Sandra not only offered encouragement but financial support to this project. It seems that every time you look around, you need more ink or other supplies. She and I have had a thousand conversations that have helped in the formation of many of the topics discussed throughout the writing of *Footprints of the Montford Point Marines.* Sandra has a way of pushing me to stay on task; she thinks I don't know, but I do. So let me assure her that her contributions and insights to this endeavor were greatly appreciated, even more than she realizes. Additionally, she was there in the time of most critical need for our dad.

Annette, another of my sisters, was helpful with getting photos from our dad—even when I could not get them myself. We've also had many discussions regarding various aspects of our dad's life and realized the significance of Montford Point in helping to shape him as a human being. Montford Point Camp and his experience overseas shaped and molded his character and thoughts as a family man after Montford Point. Annette also contributed ideas that helped configure certain parts of this material.

My daughter Suhir Mosley was just all smiles and beams. I could see her pearly whites when she and I first started discussing this material after she had seen the first draft. After all, she could not have conceived in her wildest imagination how such a large portion of her grandfather's life would unfold. For me, to see and feel her expressions was unreal. She was encouraging and held nothing back at all. She offered suggestions and ideas that had never occurred to me.

My daughter Hannan is quiet and unassuming but had a way of getting her encouragement to me as well. She has subtle ways of validating or invalidating what you say. With Hannan, you know right away if you are on the right track or just spinning your wheels. Her excitement with the project was great encouragement for me.

I also thank my two brothers, Thomas Edward and James, for their encouragement. Knowing the importance of the award, we spent hours discussing how dad's military training had influenced all our lives.

My nephew Gregory: thanks for all the words of reassurance. I want all of my nieces and nephews to know that your words of encouragement go a long way with me, and for those I am always indebted.

My niece Jade, the doctor, has always been a smooth operator, and I thank her, as usual, for her words of support. Jade had me chomping at the bit to do some writing several years before the advent of this book when I saw what she produced in her special documentation from her trip to Rome.

Thank you to all the Montford Pointers who supported my efforts, and the Montford Point Marine Association, who helped me better understand who the Montford Point Marines are. With that in mind, the support and friendship of Chief Warrant Officer 5, Dr. James Averhart, National President of the Montford Point Marine Association, who oversees forty-five active chapters nationwide, has been unbelievable and invaluable. CWO5 Averhart's decorations include the Legion of Merit Navy and Marine Corps Commendation Medal (with four gold stars instead of a fifth award), the Navy and Marine Corps Achievement Medal (with a gold star in lieu of a third award), the Combat Action Ribbon, the Marine Corps Good Conduct Medal (with three bronze stars), and the Marine Corps Outstanding Volunteer Service Medal (with a gold star in lieu of a second award). These are just a few of Dr. Averhart's many accomplishments. He has been an outstanding civilian and Marine, having received a myriad of awards both civilian and military.[2]

He is such a humble man, and I thank this officer and friend who actually gave me hours of phone time while he was totally absorbed in developing and working around the clock to help bring "gold" to these men. I will forever owe a debt of gratitude to him. He always brought me up to speed on any current development that was occurring during this process, even if he had just received the information himself; that is to say, all information except matters of security.

Many thanks to Master Gunnery Sergeant Joseph Geeter, past National President of the Montford Point Marine Association, from 2005 to 2009, who stepped down from that position to go after the gold—and "the do all you can man" for the organization and the Montford Pointers. Geeter also served as the National Legislative Officer and the National Public Relations Officer for the Montford Point Marine Association. Master Gunnery Sergeant Geeter was inducted into the Montford Point Marine Association Hall of Fame in 2010. He works tirelessly and encourages me with his energy in keeping this legacy in the forefront.[3]

In 1998, Master Gunnery Sergeant Geeter received a Special President's Award from the National President of the Montford Point Marine Association for his work with the Beaufort Chapter, and the James Calendar Award in 1999 for his continued efforts on a national level for the Montford Point Marine Association. He was honored with the prestigious NAACP Roy Wilkins Renown Service Award for his significant contributions to the Marine Corps in the area of equal opportunity and community involvement. Master Gunnery Sergeant Geeter's military honors include the Meritorious Service Medal (with Gold Star), the Navy/Marine Corps Commendation Medal, the Navy/Marine Corps Achievement Medal (with Three Gold Stars), the Marine Corps Good Conduct Medal, and the Military Outstanding Volunteer Service Medal.[4]

My daughter Suhir's fiancé, who is a mentor and consultant to me, is Gregg Bruce. A CWO3 and a helicopter pilot and instructor during the Iraqi War, Gregg proves to be an unwavering support. While working on this story and experiencing the road to the gold, Gregg supported and encouraged me with ideas and directions to help make my story a reality, even though his hands were absolutely full of his own projects. Thank you.

I do have some longtime friends that I want to acknowledge. I begin here with a native of Philadelphia named Ken Knight who was a part of the Miami, Florida, wave and did some great things there. Ken and I knew each other for many years, and he always had confidence in my abilities, and I in his. When he first heard of the Montford Point Marines he was instrumental in taking this story to his community and the customers of his favorite restaurant,

Jumbo's Restaurant. He was a longtime activist and community developer there and in Philadelphia and did everything that he could do to project the story of the Montford Point Marines in that part of the country. Many thanks and kudos go out to him.

As life goes, many times we tend to have nagging doubts no matter how much support we receive. Ken Nixon, a financial and business professional and friend who now resides in the Princeton, New Jersey, area, gave me a perspective on one of my nags that was bugging me at the time, and because of his enthusiasm, allowed me to leap over some crossroads in the book. Ken and I did our own integration story when we were fifteen or so years of age. Ken grew up in Macon, Georgia, and I grew up in Harrisburg, Pennsylvania, and moved to Macon when Olmstead Air Force Base in Middletown, Pennsylvania, was phased out and my dad chose Georgia as our new home. We integrated a long-standing all-White military ROTC school where I did not fare so well initially because I did not fall in line. The administration did not really want us there. Ken did fantastic because he already knew the deal and was able to have much success.

When I told Ken that I was writing a story about the Montford Pointers, he said, "Well, Mosley, you always have been smart. They kept you fighting so much of that bull____ over there at the school that you just couldn't get your concentration on."

I was almost flabbergasted with surprise with that particular comment, coming from someone who has always had a pencil behind his ear and who I've always looked up to when it came to academics. That he felt this reversal toward me was really a boost for my ego. I needed that as I continued working on my story.

Many times, people are inspirational and insightful in their encouragement, and it has an overall effect in helping you with motivation and confidence. Another such friend is J. T. Thomas, former NFL player with the Pittsburg Steelers for nine years, who has four Super Bowl rings. He has always been willing to go the extra mile in his explanations to me of reaching milestones. His friendship has been invaluable to me over the years. His uniqueness is that he encourages one to look at other perspectives while analyzing a particular subject. Hence, I was able to tie in some sinewy areas, and his advice helped to guide another aspect of the story from the viewpoint of a son, and then from a spiritual perspective as an observer, and looking at how fate guided these Montford Pointers to this remarkable position.

Master Gunnery Sergeant Mel Ragin of the Chapter 35,

Warner Robins/Macon, Georgia, Montford Point Marines, including Sergeant Joshua Dixon and the other members there, had been outstanding in their treatment of my dad. I also learned about a different level of respect that Marines share with one another while I was at a chapter meeting one evening in Macon. Sergeant Ragin began talking with Dad about getting in touch with Mr. Frank Johnson, a Montford Pointer but also a recent amputee who resides in Macon. Dad, when told by Sergeant Ragin that Ragin would be calling Mr. Johnson and his wife to make arrangements to go to Washington, D.C., to receive his Congressional Gold Medal, responded by questioning whether Mr. Johnson would really think about making a trip such as this in light of his recent medical status. Sergeant Ragin said, "That's no problem; that's why we're here. Whatever it takes, a wheelchair, no problem. Someone to man him the entire time, no problem. We will cover it all." His continued words to my dad were "We are Marines. No man left behind, right?"[5]

The words still touch my heart. At the same time, it made me reflect on the fact that Sergeant Ragin was letting my dad know that not only was he a Marine who was willing to go the extra mile but that he was a Master Gunnery Sergeant, and that he had the power to utilize forces under his command to accomplish this task, which in his mind was a small one. At the same time, the respect and honor that he wanted to show my dad for the Montford Pointers was staring him in the face, and there was no way that he would let this ball drop. He knew that these men had sacrificed their lives for people like him and others to rise up the ranks of the U.S. Marine Corps, and it would be a dishonor for him to respond in any fewer manners than he was responding. Here was a Master Gunnery Sergeant, and he was not going to let any doubt creep into the room regarding an original Montford Pointer. It was almost like, *Are you kidding me? Do you know who I'm looking at, and who I am responding to, sir? You, Mr. Mosley, are an original Montford Pointer. What fate has brought us together? What is the possibility for me to have ever had the privilege of meeting one of my Founding Fathers of African American Marines? You paved the groundwork for me and the other African American Marines who have followed you.* However, his response was said with utmost total respect and in the gentlest of fashions. He was letting my dad know that this was not a problem in the least. This to me was diplomacy at its highest level, and he said it all with a smile. My hat is definitely off to Sergeant Ragin. All I could do was find a corner for a few moments of solitude to weep.

Thanks for the sincere support to all the members of Chapter 35, Warner Robins/Macon, Georgia, of the Montford Point Marine Association, including Joshua Dixon and Nathaniel Royal.

Mr. Joshua Dixon, who, before the end of this writing, succeeded Gunnery Sergeant Mel Ragin as Chapter 35 President and who spent as much time assisting Dad as he possibly could, no matter the task or time. Dixon was always at the ready as well as anyone else up to and through my father's passing. From my family: Thank you, members of Chapter 35, for all that you have done over the years in assisting our wonderful dad. He always spoke highly of each and every one of you guys.

I wish to thank Bernard C. Nalty, author and military historian, who immediately offered to loan me a personal copy of his documents for part of my research and sent it out to me right away, along with his *Strength for the Fight* and *The Right to Fight.* The personal copy of Mr. Nalty's documents, which was loaned to me for research, was volume VI of his personal thirteen-volume set from his own library. There were thirteen volumes of documents that were edited by Mr. Morris J. MacGregor and Mr. Bernard C. Nalty and published in 1977 by Scholarly Resources of Wilmington, Delaware, as *Blacks in the United States Armed Forces: Basic Documents* that also served as a major source of information for this book. Mrs. Bernard Nalty, after Mr. Nalty passed away, so kindly and generously gifted this invaluable copy and source of letters and records as well as secret clearance documents during World War II—at the very formation of Blacks entering into the United States Marine Corps—to me so that I might continue to have this much needed source of information. I will truly miss the conversations Mr. Nalty and I had as well as his unbelievable knowledge regarding the Montford Point Marines that he was always willing to impart to me. He also gave me great words of encouragement and useful advice on several occasions during this process. I thank you so much. I also appreciate the great advice from Mr. Nathan McCall, author of *Makes Me Wanna Holler* and *What's Going On,* on some great directions with my work.

I'd like to express my deep and sincere gratitude to the Tubman Museum of Macon, Georgia, and Dr. Andy Ambrose and Mr. Jeffrey Bruce, Director of Exhibitions. I especially thank Mr. Bruce for understanding the importance of acknowledging the roles our veterans have had in the weaving of the fabric of this great nation. He was immediately receptive to the idea and not only wanted a display, but wanted a permanent exhibition of, Thomas Mosley, and went on to include others in the display as well.

The exhibition holds a photograph of Thomas Mosley as well as a replica of the Congressional Gold Medal, courtesy of Sandra Mosley Walker and Eugene Mosley, expressly for the Tubman Museum. It reads "This Congressional Gold Medal was awarded to Thomas Mosley on June 27, 2012." The inscription on the back reads: "For Outstanding Perseverance and Courage that Inspired Social Change in the Marine Corps. 2011, Act of Congress." The Tubman Museum happens to be the largest museum in the Southeastern United States that is dedicated to African American art, history, and culture.

I'd also like to give an enormous thank you to Houston Shinal, CW05, United States Marine Corps, director on the dedication of the Montford Point Marine Memorial Project built on Camp Lejeune in Jacksonville, North Carolina. The dedication was held July 29, 2016. The project was a successful $1.8 million fund-raising effort. When I asked Mr. Shinal to join me in formulating ideas for the exhibition of my dad at the Tubman Museum, he immediately partnered with me and shared his intricate ideas and building blocks for our project at the Tubman and elsewhere, even though, at the time, he was also the Director of the Montford Point Marine Museum.

Thank you to Past National President of the Montford Point Marine Association, Retired Mastery Gunnery Sergeant Forest E. Spencer Jr. I've had the pleasure to meet him on several occasions. He was always ready to impart a smile, kind words, and encouragement. That meant a lot.

On behalf of my family, we'd like to thank David Booker, Branch President; Mrs. Carrie Britt, Chairperson; Gwennette Westbrooks, Co-Chair; Maia Scott, First Vice President; and the others of the NAACP Macon Bibb Branch for bestowing my father with the Earl T. Shinhoster Award. This award was given for community service. Also, it is with warm hearts that we also recognize the Thomas Mosley Veterans Award, created on behalf of dad. Thank you so kindly!

Two longtime friends that I want to acknowledge who were very encouraging to me were William Clarence Cole and Charles Pleas, both of Macon, Georgia, and both longtime friends.

My son, Brian, my rap buddy, and I had many discussions regarding this book. He has a tremendous amount of appreciation and respect for his grandfather. When he saw the first draft in book form, the intensity of his response was motivation for me to continue. Whether he knew it or not, he stood about six feet from my face with an intense stare during that conversation. He is a great son.

DeYonte, my grandson, is very inspiring to me. Sometimes people don't know that they help send you on a mission. My love for him played a major role in being inspired to accomplish this goal. "I'm doing my thing, DeYonte; now you have to keep doing your thing." We bounce off one another. You have more than you need. Continue to create your world. I'm looking for great things from you because you are a great human being. Don't forget your great grandfather has a Congressional Gold Medal. He also has the Earl T. Shinhoster Award from the NAACP and countless other certificates, plaques, and decorations. It is in your blood.

Thomas McSween, longtime friend and mentor from Philadelphia, has been helpful and encouraging in my life before the advent of this book, and he continues to be. The same applies to Luciens Bowens Jr. III, of Philadelphia. I wish you the best. Keep striving and you will reach your goals.

Shout-outs to Da'ood Nasir and Doug McGraw.

A particular thank-you and shout-out goes to my siblings for their support and love of our dad: James, Helen Akins, Thomas Edward (Kariym) Mosley, Karen Coates, Annette Davenport, and Sandra Walker.

I'd like to give a huge thank you to my cousin Eugene "Tex" Mosley, for his continued support throughout my journey of this story.

Thanks to Rubin Bashir, author, who took time from his very busy schedule to entertain a variety of my questions. He was excellent at discussing and explaining better ways of arriving at completion of an undertaking such as this.

Thank you to all who gave me encouragement along the way even though I may not have mentioned you. Believe me, it was an oversight. Please forgive me.

There is another very close friend that I would like to mention. Thanks Bob Morrow and your favorite line of wisdom that "No one understands life like a father understands, exactly what it takes to turn a boy into a man."

Thanks for the smiles from my mother during this process, and my maternal grandmother, Cecelia Pearson, and my grandfather, California Pearson. All my love also to paternal grandmother Lula Mae Boone Mosley and grandfather Henry Mosley.

Dad, thanks again for your many, many hours of patience with me on this story and the love that you emanated to me during this process and always. There was never a time that dad seemed bothered as I gleaned information from him, even though I knew that many, many times he was not feeling his best. As you know, I have always loved you and always will. We all thank you for your service to your family, to your community, to the United States of America, and to the United States Marine Corps.

Footprints of the Montford Point Marines

Introduction

A-Ten-Hutt!

This is the true story of a significant aspect of the life and times of Corporal Thomas Mosley. He was an original pioneer and trailblazer of the Montford Point Marines. Known to many as Tommy, Dad, "Bruh," or Grandpop, he was awarded the Congressional Gold Medal by the House of Representatives, the Senate, and the President of the United States, Barack Obama. The bill was signed into law on November 23, 2011.

CHAPTER 1

It All Starts at Home

When we follow the trail of some true American heroes, one makes up a large part of this group. No, I'm not talking about made-up characters or fictitious entities where all the necessary blanks are filled in to portray something that is not real, but some in which most people would never expect, at least by outward appearances, to be created by circumstances of the centuries and tempered by the Lord to be some of the greatest men who have ever been on the earth. Even we humans have given them a name—we call them giants.

We, as a people in general, and younger people in particular, need to realize that our history has always been shaped by extenuating circumstances. We need to realize that it takes not only hard work but a will, a desire, and a drive to succeed no matter what the circumstances are. We are only a part of the whole. You can be successful in your endeavors and be able to succeed, but you must have character and determination. You must realize that you are a part of the whole, and the success you have achieved, or may achieve, is primarily due to those who have come before you and those who have already sacrificed and beat the path so that we can all enjoy a part of what we call the American dream.

We must also realize that we need to have knowledge of our history as a people and of our elders, and to respect the roles that many of them have contributed. Many of these great men and women have played major roles in our development and sacrificed so that our lives could be richer—so that we could have a greater share of what life has to offer. I am certainly not a Pulitzer Prize winner in writing, or even a great writer. However, without reservation, I think about and then take my pen to paper to give acknowledgment to a great hero that happens to be a part of us—a son, a brother, a cousin, an uncle, a friend, a coworker, an associate, and a dad. Surely, without reservations, I do this.

Thomas Mosley was born in Steelton, Pennsylvania, son of Henry and Lula Mae Boone Mosley. Thomas was one of thirteen children. Steelton is a town in central Pennsylvania that is bordered by beautiful mountains, rolling hills, cascading streams, and one huge river that runs for miles called the Susquehanna. My brother, Thomas Edward, and I spent many days and nights fishing along the Susquehanna during our youth. This area has beautiful architecture and other sights to behold, including dozens of churches. However, life for many around this beauty was a series of challenges, ebbs, and tides. Although challenged, life would not stand still for the Mosley family. For in this family was pride, dignity, and a sense of great worth.

Steelton was once called Steeltown because Bethlehem Steel was the primary employer for people there and in many surrounding areas, including Harrisburg, the capital of Pennsylvania, which borders Steelton. Bethlehem Steel was once one of the largest steel manufacturing plants in the Northeast region, once employing thousands and thousands of people. However, working in a steel plant was risky and caused many people to have medical problems later in life. In addition, it was extremely hard work, and people had to work long hours in a sweat box because of the extreme heat and fire that it takes to manufacture steel.

As a young boy, Thomas no doubt had aspirations of wanting to do more in life than to work at the steel plant, which many of his family members had already done or were still doing. Of course, the Mosley family was deeply entrenched in religion and most of them were members of Beulah Baptist Church of Steelton. Thomas was also a member since the age of fifteen, and no doubt had been saturated in the church from many years before.

"I was always active in Sunday school and became a teacher for the Sunday school class at an early age. I was also a member of the choir and served on the usher board. Soon I became a trustee, and before long I was a deacon," he said.[1] There is no doubt that family and church played a significant role in Thomas Mosley's growth, development, and loyalty to his family.

As an interjection to this point and of his life, I offer that as a child, my father would take our family to Beulah Baptist Church, and it seemed as though everyone there was related to us in one way or another. My Aunt Mary played the piano and sang. My Aunts Agnes, Christine, Beatrice, and Gloria were in the choir or served in some other major capacity. My Aunt Lillie Mae also served in many capacities. Besides that, there must have been about fifty children at Beulah Baptist Church of various ages who were related to us as well.

Many of the household conversations were steeped in religious overtones. Based on religious aspects, and the fact that my grandfather passed away at such an early age, coupled with my grandmother's expectations of my dad needing to contribute in more ways than one, I think his main mission in life became seeing himself as an example to others by doing work and serving in the community and church. Anyone who knew Dad knew that he had always been willing to go the extra mile and do the extra things in someone's time of need. I don't think many people can dispute that. Even to the day he passed, he was willing to go to great lengths to explain how a particular thing should be or could be done, or how he completed some task or work that he performed, or even with him discussing how to become better off financially.

I don't remember very much about my father's dad as he passed away in 1953. I was born shortly before his passing and was still just a baby when he passed on.

Of course, I remember my father's mother, Grandmom, whose name was Lula Mae, and spent many years in her company. She was nice but also stern at the same time, meaning that with six sons and six daughters, she had to really be on top of things in order to feed, provide clothing for, and take care of such a large family. Dad told me that my grandmother had to "lay down the law" many times while they were growing up. However, I don't remember any serious insolence between her and her children whenever I was around, many years later, either at her home or during one of our many family reunions. There were discussions from her children: slight disagreements, yes, but disrespect, never.

During our family reunions there was much talk about some of the relatives who had passed on or about those who were currently nearby or living out of town. There was a lot of critiquing, but mostly there was enough love and respect regarding these family members that the discussions were about the positives that they brought into the family. Although I never truly met my grandfather in the sense of knowing him, I have heard and listened to so many stories about him that I truly revered him in so many ways, just as my dad did in his own ways. Why? It is because my father never said a word of harsh or negative criticism about his father. As a result, all I know are the aspects that would add many positive influences on my life as relayed to me by Dad. With that being said, I have had a very positive relationship with all of my aunts and uncles.

To not show an indication of a very positive side of my grandmother would be to leave out a very important aspect of her makeup. My wonderful Aunt Beatrice, who would always invite my wife and I to her house every Thanksgiving, had once again invited us; Aunt Mary and Aunt Agnes were there as well. My wife and I had a gift for my Grandmom, and it was wrapped, although I can't say it was exceptionally wrapped. As Grandmom was unwrapping the gift, Aunt Mary took the gift paper and began discarding it. Grandmom asked Aunt Mary what she was doing with the wrapping paper. Aunt Mary said she was throwing it away. Well, with that said, Grandmom took some serious offense to this and told Mary in no uncertain terms that the paper was as important to her as the gift itself.

"Well, Mom, I didn't think you'd want the paper," Mary said.

"Well, I do," replied my grandmother. Needless to say, Aunt Mary apologized (while turning red) as Grandmom muttered a few extra words to her in a low voice. This was a special moment for me and stayed with me for years, for it showed me the importance Grandmom had felt even for the paper that wrapped the gift my wife and I had given to her.[2]

Dad used to tell me stories about his life and related to me once about going after a job at the Alva Restaurant in Harrisburg, Pennsylvania. It was a small but very popular restaurant near the train station. It was also located near the Capitol Building complex there, which meant that legislators, senators, and lawmakers could be there to eat on any given day. The competition there for a job was indeed high-ranking. Dad noted that he was in competition with another person he knew, by the name of William Lee, who wanted a job there as well. He said that when Mr. Lee was asked what type of work he could do, he told the potential employer that he could do anything. When the employer asked Dad what he could do, he went into very specific topics, yet didn't say he could do it all. As a result, Dad was the one to secure the employment. Knowing him as I did, I realize why he spoke of the specific things that he could do. I can tell you that he had always been a detail-oriented person. I think having this mind-set of breaking things down, and not lumping things together, demonstrates to other people that you are aware of the tasks required of a particular job, and that you respect the various levels of a profession, whatever that profession may be.[3]

CHAPTER 2

Life One Step at a Time

Dad said, "After a brief stint at the Alva Restaurant, beginning in June 1942, I began my civil service career with the U.S. government, in Middletown, Pennsylvania, by attending the Pennsylvania School of Aeronautics for three months, learning about aircraft sheet metal and the dynamics for its uses pertaining to aircraft. It was not very long before I went from a learner to a helper, to a junior mechanic, then I was promoted to master aircraft sheet-metal mechanic. The year was now 1943 and there were to be some additional major changes in the life of many more Americans. Needless to say, while I was advancing my life and had gained a somewhat secure position with a government job, life was still uncertain for many, and millions of African Americans faced hardships with employment, discrimination, and lack of food, health, and medical attention."[1]

At the same time there was another war underway overseas that was to remove many people from the rank and file of a life in and around home to the overseas front. World War II had begun in 1939, and it was a war that was involving many of the nations of the world, including all of the great powers.

The United States was reluctant to go to war because it was not ready for the production of those necessary items needed for a mobilization of this size. Jobs were increased multifold as war production changed everyday manufacturing companies into defense manufacturing. President Franklin Roosevelt felt that the enemy had to be outproduced overwhelmingly in order to defeat them soundly. In his own words, he firmly stated, "Powerful enemies must be outfought and outproduced." President Roosevelt told Congress and his countrymen less than a month after Pearl Harbor:

> It is not enough to turn out just a few more planes, a few more tanks, a few more guns, a few more ships than can be turned out by our enemies. We must outproduce them overwhelmingly, so that there can be no question of our ability to provide a crushing superiority of equipment in any theater of the world war.[2]

Only two years earlier, the United States ranked 39th in nations' preparedness to go to war, according to the same article:

> The United States knew they had to step up production in all areas of whatever would be utilized in defense as well as offense. According to this report, there were to be 60,000 aircraft built in 1942 and 125,000 in 1943; 120,000 tanks in the same time period as well as 55,000 antiaircraft guns.[3]

This nation, after reeling from a decade-long depression that removed almost all of the lifeblood, had to revive itself if it were not to be desecrated. The auto industry, General Motors and others, was transformed completely. For example:

> General Motors would make airplane engines, guns, trucks, and tanks while Chrysler would focus on airplane engines. Now Packard would make Rolls-Royce engines for the British air force. On and on the list went.
>
> While 16 million men and women marched to war, 24 million more moved in search of defense jobs, often for more pay than they previously had ever earned. Eight million women stepped into the workforce, and ethnic groups such as African Americans and Latinos found job opportunities as never before.[4]

According to Doris Goodwin, in her article "The Way We Won," the United States created 17 million new civilian jobs. However, "When large numbers of African Americans moved to cities in the North and West to work in defense industries, they were often met with violence and discrimination."[5] As Goodwin explains, there were 17 million new civilian jobs that were created in the country. The very fact that there was such systemic violence that happened as a result of minorities seeking employment of some of those jobs, in order to take care of their loved ones and families, is what prompted A. Philip Randolph and others to seek an audience with the President of the United States. As is indicated, preceding Executive Order 8802, but later an attachment to it, was a list of grievances regarding the civil rights of African Americans, demanding that an executive order be issued to stop job discrimination in the defense industry. Randolph and other Black leaders stated that, "In early July 1941, millions of jobs were being created, primarily in urban areas, as the United States prepared for war."[6]

Certainly, people in influential positions, both in the U.S. military and in the halls of Congress, were fully aware of the discontent that African Americans were showing around this time. After all, many White Americans, who recently had been unemployed, and in many cases were in soup lines, were now able to sustain themselves because of the boom in manufacturing and the excessive amount of jobs because of the war effort that was underway. "Over 15 million Americans had left their hometowns to work in war plants and shipyards and were living in a different state … than the place of their birth."[7]

It would seem that this very group of citizens, who just recently were experiencing the hunger and hearing the cries of their own families, would have no objections to sharing their windfall with other less fortunate people and their families, but shockingly, this was not the case. Although beginning to emerge from the Great Depression, with many American citizens gaining opportunities, life was still in the bowels for most African American workers. While the unemployment rate, although rising rapidly for Whites, was a tremendous 17 percent, for Blacks, it was well over twenty percent, according to Andrew E. Kersten in his book *A. Philip Randolph: A Life in the Vanguard.* He cited that although Blacks made up over 16 percent of those on public relief in 1930, for example, they made up only 9.7 percent of the American population. The positive New Deal opportunities that were being produced at this time were not benefitting this segment of the population. He also states, "The old saying still rang true: Blacks were the first fired and the last hired for any jobs, even government work."[8]

This was not the major problem: the major problem was that the government did not seem to care about the plight of the less fortunate African Americans, or so it would seem, because they were aware of where the shortcomings were regarding the lack of federal jobs for minorities.[9] At the same time, the government was dealing with many issues regarding the Armed Forces. Therefore, they were feeling the heat on numerous fronts.

Another problem was that there were legions of people putting pressure on those who held sway in the government, including pressure on those who controlled the military. The pressure was high from all sides. An example of the military problem was duly noted when the Secretary of the Navy received a letter dated December 10, 1941, from W. R. Poage, a congressman from the 11th District of Texas, which left no doubt as to his position with regard to a letter he had received from the National Association for the Advancement of Colored People (NAACP). Congressman Poage had transmitted this letter along with some documents that were in regard to Harold J. Franklin, who had been rejected by the Navy. The congressman stated that "while this association criticizes you for discriminating against Negroes, I noticed that you state that you were not discriminating. I have no objection to you stating that you were not discriminating. I have no objection to your statement, provided you do not carry out the wishes of the association."[10] Furthermore, this letter stated:

> In this hour of national crisis, it is much more important that we have the full-hearted co-operation of the thirty million white southern Americans than that we satisfy the National Association for the Advancement of Colored People.... You know that our people have volunteered for military service more readily than the people of any other section of the Nation. If they be forced to serve with Negroes, they will cease to volunteer; and when drafted, they will not serve with that enthusiasm and high morale this has always characterized the soldiers and sailors of the Southern states.[11]

In regard to the military, whether it be Navy or Marine Corps, it was clear to see the position that the congressman had for this branch of the government. To feel that this was harsh criticism coming from a U.S. congressman to the Secretary of the Navy was only the beginning. He went on to declare: "To assign a Negro doctor to treat some Southern White boy would be a crushing insult and, in my opinion, an outrage against the patriotism of our Southern people."[12]

There certainly was an onslaught of letters to the Secretary of the Navy at this critical juncture of time, though the Secretary was sympathetic to the viewpoints of those who felt that this was not the time for advancement in the Navy for Blacks, even though they were already serving, be it in lower positions and rank. Blacks in the Navy were serving as messmen. On January 19, 1942, in a letter mailed to Gifford Pinchot, a onetime politician, Secretary of the Navy Frank Knox stated that he was embarrassed by the efforts of a small class of Negroes who were upset that the Navy was only accepting enlistments for the messmen branch. He said that it was a hard experience he encountered in trying to make Black and White men live together in close proximities aboard ship.[13]

The letter from Congressman Poage was obviously fresh in his mind. The Secretary responded by saying, "So many of the recruits of the Navy come from southern states where the prejudice over the color line is inbred in that all efforts to have mixed crews have resulted in trouble, sometimes of serious proportions." In another line of the same response, he continued with:

> People who are not familiar with Navy conditions frequently ask why we don't man ships entirely with Negroes. You could not possibly find all the skills and crafts that are necessary if you had the entire Negro population of the United States to choose from.... Using Negroes solely as messmen enables us to quarter the Negroes together on the ship and limit their advancement to ratings within that branch, thus avoiding the promotion of Negroes to command white men, a thing which instantly provokes serious trouble.[14]

The mind-set permeating the top brass throughout all branches of the Armed Forces was the same. So much so that duplicate copies of directives had been sent to the Commandant of the U.S. Coast Guard and to the Commandant of the Marine Corps, and the only wording changed was the branch of service that the letters had been sent to. The key words were "would not inject into the whole personnel ... the race question." Paramount to this was the statement within the document that indicated, "The Commandant takes further cognizance of the opinion of the general board that it is unnecessary and inadvisable to repeat or further emphasize the undesirability of the recruitment of men of the colored race."[15]

During this period of time, there was a black woman by the name of Mary McLeod Bethune who was the Director of the Division of Negro Affairs of the National Youth Administration.[16] She was appointed to this position by President Roosevelt and held this position from 1936 to 1943. Mary Bethune was friends with Eleanor Roosevelt, wife of and First Lady to the President. She was influential to Mrs. Roosevelt and also to the President. Roosevelt considered Mary Bethune to be one of his foremost advisers in the unofficial "Black cabinet."[17] In his administration. Mary Bethune was also a Special Assistant to the Secretary of War and was an extraordinary educator, spokesperson, civil rights leader, and government official. President Roosevelt often consulted with her on minority affairs and interracial relations. Mary Bethune was a major advocate of opening military occupations to African Americans. Her close friendship with Mrs. Eleanor Roosevelt provided an opportunity for her to inject her persuasions to Eleanor that it was the right time and a good idea to allow Blacks and other minorities into the Armed Services as part of developing Armed Forces advances during the 1940s.

Mary McLeod Bethune founded the Daytona Educational

and Industrial Training School in 1904. The school underwent several stages of growth and development through the years, and in 1923 it merged with the Cookman Institute of Jacksonville, Florida, and became a coed high school. A year later, in 1924, it became affiliated with the Methodist Church. By 1931 the school had become a junior college. The school then became a four-year college in 1941 when the Florida Board of Education approved a four-year baccalaureate program in liberal arts and teacher education. The name was changed to Bethune-Cookman College. On February 14, 2007, the Board of Trustees approved the name Bethune-Cookman University after the institution established its first graduate program.[18]

Mary McLeod was an extraordinary woman who accomplished so many great things for which additional reading and studying is highly recommended. For a woman of her time, and a child of former slaves, her accomplishments were remarkable. I wish the possibility were here for me to devote more time to this outstanding woman.

During one of my conversations with Dad, he was resolute in raising her to the forefront as a person that was inspirational to him. "You make sure that if you are going to write anything about me, that you also include information about Mary Mcleod Bethune. She was a great woman, and no one can talk about great people unless they include her in that body of work as well."[19] He wanted to make certain that I made mention of her if I decided to write about his life experiences, Montford Point Camp, and the influences she has had in his and others lives.

As one writer, Audrey Thomas McCluskey, described Mrs. Bethune:

> Having forsaken conventional family life—although she espoused it for race uplift—Bethune contented herself with being the symbolic "Mother Bethune" to a whole race. Except for her son, Albert … her own family life was mostly nonexistent. She was, however, quite supportive of a large extended family, some of whom she helped educate at her school. She said Albert was her first child and Bethune-Cookman College her second.[20]

While William Franklin "Frank" Knox, Secretary of the Navy, was busy receiving letters from one side of the field regarding the "race issues," he would also receive another letter that would, no doubt, make him ponder issues regarding the other side of that race. On June 4, 1941, A. Philip Randolph, along with members of the Negro March on Washington committee, would also construct a letter that would shake up this country down to its fiber.

The letter was extremely diplomatic in its content and acutely respectful, but at the same time the picture it laid out was crystal-clear in its definition of what needed to happen. The letter read in part:

> Because the Negro people have not received their just share of jobs in the national defense, and our young men have not been integrated into the Armed Forces of the nation, including the Army, Navy, Air Corps and Marine, on a basis of equality, some of the Negro leaders have formulated plans and set up the necessary machinery in the various sections of the country for the purpose of mobilizing from ten to fifty thousand Negroes to march on Washington in the interest of securing jobs and justice in national defense and fair participation and equal integration into the Nation's military and naval forces.
>
> This movement has been initiated by the officers of the National Association for the Advancement of Colored People, the National Urban League, the Brotherhood of Sleeping Car Porters, the Young Men's Christian Association's branch of the Harlem Community, the Negro Labor Committee of New York, the Elks, and a number of other groups.[21]

Certainly, the mobilization, support, and mention of so many influential groups were enough to grab the attention of the Secretary. That, and no doubt this information having had to have been discussed with others in the Secretary's Cabinet, meant that it had to have been taken seriously. It went on to state:

> A call for the march, to take place July 1, 1941, is signed by Walter White of the National Association for Advancement of Colored People, Reverend William Lloyd Imes of the Presbyterian Church of Harlem, Frank R. Crosswaith, Chairman of the Negro Labor Committee of New York, Layle Lane, Vice-President of the American Federation of Teachers, Dr. Rayford Logan, Chairman of the National and State Committees for the Participation in Negroes in National Defense, Henry K. Craft, Secretary of the 135th Street branch of the YMCA, J. Finley Wilson, Grand Exalted Ruler of the Independent Benevolent Order of Elks of the World, Reverend Adam C. Powell Jr. of the Abyssinian Baptist Church of Harlem, and the undersigned.[22]

If that were not enough to grab his attention, Mr. Randolph also stated that there were local committees that were being mobilized and set up throughout the entire country that were developed for the sole purpose of recruiting marchers. These marchers were working with an interest only in demonstrating to appeal for Negroes to receive access to full participation in the national defense program.

Mr. Randolph then indicated that a week prior to this march on Washington, plans had been developed for staging marches in different cities for the express purpose of calling on mayors and city council members to appeal to President Roosevelt to override the discrimination happening across the country, including in the military and in federal workplaces. Within the body of the letter, he also stated that there were plans to have a rally at the Monument of Abraham Lincoln, "because of its historical symbolism in relation to the issuance of the Emancipation Proclamation for the liberation of the Negroes from chattel slavery."[23]

He further went on to ask that the Secretary himself address the rally from the Monument of Abraham Lincoln, "where a great throng of Blacks from all parts of the country will be gathered," also stating that nothing that has happened since the great Emancipation has "gripped the hearts and caught their interest and quickened their imagination more than the girding of our country for national defense without according them the recognition and opportunity as citizens, consumers, and workers they feel justified in expecting."[24]

The letter and request were written on June 4, 1941.[25]

A major catalyst for the march began back in mid-September 1940, when Congress was passing the Burke-Wadsworth Selective Service Act.[26] At the same time, the Brotherhood of Sleeping Car Porters were having its annual convention in Harlem, New York, at the YMCA and had as its guest speaker, Eleanor Roosevelt, the President of the United States' wife, where she was serving as the President's representative.

The most important issue that night at the convention was that the delegates had passed a resolution reflecting Randolph's thrust to the United States government that there be no discrimination against Blacks in the U.S. Armed Services. As an advocate for Blacks in the military, the First Lady, somewhat sensitive to the issue, was able to secure a meeting for Mr. Randolph at the White House with the President.

Just a couple of weeks later, Mr. Randolph and a small delegation of his top aides were able to meet at the White House with the President. Because of the success of the resolution at his convention, Asa Randolph felt confident in being able to have the President side with him regarding avoiding discrimination against Blacks in the military. Although confident, still he could not forget a meeting he had attended in 1925.

So there would be great challenges in this meeting, but Randolph and his delegation felt that they were armed well enough to get through to the President. Also, because Eleanor had been reaching out to Black Americans, there seemed to be hope, although very little had changed in the two terms that Roosevelt had inhabited the White House as related to Black servicemen. As a matter of fact, very little has been achieved since Calvin Coolidge's time.

With a meeting encouraged by Eleanor Roosevelt, there was much less reticence for Randolph meeting with President Roosevelt than there was in 1925 when Mr. Randolph had attended a meeting at the White House led by William Monroe Trotter. Mr. Trotter was an advocate of civil rights for African Americans and had also graduated from Harvard University in 1895 with a bachelor's degree in international banking with honors (magna sum cum laude) and also a master's degree in 1896 in finance. He was also the first African American to earn a Phi Beta Kappa key.[27] However, after Mr. Trotter asked then-President Calvin Coolidge to work for federal legislation outlawing lynching, Coolidge gave no encouragement nor support.[28]

As Andrew E. Kersten describes in *A. Philip Randolph, a Life in the Vanguard,* there were the strongest reasons for confronting President Franklin Roosevelt and the U.S. policies regarding African Americans. Even on the doorsteps of a world war, many of the United States' major companies continued to lock out employment, education, and other opportunities against African Americans. Racial policies were still as prevalent now as they were before, but now they were even more firm and systematic.

The meeting took place as planned on September 27, 1940. The President seemed to be receptive to listening "more closely to minority views on greater participation for Blacks within the military." It was also during the period of upcoming elections. The meeting seemed even more hopeful to Mr. Randolph because included in the meeting was Secretary of the Navy Frank Knox and assistant Secretary of War Robert Patterson. Walter White, Executive Secretary of the NAACP, was also in attendance as one of Randolph's top associates. White forwarded the idea to the President that an army fighting for democracy "should be the last place in which to practice undemocratic segregation."[29]

However, in less than two weeks, on October 9, the White House announced a policy of strict segregation for Negro units in the Army. It seemed, according to the information written by William Percy, that the President's advisers had warned him that there would be gruesome race riots in an integrated army and that the President had gotten cold feet.

After feeling betrayed from this prior meeting, A. Philip Randolph was determined that the outcome would be different this time with his new strategy of a march on Washington.

On June 18, 1941, there was a meeting at the White House regarding the anticipated March on Washington. The meeting included A. Philip Randolph, Franklin D. Roosevelt, Walter White, and Fiorello La Guardia. The text of the meeting is as follows:

A. Philip Randolph: "Mr. President, time is running on. You are quite busy, I know. But what we want to talk with you about is the problem of jobs for Negroes in defense industries. Our people are being turned away at factory gates because they are colored. They can't live with this thing. Now, what are you going to do about it?"

Franklin D. Roosevelt: "Well, Phil, what do you want me to do?"

Randolph: "Mr. President, we want you to do something that will enable Negro workers to get work in these plants."

Roosevelt: "Why, I surely want them to work, too. I'll call up the heads of the various defense plants and have them see to it that Negroes are given the same opportunity to work in defense plants as any other citizen in the country."

Randolph: "We want you to do more than that. We want something concrete, something tangible, definite, positive, and affirmative."

Roosevelt: "What do you mean?"

Randolph: "Mr. President, we want you to issue an executive order making it mandatory that Negroes be permitted to work in these plants."

Roosevelt: "Well Phil, you know I can't do that. If I issue an executive order for you, then there'll be no end to other groups coming in here and asking me to issue executive orders for them, too. In any event, I couldn't do anything unless you called off this march of yours. Questions like this can't be settled with a sledgehammer."

Randolph: "I'm sorry, Mr. President, the march cannot be called off."

Roosevelt: "How many people do you plan to bring?"

Randolph: "One hundred thousand, Mr. President."

Roosevelt: "Walter, how many people will really march?"

Walter White: "One hundred thousand, Mr. President."

Fiorello La Guardia: "Gentleman, it is clear that Mr. Randolph is not going to call off the march, and I suggest we all begin to seek a formula."[30]

After consultation with his advisers, Roosevelt responded to the Black leaders and issued Executive Order 8802 on June 25, 1941, less than a month later, which declared, "There shall be no discrimination in the employment of workers in defense industries and in government, because of race, creed, color, or national origin."[31] It was the first Presidential directive on race since reconstruction. The order also established the Fair Employment Practices Committee (FEPC) to investigate incidents of discrimination.[32]

Although Executive Order 8802 forced the Marines to accept African Americans, the Corps also allowed the continuation of the racist policies of segregation to exist. Executive Order 8802 was a long time in the making because of the racist policies that were in existence in the branches of military history since their beginnings. African American civil rights groups were exasperated and frustrated with the way their servicepeople were being treated once they returned from war overseas. This was especially true after having served in the Army and Navy for decades, and particularly in the Navy, dating back to the Civil War.

There was so much pressure on President Franklin Roosevelt to remove the status of second-rate citizenship from these honorably discharged African American military men that the president essentially caved and signed Executive Order 8802. Nevertheless, from the onset it was the senior officials inside the Corps that were opposed to Blacks in the Marines, although they had to comply. They decided the best way to comply was to accept the mandate but continue to keep Blacks and Whites separate.

Although many in the Black community thought Executive Order 8802 was concrete and tangible, as Mr. Randolph had asked for, it was minute compared to what was really needed to establish racial integration in the military. As Major Christopher A. Browning, USMC, describes in his report:

> The President was very careful in selecting his words. While this order established the foundation for racial integration in the Armed Services, its wording left its implementation open to broad interpretation. By doing so, it allowed him to appease the pro–civil rights population who pushed for this order while still pandering to those who believed segregation was the correct policy for the United States. While it can be argued this order fell well short of its original intent, it opened the door for the African American community to equal opportunity in the Armed Services.[33]

All departments within the Corps felt that they were being forced to comply with integration, although there were no signs that they were moving or even wanted to move in that direction. In fact, the entire chain of command in the Corps was determined not to comply with what they felt was being forced upon them. This was apparent from the Commandant, General Holcomb, and on down the chain. The Marine Corps did not feel it had to follow the dictates of the president or any other department within the Navy Board. Be that as it may, the progression of pressure continued even after World War II, and it was President Harry S. Truman who circumvented all opposition and issued Executive Order 9981 on July 26, 1948, integrating all branches of the armed forces of the U.S. military.

Earlier, in 1943, the FEPC was greatly strengthened with Executive Order 9346. This order required that "all" government contracts have a nondiscrimination clause. There was so much work to be done and such an abundance of jobs that there truly was work for almost anyone who wanted it. Unfortunately, in spite of all of the opportunities given to so many others, there were still many that did not want to work with minorities. During World War II the federal government operated shipyards, airfields, ammunition plants, and thousands of other facilities that hired and employed people on an unprecedented scale. Here the FEPC rules were applicable and guaranteed the equality of employment rights.[34]

It did not mean people were happy, even though the jobs were plentiful, and the employment produced by the war effort allowed many families to become independent of the soup lines once again. It was in this type of example where the FEPC had to step in. The FEPC was able to enforce the laws in the North primarily but did not do much challenging when problems arose in the South.

Even after all the work President Roosevelt did to compose Executive Order 8802, Congress subsequently never enacted FEPC into law. Thus, it was President Harry S. Truman, in 1948, who called for a permanent FEPC, antilynching legislation, and the abolishment of the poll tax. Previously, these initiatives had been prevented by the conservatives in the Democratic-controlled Congress. It was not until 1950 that the House approved a permanent FEPC bill. Unfortunately, the Southern senators were able to filibuster the bill, and it failed. At this time there were five states that enacted and enforced their own FEPC laws. They were New Jersey and New York in 1945, Massachusetts in 1946, Connecticut in 1947, and Washington in 1949. Even though there was much strife and turmoil regarding this bill, it was an effectively used tool in preventing much racial discrimination during the war.[35]

CHAPTER 3

Orders from Franklin D. Roosevelt

opy of the transcript as issued:

Transcript of Executive Order 8802: Prohibition of Discrimination in the Defense Industry (1941)

Executive Order

Reaffirming Policy of Full Participation in The Defense Program by All Persons, Regardless of Race, Creed, Color, or National Origin, and Directing Certain Action in Furtherance of Said Policy

June 25, 1941

WHEREAS it is the policy of the United States to encourage full participation in the national defense program by all citizens of the United States, regardless of race, creed, color, or national origin, in the firm belief that the democratic way of life within the Nation can be defended successfully only with the help and support of all groups within its borders; and

WHEREAS there is evidence that available and needed workers have been barred from employment in industries engaged in defense production solely because of considerations of race, creed, color, or national origin, to the detriment of workers' morale and of national unity:

NOW, THEREFORE, by virtue of the authority vested in me by the Constitution and the statutes, and as a prerequisite to the successful conduct of our national defense production effort, I do hereby reaffirm the policy of the United States that there shall be no discrimination in the employment of workers in defense industries or government because of race, creed, color, or national origin, and I do hereby declare that it is the duty of employers and of labor organizations, in furtherance of said policy and of this order, to provide for the full and equitable participation of all workers in defense industries, without discrimination because of race, creed, color, or national origin;

And it is hereby ordered as follows:

1. All departments and agencies of the Government of the United States concerned with vocational and training programs for defense production shall take special measures appropriate to assure that such programs are administered without discrimination because of race, creed, color, or national origin.
2. All contracting agencies of the Government of the United States shall include in all defense contracts hereafter negotiated by them a provision obligating the contractor not to discriminate against any worker because of race, creed, color, or national origin.
3. There is established in the Office of Production Management a Committee on Fair Employment Practice, which shall consist of a chairman and four other members to be appointed by the President. The Chairman and members of the Committee shall serve as such without compensation but shall be entitled to actual and necessary transportation, subsistence, and other expenses incidental to performance of their duties. The Committee shall receive and investigate complaints of discrimination in violation of the provisions of this order and shall take appropriate steps to redress grievances which it finds to be valid. The Committee shall also recommend to the several departments and agencies of the Government of the United States and to the President all measures which may be deemed by it necessary or proper to effectuate the provisions of this order.

Franklin D. Roosevelt, The White House, June 25, 1941.[1]

"Although I had begun my civil service training," said Thomas Mosley, "I was about to embark onto another life journey. This journey would take me away from the comforts of home and my loved ones and prepare me for battle along with thousands of other young men and women. This journey would take me to the other side of the world.

"On November 16, 1943, I was enlisted into the Marine Corps in Philadelphia. I would be the first Black man to enter the Marine Corps from Steelton, Pennsylvania. There were others that went into the service from Steelton, but I was the first Marine. Even though life had held many challenges for me and my family members while growing up, I had no idea that life for me was about to drastically change even more."[2]

For many others it meant that opportunities were now on the table. This was a huge advancement for all people in all aspects of the U.S. government. The soup lines did not need to exist anymore.

The borrowing of a cup of soup or flour or sugar from your neighbor could now be eradicated.

So, it was with this executive order, which now created opportunities that had never been in existence in the United States of America before, that demanded that all hiring in the federal workplace be based on qualifications and not racist practices as had been the customary practice for decades. The issuance of the executive order also established the creation of the Fair Employment Practices Committee (FEPC). Not only did this Executive Order establish fair hiring practices within the federal workplace, but it also extended itself to corporations that received federal contracts as well. Finally, the economic law of supply and demand helped to tip the scales in the favor of justice and prosperity for all.

CHAPTER 4

Chosen, Accepted, but Unwanted Marines

After President Franklin D. Roosevelt issued Executive Order 8802 in 1941, Montford Point Camp, a part of Camp Lejeune but separate, located in Jacksonville, North Carolina, was to serve as one of the military training camps for new Black Marine recruits. I am certain there was much apprehension on the part of many of these new recruits, but for some others it was an opportunity to finally feel that they were beginning to be accepted as equals in this country. After all, many of their predecessors, past and present, had seen some of the worst that this country had to offer, but had also heard of the opportunities and stories that had arisen through their families and other families during times of war.

"For years, history has described how many Blacks, as far back as slavery, had gained freedom from bondage by participating in some form of fighting for the slave masters. During the Centennial Celebration of the Revolution in Philadelphia that took place in 1876," said Edward Ayres, Historian of the American Revolution Museum at Yorktown, "not one speaker mentioned that by 1783 there had been thousands of African Americans that had been involved in the war in helping to establish our nation." He further stated, "Many were active participants; some won their freedom and others were victims, but throughout the struggle Blacks refused to be mere bystanders and gave their loyalty to the side that seemed to offer the best prospect for freedom."[1]

Many who were enslaved and many who were free knew that in many cases freedom came as a result of participating in war. Half a million enslaved African Americans in the thirteen colonies were looking for any way possible to get out of the horrible and wretched life and conditions that they found in slavery. Edward Ayres also said, "Widespread talk of liberty gave thousands of slaves high expectations, and many were ready to fight for a democratic revolution that might offer them freedom."[2]

Although the promise of freedom had eluded them many times, and for just as many years, nevertheless Blacks were still willing to lay their lives down with just the thought that this time, freedom may be theirs. Somehow, although told in most cases that they were not wanted, or because of the fear of the military arming them, African Americans were still willing to take up arms to fight on the behalf of democracy, and they continued to. Fortunately for Blacks, many states were unable to fulfill their enlistment quotas with White citizens and had to turn to those enslaved Blacks for the help needed in this drastic cause. "Eventually every state above the Potomac River recruited slaves for military service, usually in exchange for their freedom."[3]

After all, it was now 1941 and not 1741. With the world at war, and knowing that times had changed, and circumstances had changed, maybe this time the opportunity to serve this government would end up bringing the desperately needed freedom and respect that was craved for and needed by the African American. It always seemed that freedom was just over the hill, or just one more ridge to cross, or maybe one more cross to bear. The African American family hoped that they could cross the finish line this time. Even though it may not have completely worked in the past, this time they would "be accepted for sure." It was now not just war with Native Americans in the United States, or White settlers, or even with the British; it had stretched around the entire globe and the stakes were higher. World War II was on the horizon!

Still worth noting, however, in early America, Blacks were looking for just ways to gain their freedom, and one of the ways was to fight for that cause. Sometimes they would fight with the Native Americans against the settlers; sometimes they would fight with the settlers against the Native Americans. Nevertheless, they wanted their freedom.

It is well worth noting that initially, in many areas of the United States in the early 1700s, where Blacks and Native Americans shared close proximity, there was extensive relationships and mixing among the Native Americans and the African Americans. Gary B. Nash, in his historical studies of early America in his book *Red, White, and Black,* describes in great details many of the relationships between the early settlers, the Native Americans and the

African Americans. In his book *Red, White and Black: The Peoples of Early America,* he goes into great length regarding the relationships.

In New England for example, the coastal tribes had been killed off before a few of the African Americans arrived, and therefore not much mixing occurred amongst the two peoples. However, it is well worth noting that in a few places such as Cape Cod, where many of the Native Americans did survive, there was intermingling between them and a small group of Blacks, and it became extensive by the end of the century. In many of the coastal areas this also occurred. The reason behind this was that many Native American slaves had been removed and transported early in the eighteenth century from South Carolina.[4]

A census in South Kingston, Rhode Island, in 1730 showed 333 Negro slaves and 223 Indian slaves; the resulting intermixture is not to be wondered at. It was reported that in Massachusetts in 1795 that the Blacks "have generally left the country and resorted to the maritime towns. Some are incorporated, and their breed is mixed with the Indians of Cape-Cod and Martha's Vineyard," as stated in Nash's *Red White and Black.*[5]

It is said that in New York, which had the largest population of slaves north of the Chesapeake, intermixture of enslaved people and Native Americans was not unusual. In 1712 there had been an insurrection in New York City, and in what was known as a "blood bond," the Native American slaves and the Negroes joined together. From that time on, whenever officials were looking for escaped slaves, they knew that the best place to look for them was the local tribes that remained on Long Island and in the Hudson River Valley. In many instances, it can be noted that Native Americans of the coastal tribes gave refuge to many runaway slaves.[6]

In South Carolina and Georgia, Native Americans and Africans, who were in substantial numbers, found themselves face-to-face with the fears that Europeans had regarding them joining forces to overthrow them. It was with this thought in mind that it was determined a necessity by the settlers to keep them apart. During the Pre-Revolutionary period, the Native Americans of the Southeast remained numerous in the areas that Whites had settled in. Between the Native Americans and the Black slaves and the free Native Americans, the White settlers were outnumbered by a ratio of three or four to one throughout most of the early period of colonization. Even during the middle eighteenth century, only about 25,000 Whites inhabited the colony along with 40,000 Black slaves and 60,000 Native Americans, who were a part of the Creek, Cherokee, Choctaw, Chickasaw, and other tribes. Even as the White population grew, the slave population grew as well. Although they were able to nip it early on, the Native American uprisings at the onset of the colonial period and the progression of the slave risings made the South Carolinians keenly aware at all costs that they must keep the Negro slaves and the Native Americans apart. The South Carolinians were surrounded on all sides by African slaves and Native Americans, and the deepest fear was that those two would come together in a collaborative effort and annihilate them.

The fact that they were able to control the situation shows that they were at least wise in their abilities to work one Native American tribe against another and in keeping the Native Americans and the slaves divided. There were several methods that the settlers used to achieve their goals. Laws were passed that prevented Negroes from traveling in Native American country, whether they were free or not, as traders or trader's helpers. There were treaties signed with Cherokees, Creeks, and other tribes with a clause that usually included a part that asked that slaves be returned to the South Carolina government. Then there was the suspicion that was fostered to the Native Americans regarding the Negroes that furthered the divide. Another thing that was used in many cases was a bounty placed on the heads of the free Blacks or the slaves.

Once this went into effect with the Native Americans and apprehensions ran high, the settlers put another plan into use that would work against the Native Americans. During the Indian Wars, South Carolina incorporated Black slaves into their militia. Without using them it would have been virtually impossible to have defeated the Tuscarora, Yamasee, or Cherokee forces. This strategy also served as a reminder that the Africans were not their friends. In 1715, the governor of South Carolina led forces against the Yamasee people, and at least half the force comprised Black troops. There was also a Black company in the same offense that was led under Captain Plight.[7]

Because there was no real ongoing solid and binding connection between the Africans and the Native Americans, and both were being used against the other, the relationship between the two floundered at times. There was a cultural barrier, and there was a language barrier. For the slaves, in most cases, it was the aspect of possible freedom through a militia or a military. It seemed to be the only way out for some slaves, and it was a chance worth taking. For both the Native Americans and the slaves, fighting one another was mostly in response to major gains from the White settlers. For the Native Americans it was to gain trade items as well as monetary wealth. What they stood to gain seemed enormous, and although they at times sympathized with the slaves, they also did not want to give up those items gotten from the settlers. Some of those items included tools, new techniques, clothing, firearms, alcohol, and opportunities to acquire wealth of a different nature.

Another example shows how rapidly the Native Americans would seem to forget the relationships that did exist on occasion between them and the slaves. For instance, in 1739 there was an enormous revolt by Black insurrectionists called the Stono Revolt. The slaves had eluded capture while headed to Spanish Florida. The South Carolina government supplied the Native Americans with clothing, guns, and ammunition, and also promised a specific sum of money for each slave brought back alive or half that amount for each returned dead.

Although the exchanges took many forms and lasted for years going back and forth, once again it was the slaves that were looking at ways of freedom, and the majority of time it was the enlisting or the services performed during battle that were the means of exchange that the slaves used in order to try to gain that freedom. These facts are well documented in military history. Hopefully, this time, fighting and winning against Japan and Germany would mean true freedom for the African American. After all, this was the big stage; all eyes were watching, and especially for the African American families, hoping.

Moving forward to modern historical times, imagine being an African American and enlisting into a segregated branch of the military. At the time the Marine Corps was the last branch to integrate. In the words of Major General Commandant Thomas Holcomb, while at the Marine Corps Headquarters, in testimony before the General Board of the Navy on January 23, 1942:

> As Commandant of the Marine Corps I would like to say this is not a new question with me. I have thought of it for years and have talked it over and I know I speak not only for myself but for all the officers I know, that we believe there would be a definite loss of efficiency in the Marine Corps if we had to take Blacks; I hope very much that the General Board ... will see its way clear to stating that no plan can be made for the employment of Blacks in the Naval Service that will not serve to reduce the efficiency of that service.[8]

This was specified because there was serious doubt that Blacks would meet the high standards of infantry in the Marine Corps.

General Holcomb also indicated that it was not only him that felt this conviction, but also that this was the conviction that all of the other officers he knew felt.[9] This set the tone for the way these new recruits were to be treated, and at the time there was no Dr. King or others to lobby on their behalf because of mistreatment. And if there were, the voices were not being heard very loudly. Concluding his remarks, Major General Commandant Thomas Holcomb said, "the Negro race has every opportunity now to satisfy its aspirations for combat, in the Army—a very much larger organization than the Navy or Marine Corps—and their desire to enter the naval service is largely, I think, to break into a club that doesn't want them."[10]

It was realized that no matter how outspoken these opposition leaders were, the executive order had been written and signed by President Roosevelt, and the orders had to be carried out. Realizing that all they could do would be to try to get the best recruits, the word was put out by Lieutenant Colonel Campbell C. Johnson that, "if you want to die young, join the Marines." This was being said as a psychological ploy, "so that anybody that joins has got to be pretty good."[11]

Also, in regard to Major General Commandant Holcomb's testimony before the General Board of the Navy, one may ask the question: Why would a general for the Marine Corps testify before a Navy Board? It is because the U.S. Department of the Navy (DON) was established by an act of Congress on April 30, 1798, to provide a government organizational structure to the U.S. Navy and, from 1834 onward, for the U.S. Marine Corps. According to Wikipedia, the highest-ranking military officers in the Department of the Navy are the Chief of Naval Operations and the Commandant of the Marine Corps, who are the principal military advisers to the Secretary of the Navy. They supervise their respective military services of the Department of the Navy, and in a separate capacity serves as members of the Joint Chiefs of Staff.

Prior to this, keep in mind that the prewar policy was designed to alienate and keep out the Blacks. General Holcomb, under normal standards, being the commandant, set up his own policies; nonetheless, when President Roosevelt issued his proclamation, the general eventually had to fall in line. Commandant Holcomb did not want Blacks in the Marine Corps, insisting the Corps was too small to break the units down in the manner he would insist upon to maintain racially distinctive units. One senior recruiter even indicated that the applicant should be disqualified by the medical examiner "during the enlistment physical."[12]

Realizing that he had no control over stopping the movement of Blacks into the ranks of the Marine Corps, Holcomb came upon other ideas to exclude Blacks from the general population. One major proposal is that they allow one thousand men into the volunteer Marine Corps Reserve for duty in a segregated composite defense battalion. This was to consist of a rifle company with a light tank platoon, seacoast and antiaircraft artillery, and whatever other components that might be needed to make it a self-sustaining unit.[13]

Although segregation was a part of all branches of the military at this time, it was more obvious in the Marines than in any other branch of the service. The reason for this was because the Marines were a small, specialized branch of the military, and it was more difficult to hide unequal treatment. Blacks in the Marine Corps could not be hidden and stood out like a sore thumb, to use a metaphor. In the other branches of service, unequal treatment could be hidden in many obscure ways, but not in the Marines. The Blacks were there, and they had to be dealt with, but the Marine Corps did not have the experience to do that. What they did, though, was to utilize the patterns that were already previously established by the Army and Navy as best they could. The enlistment of Black Marines began on June 1, 1942, but they placed the reservists on inactive status until a training-size unit could be enlisted and a training facility built at Montford Point.[14]

It was the segregation that forced the Marine Corps to find new jobs and units so that the Black inductees could be absorbed into the Marines. Thus began the opening of areas such as messenger clerks, janitors, chauffeurs, and more defense battalions. Even though these were the areas opened, these were not the areas in which the recruits were used. Instead, they placed most of the recruits in defense battalions.

Not only were these men placed primarily in defense battalions, but in order to keep the units segregated, plans had already been made to remove the white drill instructors from these units as quickly as possible. The reason stated by Major General Harry Schmidt, in a letter to Marine Commanders, was that Blacks should be under the command of Black officers because they knew the racial qualities and characteristics of their people.[15]

General Holcomb was also aware that White noncommissioned officers had an adverse effect on Black self-esteem, and this in part was the other reason for removing them from these segregated units. With this new departure from the standard Marine Corps regulations, Holcomb needed to be constantly informed on how these new changes of departure were progressing.

While most inductees and the civilian population had a limited amount of knowledge regarding the foundational setup and the structure that would take place for the new Black recruits, the Secretary of the Navy, the Commandant of the Marine Corps, and others in the hierarchy knew exactly what the plans were to be. At least in theory, it was an idea that had some strategies that would come into play because they had been utilized previously. It was a combination of ideas that were wrapped around tradition in the old segregated ways, plans that had been formulated by the command structure and employed in structuring the intake and the utilization of Blacks in the Navy and the Army.

The most important factor that was to be adhered to by the command structure of the Marine Corps, according to secret documents and information at that time and compiled by MacGregor and Nalty, was to keep the "racial question" out of the Corps.[16]

On February 27, 1942, the Commandant of the U.S. Marine Corps, General Holcomb, sent a letter to the Chairman General Board regarding where the men of the colored race may be assigned, other than the messman branch. The letter also indicated that there was no need to reiterate the fact that these men were not wanted but had to be employed at some location. Anyone on the outside looking in may not have had the true understanding of the term "racial question," but even this was understandable because it seemed to be such a misleading phrase, except to those charged with its secrecy and deemed with the responsibility of carrying out those orders. The clearest meaning of this term, without injecting the race question, meant "Keep the colored personnel segregated from the White personnel.[17] In its simplest terms, the memorandum indicated that the new African American recruits, one thousand per month, were to be kept separated from the White personnel.

Although a problem for the Corps, nevertheless, President Roosevelt had given the order, and it had to be carried out. The Corps would get these new recruits from Selective Service in order to maintain the necessary quotas that were prescribed. Along with this phase, they would also fall into categories that were already set up to describe the "intelligence levels" that they would fall into.

Indicated by the command structure as to how best to utilize the men and to see where their intelligence level was, the Corps would use the same stereotype tables from the Army that had been used in previous years. Broken down into percentages, it showed the so-called "distinction and probabilities" of African Americans and Whites into classifications:

1. Superior: the Negro having 0.6 percent to the Whites having 7.6 percent
2. Above Average: the Negro having just 5.0 percent to Whites with 29.2 percent
3. Average: the Negro having just 16.5 percent to Whites with 32.7 percent
4. Below Average: the Negro having 30.4 to Whites with 21.6 percent
5. Inferior: the Negro having 47.5 percent to Whites having 8.9 percent.[18]

Almost half of the new black inductees were predisposed to being categorized as inferior based on the Army table of statistics. That coupled with the already existing racially superior mind-set, it was no wonder that there were so many problems in how to absorb and how to relate to the thousands of new recruits now pouring in to Montford Point Camp.

The Marine Corps's answer to the problem was to form composite battalions, which initially were designed to absorb 1,200 or so new recruits per year, train them, move them out once trained, and deploy them overseas. The other assembly of inductees, once inducted, would be a part of the messmen's group, and that was designed to hold another 3,500 men. Then there would be the chauffeurs, the postal exchange workers, janitors, maintenance men, and so on.

The top brass was not able to stop the incoming flow of colored troops coming into the Corps, and they projected that the coloreds were not intelligent enough for the combat units as a whole. However, they could be contained in this quasi-structure that would look like a part of the organizational structure but not disturb the "racial question." This was the key element regarding the African Americans at the beginning of World War II.

The use of the composite battalions was multifaceted from the beginning. Not only was it theoretically designed to train men to become fighters in combat units, with the use of specialized training in the occupation in which they were desired, it was also designed as a catch-all for African American Marines. No matter what station he was derived from within a unit, he was deemed sufficiently capable to be promoted to noncommissioned officer rank, and he was transferred for duty with a composite company. This type of setup seemingly gave the Marine Corps a way out in that it could not be charged with racial discrimination. But it was racial discrimination, because the primary motive was in the fact that there were to be no African Americans of equal rank to a white officer serving in the same company as that white noncommissioned officer at Montford Point Camp, unless it was temporary.

Once again, try to imagine being the first Black man to set foot inside a Marine Base in this country since 1776–1777, where only a dozen or so Blacks were known to have served in the American Revolutionary War. In 1942, the number was at zero, even after 167 years. The fear and the anxiety that must have weighed on that first Black person must have been without comprehension. Above all, the courage that this person had to have had must have been astounding. For no one to have gone before you as a vanguard in 167 years to have tested these frigid waters was mind-boggling. Watching the eyes watch you as you entered Montford Point ready to serve as that first Black recruit had to have been a major mental challenge. There could have been no greater test or challenge for one man in modern history with respect to the U.S. military and its operations.

Let's remove the imagination. After much ado about who the first African American Marine to be sworn in was, I decided to call Master Gunnery Sergeant Joe Geeter to get the definitive answer. Sergeant Joe Geeter, who currently holds four posts as the President of the Philadelphia Chapter (Chapter 1, Philadelphia), was all too happy to make the distinction between the two men that seemed to hold that title.

He immediately knew where I was going with my question as I asked, "Sergeant Geeter, there seems to be a slight controversy in books and writings that indicate someone other than Howard Perry was the first African American to be sworn in at Montford Point Camp." Before I could get the question out thoroughly, Master Gunnery Sergeant Geeter gave me my answer. His reply set the record correct in my mind.

"Alfred Masters was the first to be sworn in on June 1, 1942, but Howard Perry was the first to step foot on Montford Point Camp. He reported to boot camp on August 26, 1942, and as is customarily said, 'the rest is history.'"[19]

CHAPTER 5

All Might Needed Against Hideki Tojo

For men in the Marines such as General Thomas Holcomb or other brass who opposed Blacks in the Corps, who also tried to prevent Blacks from joining and serving in the Corps, the need to have them as support and help was greater than the false resistance displayed, as history would later confirm. So whether or not their reluctance was to go along with the status quo, or that they truly believed Blacks were an inferior lot, history would later prove, no matter what the reluctance may have been, their tactical calculations were completely off the mark.

There is no question that keeping African Americans out of the Corps was just a premise of keeping a good ol' boys club secluded from some, because generals in the military at that time, and other top brass, had to know the illustrious history of African American soldiers in these United States of America.

For example, author Herbert Aptheker's qualified studies presented the latest revised official casualty figures for Negro troops in the service of the United States Army during the Civil War. According to his data, there were a total of 186,097 troops that included 7,122 officers and 178,975 enlisted men. Within this striking statistic there were "a total of 324 officers and 36,523 enlisted men [that] lost their lives, from all causes, known and unknown." He goes on to state, "making a grand total of casualties, in the form of deaths, among what we referred to as the United States Colored Troops, of 36,847. Of the total number of deaths, 2,870 were killed in action or mortally wounded, while 29,756 died of disease."[1]

Many more also served in the Union Navy. On the Confederate side, the issue was whether to arm them or not, although most were used as labor forces.

Later on, the Buffalo Soldiers had stellar notoriety. No one could deny the fierce fighting abilities that these men had; the name was possibly given by the Native Americans themselves. There were three or four ways that the attribute could have been given to them, but no one can deny the fortitude these men had or the sacrifices they made in the defense of this country.

The Buffalo Soldiers were originally members of the U.S. 10th Cavalry Regiment of the U.S. Army. They were originally formed on September 21, 1866, at Fort Leavenworth, Kansas. The Buffalo Soldiers seemed to be the name given to the Negro Cavalry by the Native American tribes they had done battle with or because of the Native American rumors spreading regarding their ferociousness as well as their savvy and gallantry on the battlefield. Eventually this is the name that became synonymous with all of the African American regiments formed in 1866.[2]

> During the American Civil War, the U.S. government formed regiments known as the United States Troops, comprised of Black soldiers. After the war, Congress and the Army authorized the formation of two regiments of Black cavalry with the designations 9th and 10th U.S. Cavalry, and four regiments of Black infantry, designated the 38th, 39th, 40th and 41st Infantry Regiments (Colored). The 38th and 41st were reorganized as the 25th Infantry Regiment, with headquarters at Jackson Barracks in New Orleans, Louisiana, in November 1869. The 39th and 40th were reorganized as the 24th Infantry Regiment, with headquarters at Fort Clark, Texas, in April 1869. All of these units were composed of Black enlisted men commanded by both White and Black officers. These included the first commander of the 10th Cavalry Benjamin Grierson, the first Commander of the 9th Cavalry Edward Hatch, Medal of Honor recipient Louis H. Carpenter, the unforgettable Nicholas M. Nolan, and the first Black graduate of West Point, Henry O. Flipper.[3]

There has never been a major war in this country that African Americans, Colored, Negroes, or whatever name was used at the time, were not a part of as soldiers and that there was not a substantial amount wounded or killed in action. Regardless of the opposition, these African American troops stood, whether it was against the enemy at home or the enemy abroad. It did not stop them. These men, these fearless warrior soldiers, stood tall with pride and dignity and were determined to make their country, their families, and themselves proud in spite of every obstacle that came their way.

There was an absolute need to have as much help, support, and experience as the United States could stand because Hideki Tojo had already made his move against the United States. On July 22, 1940, Prime Minister Tojo was appointed War Minister of Japan by Prime Minister Konoe. Prince Funimaro Konoe, as he had been known at one time, was a politician and served as the 34th, 38th, and 39th Prime Minister of the Empire of Japan. Minister Tojo, as he was now known, was instrumental in forming an alliance between Japan, Germany, and Italy. Minister Tojo was not one to procrastinate or to sit back and wait for others to make their move. In fact, he was nicknamed Kamisori, which means "razor." He was known for his decisiveness,[4] as noted by C. Peter Chen, a historian and managing editor of the World War II database, and was also on the staff of the Imperial Japanese Navy.

For Tojo's part, he had had a long existence with Japan and its war machine. He had also been instrumental in Japan's war effort against China and Russia. On December 1,1935, he was promoted to the rank of lieutenant general. During a February 26, 1936, coup attempt, he stood against the rebels and emerged as the Army's leading political figure. On March 1, 1937, he became the Chief of Staff of the Kwantung Army. He led units of the 1st of the independent mixed brigade during Operation Chahar in July 1937, and deployed his troops to Hebei Province, China, after the Second Sino-Japanese War began with the Kwantung Army. He also played a key role in efficiently utilizing Manchuria's natural resources to feed the hungry Japanese industrial machine. Returning to Japan in May 1938, he became Vice War Minister and Chief of Army Aviation under War Minister Seishiro Itagaki, who was a member of Fumimaro Konoe's cabinet. As head of the Japanese Army's aviation program, Tojo adopted an aggressive stance in conducting preemptive strikes against China and Russia.[5]

General Tojo, in Emperor Hirohito's mind, was the strongest mouthpiece for war and was outspoken in not reducing troops in the war against China. Although there were others in the lineup to possibly become prime minister, Tojo was firm in projecting that troop withdrawal would not solve any problems in the relationship with China and also not ready to acquiesce to any problem-solving aspects of the United States, figuring that would only serve to give the United States an upper hand. These were things that pleased the emperor. Although General Tojo did not anticipate being chosen as the prime minister, nevertheless he was chosen by the emperor on October 18, 1941, to be the 40th Prime Minister of Japan.[6]

In the Far East, before the war with the Western Powers, Japan had been at war with the Republic of China. Japan colonized Manchuria and wanted to dive deeper into China. They tried this on July 7, 1937, at what is called the Marco Polo Bridge Incident.[7] Japan was pushing its luck during this period because in their maneuverings, they also had attacked some American warships. Because of their aggression, world opinion condemned Japan.

Japan was far from satisfied with aggression, however, and in 1939 they decided to push into the Soviet Far East from Manchuria. The Soviets and the Mongolian forces teamed up and soundly defeated the Japanese. Still not satisfied, they decided to block China's only land route to the outside world by seizing Indochina. At the time Indochina was controlled by Vichy France. Japan was under agreement with Vichy France, and thus the terms of the agreement had been broken. Fighting broke out, and Japan did win this battle. Japan was never truly successful in conquering much of China because they were not able to control the vast Chinese countryside or other holdings that would secure an overall victory.

They did, however, sponsor several puppet governments, but they were so brutal against the Chinese people that it did not work, and they would not relinquish any real power to the mock government they set up. All in all, the Japanese armies were so brutal against the Chinese that nothing the Japanese did made the Chinese population submit to their rule. From time to time the Japanese rulers of the armies sought to appease those under their command within the Shanghai Chinese population. Not only did the Chinese population resist, but they also became more nationalistic.[8]

Once the Japanese felt that the nationalist government would not yield to their demands, it was all-out massacre time, and nothing was held back or barred. In the city of Nanking (now Nanjing), "the liquidation of that city and its inhabitants became known as the Nanjing Massacre. As many as 300,000 Chinese civilians and surrendered troops were killed. [There were] tens of thousands of women that were raped on the orders of Japanese commander Matsui Iwane."[9]

Japan's expansionist philosophies, which became heavily influenced by Tojo, eventually led to economic sanctions conducted by several Western powers, including the United States and Britain. Trying to discourage Japan from further militaristic aggression, Western powers, including the United States, Australia, Britain, and the Dutch, decided to stop selling steel, iron ore, and oil to Japan. These were the raw materials Japan needed to continue any type of war effort and civilian efforts as well. The oil alone made up about 80 percent of its domestic consumption, and the other resources were needed for many other important facets of day-to-day life and activities. Japan looked upon these embargoes as acts of aggression because their results would bring all of its economy and military to a screeching halt.[10] In reality Japan knew it wasn't an act of aggression but part of a larger plan that was about to unfold and would be shown for what it was.

Japan had a tremendous foothold on China, but not nearly as tight as it needed to have because China was constantly resisting a tighter grip from Japan no matter the devastation being imposed. Japan knew that they had to be able to secure a stronger hold on towns, cities, bridges, and railroads because if not, these areas would fall into the hands of Chinese guerilla resistance.

Japan thought China would fold when Nanking, the capital, fell. However, that did not happen. They tried countless strategies to get the Chinese to surrender, but those strategies did not work. China was just too large and too determined not to surrender. The Chinese were as relentless in resisting as were the Japanese in advancing. It was during this time that World War II had broken out and there seemed to be brighter possibilities elsewhere.

As many other nations were witnessing acts of aggression of Japan against China, the United States was applying economic pressure against Japan in refusing to sell scrap metal, oil, and other products to Japan. Japan, on the other hand, had ulterior motives, especially when France fell. It was obvious that France could not protect its wealth in the Far East, Britain was going at it alone against Germany, and Holland was also unable to protect its holdings. This was the signal for Japan as to who the next victims would be. The only major deterrent was the United States.

Had Japan directly attacked French Indochina, the Dutch East Indies, and British Malaya, to name a few, but not attack Pearl Harbor, the U.S. Congress might have taken six months to a year to approve war with Japan. By that time Japan could have taken hold of all these possessions. However, Japan was ruled by its military and would not listen to its civilian counsel and advisers. As a result, the military felt that to attack Pearl Harbor and the United States Fleet would cripple the United States, and they would be powerless to assist.[11]

In the final days preceding the attack on Pearl Harbor, the admiral of the combined fleet and also the original planner of the attack, Admiral Isoroku Yamamoto, went to visit Prime Minister

Konoe. At this point Konoe was concerned that no matter what, even with any talks that were to be, even with President Roosevelt, war was inevitable.[12]

With the prime minister sensing that the United States wanted to annihilate Japan rather than hold any talks of peace, and even though the admiral had personally come to reassure him regarding the navy, Prime Minister Konoe was not relieved. When Japan's early October deadline for rectifying relations between the United States and Japan passed with very little progress, and also Emperor Hirohito then indicated that war was almost certain, the next day was Konoe's last cabinet meeting, but Army Minister Tojo did the majority of the talking.

> For the past six months, ever since April, the foreign minister has made painstaking efforts to adjust relations. Although I respect him for that, we remain deadlocked.... Our decision was to start the war ... if by early October we cannot thoroughly achieve our demands through negotiations. Today is the fourteenth. We are mobilizing hundreds of thousands of soldiers.... I would not mind stopping them, and indeed *would* have to stop them if there was a way for a diplomatic breakthrough. The heart of the matter is the [imposition on us of] withdrawal [from Indochina and China]. If we yield to America's demands, it will destroy the fruits of the China Incident. Manchukuo will be endangered, and our control of Korea undermined.[13]

Although Konoe recommended Prince Higashikuni to succeed him, Hirohito was not in agreement with his choice or that of others. Hirohito was well satisfied with Tojo as the new prime minister and successor, and therefore Tojo was elected. Once Tojo was the new prime minister, those around him, including the emperor, knew that war was inevitable. Still, there were rounds and rounds of talk with government leaders and senior statesmen, with many in opposition to war with America, but to no avail.[14] The Pacific War began as Japanese aircraft attacked the American naval base of Pearl Harbor on December 7, 1941. Hideki Tojo was here!

It was imperative and a must that these new Marine recruits who were soon to be at Montford Point Camp be given the necessary training and equipment needed so that they could take their part in becoming a major and integral unit of the great history that they would later be known for. It was certainly not a time for stalling.

This war, called the Pacific War and also called the Asia-Pacific War, paints a picture of the part of the world that World War

II took place in and around. This place was the Pacific Ocean, the islands that surrounded it, and also in East Asia. The term *Pacific War* encompasses those areas that are also referred to as the Pacific Ocean Theater, the Southwest Pacific Theater, the Southeast Asian Theater, and the Second Sino-Japanese War.

On December 7 and 8, 1941, with respect to the International Date Line, Japan attacked not only Pearl Harbor. "Almost simultaneously the Japanese attacked Hawaii, the Philippines, Wake, Guam, Singapore, Hong Kong, Malaya, and Thailand. All these assaults, even the one against Pearl Harbor, had been foreseen, but no one had anticipated that they would all be made at once, on the first day of war."[15]

Prior to the bombing of Pearl Harbor, with fears and embarrassment as a result of the embargoes looming on the horizon, Japan decided to take their military might in another direction: toward the Western powers. Planning began in April or May 1941. Here is where that other part of the Pacific terminology comes into play: the Southwest Pacific Theater and the Southeast Asian Theater. This plan was to be executed by the Southern Expeditionary Army Group, responsible for all army operations in Southeast Asia and southwest Pacific campaigns. The Southern Army Group was formed on November 6, 1941, as final preparations were being made for the attack on Pearl Harbor and to establish the order of battle for the group. Their mission was to occupy the Philippines, British Malaya, the Dutch Indies, and part of Southern Burma.[16]

The primary objective for the Southern Army Group was to seize economic resources under the control of Britain and the Netherlands, especially those in Malaya and the Dutch East Indies, known as the Southern Plan. Knowing of the close relationship that existed between Britain and the United States, and the idea that the United States would become involved, Japan would also require an Eastern Plan.

The Eastern Plan would mean attacks on the U.S. Pacific Fleet at Pearl Harbor, Hawaii. After this attack they would immediately seize the Philippines and then cut the lines of communication by seizing Guam and Wake.

The Southern Plans called for attacking Hong Kong and Malaya, Java and Sumatra, and some other strategic locations, and being able to isolate Australia and New Zealand. With these locations under their control, they would then hope for peace through negotiations. Unfortunately for Japan, those peace plans never materialized and remained on the drawing board.

The Japanese Empire, ready to begin a mission of overpowering and taking the necessary oil and scrap metal to continue the war, were already planning to cripple the United States Fleet at Pearl Harbor because they knew that the United States was the only obstacle in stopping them in their mission. France had already fallen in 1940, and to Japan was powerless in the Far East. The Netherlands was defenseless, and Britain was using all of its might against Germany. The military rulers, who by this time ruled the Japanese Empire, believed that the United States was the only obstacle in their path.

Also, by this time the "Civilian Council and diplomatic advisers were no longer listened to in Tokyo."[17] If respect for the Civilian Council had been acknowledged, the military rulers might have learned that under the U.S. Constitution, no matter how badly America would have wanted to declare war, it would not have happened immediately. If Japan had attacked only Malaya and the Dutch East Indies, as originally planned, the United States would still have probably taken six months to a year to join the fray. By this time Japan would have conquered all that it set out to conquer, and its mission might have been achieved.[18] However, the way the military rulers saw it in Japan is that if Pearl Harbor were removed, and if Guam and the Philippines were overpowered, America would also be powerless to stop any moves. With this rigid military, and one vision, it left a complete part of the equation—the main part—off the table.

With all of the plans Japan had on the war table, it is no wonder that they took the United States completely by surprise. America thought the Japanese military would attack only the Philippines and Southeast Asia, but how wrong they were. Almost simultaneously the Japanese attacked Hawaii, the Philippines, Wake, Guam, Singapore, Hong Kong, Malaya, and Thailand. All these assaults, even the one against Pearl Harbor, had been foreseen but no one had anticipated that they would all be made at once, on the first day of war.

CHAPTER 6

Last Stop: Montford Where?

Although the United States Marine Corps tried persistently, although unsuccessfully, to keep African Americans from the Corps, it could not be prevented. On the wings of Executive Order 8802, the first recruits were arriving at Montford Point Camp. It was August 26, 1942. Montford Point Camp is located in Jacksonville, North Carolina, a part of Camp Lejeune but without a doubt separate and apart. These were the segregated facilities that these men were arriving at this day. Montford Point Camp is located off Highway 24 and about a mile from this main road through the pinelands.

Once through, there were some buildings that were part of the facilities that these men would utilize while here at boot camp. According to reports in *Blacks in the Marine Corps* by Henry I. Shaw Jr. and Ralph Donnelly:

> There was: ... a headquarters building, a chapel, two warehouses, a theater building with two wings, which later housed a library, barber shop, [and] classification room on one side and a recreation slop chute [beer hall] on the other, a dispensary building, a mess hall, designated by the recruits as "The Greasy Spoon," quarters and facilities for the SES personnel, a small steam generating plant, a small motor transport compound, a small officers' club, and 120 green prefabricated huts, each designed for billeting 16 men.
>
> Surrounding the open spaces of the main camp area were thick pine forests. Beyond the north forest area was Highway 24, to the south the point of land that gave the area its name thrust into the New River, to the west was the river, Wilson Bay, and the town of Jacksonville, and to the east was Scales Creek, which had notorious areas of quicksand. Across the creek was an old Civilian Conservation Corps (CCC) camp area now partially occupied by a war dog

> training center. In all there was about 5½ square miles of rugged ground in the original camp site. Mosquitoes abounded, the woods were full of snakes, and bears padded about through the camp, much to the consternation of recruits who saw their tracks when they fell out for morning roll call. There was a lot of bush in the camp area to start off with, but the boots soon cleared it away or wore it away with their incessant drilling.[1]

Once at the segregated camp, called Camp Montford Point, the men began their basic training. The first 1,200 quota of men lived in Quonsets. These were not the modern-day metal corrugated Quonset huts but the compressed, almost cardboard-like type of material. One recruit named Oscar Culp described the barracks as being made out of cardboard. He said the water was bad, it was extremely cold in the winter, and that ice would be on the floor where he slept. Culp was also a young recruit who had just turned eighteen and had joined the Marines in 1943. He was from Charlotte, North Carolina.

Thomas Mosley's opinion of the interior of the Quonset hut by the time he arrived was that there was a huge potbellied stove in the middle of the barracks, and "if you wanted to stay somewhat comfortable and warm, you had to keep that fire going."[2] However, after a more thorough study of Montford Point, one realizes that by the time Dad arrived, there was another phase of building that was underway. It was in a different type of Quonset hut that Dad and other recruits were able to stay in.

Although nearby, the men from Montford Point were not allowed to enter Camp Lejeune unless they were accompanied by a White Marine or a White officer. I've read more often that it had to be a White officer that did the accompanying. Also, it did not matter what your station was in life prior to the camp. You may have been a professor at a university, or a medical doctor or any other type of professional, even so, you were given the rank of private.

While the Corps had its share of problems at Montford Point Camp in that the Black Marines were treated as inferior to White Marines, there was also the hostile climate that existed outside the base. Local business owners, eager to take the money from the

Marines, were not eager to provide the services they received the money for and also treated the Marines as second-class citizens. Some servicemen were denied service in restaurants even though they were in training and stood ready to lay their lives on the line for their country and for the very ones that were denying them a service. As an added note, many did get injuries of all types, and many did lose their lives.

> In early December, the new graduates had their first opportunity to go on liberty and poured out the front gate walking down the long road to Jacksonville. Their reception was a rude awakening to the men. The sight of a couple of hundred Blacks in Marine green coming into the little town was unnerving to the merchants, and they closed down their stores. They had no intention of staying in town. They wanted to get out, to take a bus to Wilmington, Kinston, or New Bern; larger towns with substantial black populations.[3]

Life was drab and challenging for the Black Marines at Montford Point, and the drill instructors gave the men the basic treatment as they would at all training facilities, but in addition to the basics, the negativities and hatred played a major role. The basics of this training could have been at Parris Island, or San Diego, or here with Blacks at Montford Point. However, at Montford Point, the challenges were different. The White drill instructors had never

Thomas Mosley, standing fifth from left, Montford Point Camp, January 1944.

encountered any standard routines as a guide to molding Black recruits, and also, they were not reasonable, to say the least, in working with these recruits as human beings. These recruits, like any other Marines, were capable of growing and developing and being shaped into the type of soldier desired by the Corps as any other trainee given the time and proper motivation. Given the fact that these drill instructors felt that these recruits were undeserving of being in the Corps, most restraints were lifted, and there seemed to be an overwhelming desire to treat these recruits as those who would never make the grade, and if they did make the grade, it wasn't because they were given any type of free pass, especially from these hard-core drill instructors.

However, one Marine, Oscar Culp, said that "Montford Point was hell, really," and recalled watching the rifle butt of a White drill instructor being slammed into the back of men's heads because the trainees could not keep step. "You just had to take it: take a rifle snapped across your head or be kicked. It didn't happen to me, but I saw it happen to other people."[4]

In a speech by Gunnery Sergeant Elijah Abram (USMC-Ret.), who at the time—February 28, 1998—was Vice President of the Montford Point Marine Association, Sergeant Abram reiterated that "there were five different commands that were

Thomas Mosley, standing third from left, Montford Point Camp, January 1944.

maintained at Montford Point during the war period: Recruit Depot, Headquarters, Stewards Branch, Defense Battalion, and a separate Infantry Battalion with attached Depot and Ammunition Companies, which ably assisted in landing operations of the Fleet Marine Force."[5] He went on to indicate that there were not just two Recruit Depots in the Marine Corps but actually three. In the Recruit Depot Battalion every "boot" received basic training similar to that of any leatherneck at Parris Island and San Diego. History will note later that there were not just two Recruit Depots in the Marine Corps but three: "Montford Point Camp was often left out of historical records."

The question then becomes, Why have people never heard of Montford Point Camp when almost twenty thousand African Americans spent their basic training there from 1942 to 1949? Montford Point Camp was left out intentionally from mainstream historical records, although these men were gallant soldiers with courage of steel, love of country and fellow human beings, who fought for America and were part of and supported major infantrymen all over the world.

Once again it was now time for African Americans to bring forth their courage for battle. The U.S. Marine Corps was the last stronghold of military units in the United States for the patriotism and courage of the African American to be shown to. On August

Thomas Mosley (right) instructing on drill, Montford Point Camp, January 1944.

18, 1942, the Headquarters and Service Battery of the 51st Composite Defense Battalion was activated at Montford Point. In order to keep these Black recruits and Marine soldiers away from the White Marines at Camp Lejeune, it was here at this "lonely outpost" of Camp Lejeune—Montford Point Camp was five to seven miles away and adjacent to Camp Lejeune—that these men were to be stationed. Under the firm grip of some hard-core drill instructors, these new recruits would learn from the first day varying lessons, all of which reinforced that these drill instructors would be firm and that not an inch would be given to anyone for anything. They would learn the values of the Corps or leave.

Culbreth, a cook at the camp, 1944.

The training was so grueling that even the toughest men had the most difficult times during boot camp and basic training. At the time, the first defense battalions were being developed, namely the 51st and the 52nd Composite Defense Battalions. There were twenty-three officers and ninety enlisted men called SES men or Special Enlisted Staff. Within this group of men there were a few very experienced officers and warrant officers, although the majority of commissioned strength was second lieutenants who had just recently completed officers training at Quantico, Virginia, at Marine Corps school. These men would fulfill the necessary tasks needed such as the drill instructors (DIs), clerical duties, motor transport, and other duties pertinent to completing these battalions.[6]

According to Gilbert H. Johnson, one of the first recruits, these drill instructor's "set about from the very beginning to get us thoroughly indoctrinated into the habits and the thinking and the actions of the Marine Corps. Discipline seemed to be their lone stock in trade, and they applied it with a vengeance, very much to our later benefit."[7]

However, with Johnson's background of six years in the Army as well as most of the 1930s in the Navy, he could also recognize an aspect of the shaping and molding of individual characteristics necessary for being a U.S. Marine. Hence, the added comment regarding the character of these SES drill instructors and that "the policy was to select the type of individuals who were not against the Negro being a Marine, and had it been otherwise, why, I'm afraid that we would have all left the first week. Some of us, probably, the first night."[8]

Two unidentified Marines taking a breather from training, 1944.

Overall, new enlistees for the entire Marine Corps were at an all-time high after the attack. Prior to Pearl Harbor being attacked in December 1941 there were approximately two thousand recruits per month, but following that date, according to Benis M. Frank and Henry I. Shaw in "History of U.S. Marine Corps Operations in World War II," the numbers were over twenty thousand. From a broader perspective, "The July 1941 strength of the Corps was 53,886; a year later, after the Pearl Harbor attack impelled ... Marine Corps strength had increased to 143,388."[9]

Because of the effort to reach the goals of maximum strength in a short time period, the recruit depots were bursting at the seams. As a result of this pressure, General Holcomb, on January 1, 1942, decided to reduce the training of recruits to a five-week course. Of course, within this time frame a recruit was still required to take over 188 hours of a major discipline. There were 96 hours of weapons training, 56 hours of drilling, many more hours of field training, and at least 4 hours of physical training. For a brief period of time beginning in February, the training schedule went to a six-week period, but then on March 1, 1942, went back to the seven-week schedule. The seven-week period consisted of the recruits having three weeks at the recruit depot, then two weeks at the range, and the rest of the time during boot camp at the depot. Along with more efficient time management for the seven-week schedule, more instruction on the most important subjects was given.[10]

Beginning in 1944, and especially after complaints were being lodged against the recruits from the other schools that these recruits were attending, General Holcomb established what would be called a master eight-week training schedule that was to be followed by "both recruit depots." As if the recruits at Montford Point Camp were not in the throes of the most serious thrashing, out of whatever training camps were being utilized for boot camp, they were not mentioned in all of the training sessions indicated by the U.S. Marine Corps.

Although stories abound about how tough one had to be to be a Marine, then and now, I know many never got the true picture. At Montford Point it wasn't just the roll out of bed for early morning roll call, or the up-in-the-face hollering, or even the many marching-through-the-swamps days, Thomas Mosley recalled. "It was much more than that. When the first drill instructors were there, they were all White, and there was plenty of friction and other negativities to go around. A good majority of the recruits could not wait for them to be relieved of duty and to have Black drill instructors take their place, as the formula had called for."

However, many of the men were to be in for a rude awakening. The major consensus of these enlistees was that the treatment got worse after they indeed left. One recruit, who joined the Corps in 1943, remembers when he first arrived at Montford Point Camp after being dropped off by the Marine bus. They began lining us up and asking our names," Lee Douglas Jr. said.

"And if you didn't speak fast enough, you got a slap in the face, which I wasn't used to."[11]

"And you look at the way they were handling other people, knocking them down and so on; it made me stand up and try to be strong. Because they asked you a question, you better come out with an answer, to their liking, in a hurry. One person did not speak to them right, and they grabbed him in the collar, and he grabbed one of the Marines. And one struck him in the head with the butt of a pistol. So therefore we knew that you'd got to straighten up and fly right."[12]

Thomas Mosley at Montford Point Camp, January 1944.

You were referred to as an "extra man" and you kept your own street clothes on for a few days until you were put into a platoon. He says he didn't remember the racism as much as he remembers the brutality. By not being accustomed, he says, to the Marine Corps method of being awakened with shouts and hollers, he was totally taken by surprise when mornings came initially for reveille. "If you didn't immediately rise and jump out of bed, you were snatched out of the bed onto the floor. Everything you did you did with speed. You could not walk anywhere. If you were the last man out of the barracks, you knew punishment was on its way."[13]

Isaac David Frasier, who also joined the Marines in 1943, remembers his first day at the camp as well. Apparently loving the zoot suit look, he wore his wide-brimmed hat and his large overcoat. After having to remove those items, he was told to place them between his legs, on the ground, and to commence stomping on them. The drill instructor told him he never wanted to see those items again.[14]

Truman Boone of the 5th Marine Ammunition Company described some of the rigors of boot camp. He was born in Sedalia,

North Carolina. Raised by his grandmother, he joined the Corps in November 1943 and ended up in the 5th Marine Ammunition Company. His recollection is that boot camp was about twelve weeks and was seriously rough. "Everywhere you went, you had to run. You had to run to eat; you had to run to train. When you hit the doors, you had to start running. During this period of time all you did was march, read your books, and study. It was grueling."[15] Like the other men described, he knew that after boot camp, and the detailed rifle training, he would be considered a Marine. It did not matter what anyone else thought; he and the others knew that they were Marines. "There was no denying this fact. Once you had this training; you knew you were absolutely a Marine for life."[16] Before that time, though, let us check out Montford Point Camp.

CHAPTER 7

Why Me, Oh, Lord?

Thomas Mosley enlisted on November 16, 1943, at the recruiting station in Philadelphia.[1] He was only nineteen years old. After recruitment, he boarded a train and went back to Steelton, Pennsylvania. He spent a short time there before embarking on his new and uncertain journey. Before Dad's arrival at Montford Point Camp, there were some major changes that had taken place. Most importantly, some of these changes need to be disclosed at this point and others throughout this book. Remember, this was all new, and the major changes had to do with where to install these new recruits—they could not hide them, and they had to be established somewhere. But where?

Thomas Mosley, 5th Ammunition Company, 365th Platoon, early 1944.

This journey certainly was uncertain for Dad because even though he was accepted to serve in the U.S. Marine Corps, the Marine Corps was uncertain about what to do with him as well as the other recruits that had already been inducted and were at Camp Lejeune. Fortunately, though, by the time Dad arrived, there was a formula being followed that was already in motion, and the kinks were being worked out.

According to research done by Henry I. Shaw and Ralph Donnelly, there was a study done by Brigadier General Keller E. Rockey, Director of the Division of Plans and Policies, about which area of the Marine Corps these "Negro" men might be able to fit into. He and others felt that these men could not serve in combat, and so what to do with them was something that seriously needed to be worked out.[2] They had used numbers that had been taken from the Army that showed that the test scores these men had taken during the general classification exams resulted in

These Marines of the first platoon to enter training at Montford Point were promoted to private first class a month before completion of boot camp and became assistant drill instructors. From left: Mortimer A. Cox, Arnold R. Bostic, Edgar R. Davis Jr., Gilbert H. "Hashmark" Johnson, Edgar R. Huff, Charles E. Allen.

low scores. The Marines tried to use this too, but eventually that excuse would not work.

These men were going to serve in combat: initially composite defense battalions that would contain antiaircraft artillery, seacoast artillery, and whatever was needed for the type of defense in the type of mission that these men would be embarking on. Other units had used these formulas previously, and as long as they were carried out properly, they would hopefully work for these men also, but the numbers had to be kept small for test purposes.

The study also included the name of one commanding officer

who was felt to be the one most suited for helping to work out and implement these new plans. This officer was to be the one in charge of all Black Marine training. His name was Colonel Samuel A. Woods Jr., and he was a graduate of the Citadel. Colonel Woods was from South Carolina and had at least twenty-five years as an officer. He had served in both China and the Philippines and had been in the Dominican Republic and in France during World War I.[3]

Another hardship at Montford Point: the mess hall tables. They are nothing more than four- by eight-foot pieces of plywood set atop sawhorses that take a skilled craftsman about five minutes to build.

Colonel Woods had to present his plans to the board, which was accepted, but there were modifications made. Colonel Woods wanted to start out with a minimum of one thousand Black reserve recruits, as was indicated somewhat according to plans, who would form a defense battalion and be ready for combat after six months. This tied into what General Holcomb proposed earlier before the Navy Board. They were to begin their training at Mumford Point, which later would be renamed Montford Point, at the Marine barracks in New River, North Carolina. A sum of $750,000 would be used for additional construction and modifications.[4] This site would be the only one used for training these new Black recruits.

One of the most unusual experiences Dad remembered about his arrival at the Point is that when he and fellow recruits were finally given their clothing or fatigues, they were from the previous men of the previous platoons that had already gone through boot camp. He remarked that they had to match up their sizes for all of their clothing, from top to bottom, the best they could from what was available.[5] One can only imagine the condition of the clothing after the grueling workouts the previous platoons had encountered as Marines. Fortunately, this did not last very long, and in a few days he and the other men were issued their own set of clothing.

By this time Montford Point Camp was "hot and smokin'." The standard table of organization did not apply to all aspects and details of training. "For example," Dad remarked, "Under most circumstances to receive rank, you had to earn it, and nothing was given for free. Of course, nothing here was given for free either, although some rank that may normally have taken many years to attain found its way to some of these recruits through different methods as a matter of accelerating the process of having Black NCOs in charge of these recruits." The goal once again was to have these men active and ready to ship out in the shortest time possible.

With this in mind, many of these new recruits that would eventually be selected as NCOs would have to learn on the job.

Members of the clerical pool. These men were entrusted with the most vital information.

Many of these first NCOs were selected because they were older, and of course had some things on the ball, but most of the younger guys were not selected as such. These are words that were emphasized on more than one occasion. After all, he had a bird's-eye view.

Thomas Mosley was in the 5th Ammunition Company out of Montford Point Camp and in support of the 5th Marine Division. He was in the 365th Platoon in boot camp. Dad said he left home on November 26, the day after Thanksgiving, heading for boot camp at Montford Point Camp. He was certainly not the only one heading to that hub. There were Marine recruits from New Jersey, Virginia, Pennsylvania, New York, North Carolina, South Carolina, and other states as well. Montford Point was abuzz as hundreds of Marines poured into Camp Lejeune. New recruit companies and new motor transport companies were added to Montford Point, serving the new recruits as companies.

Some of the most drastic changes taking place at the camp were the drill instructor changes. They were going from White to Black. By the end of April 1943, almost all of the Special Enlisted Service (SES) drill instructors had gone. Black sergeants and corporals took over as the senior drill instructors of the eight platoons then in training:

- 16th Platoon: Edgar Huff
- 17th Platoon: Thomas Brokaw
- 18th Platoon: Charles E Allen
- 19th Platoon: Gilbert H. Johnson
- 20th Platoon: Arnold R. Bostic
- 21st Platoon: Mortimer A. Cox
- 22nd Platoon: Edgar R. Davis Jr.
- 23rd Platoon: George A. Jackson

Some distinguished Marines that should be noted at this period are as follows:

- John T. Pridgen: member of the Black 10th Calvary in the late 1930s.
- George A. Jackson: Army lieutenant.
- Charles Anderson: graduate of Morehouse College. He became the first Black sergeant of Montford Point.
- Corporal Arvin L. "Tony" Ghazlo: former bodyguard and jujitsu instructor from Philadelphia. He was also a senior bayonet and unarmed combat instructor.
- Ernest "Judo" Jones: principal assistant to Ghazlo.
- Charles Simmons: graduate of Alcorn A&M with a master's degree from the University of Illinois. He became the Sergeant Major of the 51st Defense Battalion.

In late May, the last White drill instructor, First Sergeant Robert W. Colwell, was transferred, and Sergeant Gilbert "Hashmark" Johnson took his place as the recruit battalion's Field Sergeant Major, in charge of all drill instructors. Sergeant Thomas Pridgen was his assistant. From that point on, all recruit training at Montford Point was conducted by Black noncommissioned field officers (NCFOs). This in itself was a huge milestone, although boot camp did not get any easier. In fact, the testimony of many was that it got harder and stayed harder.

Hashmark Johnson, first as Field Sergeant Major, then as Sergeant Major of the Recruit Depot Battalion, was determined the black boots would measure up to the standard of the Marine Corps in every way. In later years, while addressing a group of veterans of that era, he made the following comments:

> I was an ogre to some of you who met me on the drill field and in the huts of Montford more than a quarter century ago. I was a stern instructor, but I was fair. I was an exacting instructor, but with some understanding of the many problems involved. I kept before me, always, that nearly impossible goal to qualify in a few weeks, and at the most a few months, a type of Marine fully qualified in every respect to wear that much cherished Globe and Anchor.
>
> You were untried. The objectives were to qualify you with loyalty, with a devotion to duty, and with a determination equal to all, transcended by none.... As I look into your faces tonight, I remember the youthful, and sometimes pained expressions at something I may have said.... But I remember something you did. You measured up, by a slim margin, perhaps, but measure up you did. You achieved your goal. That realization creates within me a warm appreciation of you and a deep sense of personal gratitude.[6]

I cite Sergeant Major Gilbert Johnson's personality, because as you read of his history and personality, you will find that he was a remarkable man. He was also one of the first Blacks to enlist in the Marines. He was born in rural Mount Hebron, Alabama, and attended Stillman College in 1922 with the aspiration of

Sergeant Gilbert "Hashmark" Johnson inspecting his troops.

becoming a minister.[7] Stillman College was founded in 1875 under the auspices of the Presbyterian Church and was chartered as a legal corporation by the state of Alabama in 1895. At that time, the name was changed from Tuscaloosa Institute to Stillman Institute. It had an established and accredited junior college. Hashmark Johnson left college the following year and joined the Army. At the end of his enlistment in 1929, he was discharged as a Corporal. After four years as a civilian, Johnson decided to join the Navy.[8]

Johnson served in the navy for almost ten years. He was aboard the USS *Wyoming* during the bombing of Pearl Harbor in 1941. The following year, after President Roosevelt issued Executive Order 8802, Johnson immediately requested a transfer from the Navy into the Marines, to serve the last seventeen years of his thirty-two-year military career in the Marine Corps.

Sergeant Major Edgar R. Huff.

According to Gail Buckley, in her outstanding national best-seller *American Patriots: The Story of Blacks in the Military from the Revolution to Desert Storm,* when referring to Gilbert Johnson on his arrival at Montford Point, said that Johnson "was so impressive in his naval uniform," standing before Huff, who was already at Montford Point, "with three stripes up and three stripes down his arm, that Huff stood at attention until Johnson said, "Son, sit down."[9]

This was a man whose military experience could be passed on to the younger and less experienced comrades. In analyzing Johnson, one gets the sense he felt that if anyone were going to build up the men in the ranks, or "break them down" to the standard of the Corps, it would be him. He had the military background and the wherewithal to understand the level that these men had to be at in order to not fall short. Sergeant Johnson without question had seen his share of racism and prejudices during his youth and time spent in the military. He had all the information at his disposal and in his mind that was needed to be able to pass on to the new Marines and knew that he could be successful at training these men. He knew because he himself had been able to pass all of the rigors that had been imposed upon him, in his previous years, and that he could pass this information on and allow his fellow brethren to be successful and worthy Marines in the United States Marine Corps. He also knew that if these men could not pass his tests that they would not be able to pass the tests that awaited them in the framework of those that had no human kindness for these men at all. With that being said, Sergeant Johnson knew that it would take all that these men could muster to meet the challenges that were at hand. However, he knew that it was achievable because when he decided to transfer from the Navy to the Corps, he gave up his pay rate, and he also gave up his rank, which was that of an Officer's Steward, First Class. This was equivalent to a Marine Corps Staff Sergeant, and he began his stint in the Corps as a private.

Montford Point Camp. The tents in the background housed the first Marine recruits.

While Dad was at Montford Point Camp, he served as a platoon guide for his platoon. Under normal circumstances, the guide is the person who is in charge when the drill instructors are not present. The guide is in charge of the squad leaders and normally gives instructions to the squad leaders as well as the recruits. During times of marching, they then repeat the drill instructors' commands when the drill instructors are there. However, I do not have the details of Dad's responsibilities as a guide while at Montford Point because these were not ordinary times nor circumstances. Typically, his job would be to make sure that his platoon was accounted for and whatever other duties were asked of him. Technically he would have ranked higher, in terms of responsibilities, than the other men of equal rank because of his duties and other requests that were asked of him, but he did not have higher rank or pay at that time. Dad said things were moving at such breakneck speed that he does not recall all of his duties that were at hand.

"Every time we prepared to march, or drill, my Company

Commander would call my name to take the position as the guide. 'Mose-lay,' he would shout, "take your position!" I would then go to the forward and right side of our platoon, and once I assumed my position, and orders given, we would begin the march. After a few times of being told, it was automatic after that, that I would take my position as the guide."[10]

One thing is certain: Dad, like so many others, had to have been outstanding in his time at Montford Point because the drill instructors were constantly on the lookout for outstanding characteristics in their men. For Dad to have been one of the ones chosen to be a platoon guide shows that his leadership abilities must have shone from the outset. Another note to keep in mind is that the drill instructors at Montford Point were extremely harsh and critical and did not cut the men any slack at all. This being said, it shows that Dad was also a remarkable Marine, as many others were, but also one that was worthy to stand in the front of the platoon, and in front of these other great Montford Point Marines, as time has now shown them to be. Of course, Dad was not the only one, but there is a special emphasis being placed on him, my dad, in this narrative.

Another aspect that Dad relayed to me as well is that at the time of his training he noticed that a good majority of the men that were selected for training as drill instructors were slightly older than most of the other men. The second factor is that Dad was in an ammunition company, and outside of the additional

Marines at parade rest on the grounds of Montford Point Camp.

training needed for handling ammo, these men were firsthand pickings for the Fleet Marine Force, and most of these guys in ammunition squads and supply depots were moved out as soon as their training was completed. These were the guys that were needed to get the ammunition out to the front line, and they were needed desperately in the South Pacific.

It had been noted with certainty through the commanding officers and Marine planners that an immensely increased and improved supply system was needed in the Pacific. Most recruits at Montford Point Camp could not be moved out fast enough to man the supplies that were being shipped to the South Pacific. Using combat troops as were used initially was a major flaw in the operation of the ship-to-shore manpower needed to handle those duties. There were too many intricate areas of details that needed

A company of the "chosen few" practicing drill techniques.

to be followed in order to have success in the various requirements of this type of operation. Organization and control were a major factor in this type of operation, and hour-to-hour management and administration was a must for the continued flow that had to take place to keep supplies of all types moving to the front line and rear support bases. Dad's skills would be used as an ammunition specialist in the South Pacific, not at Montford Point.

With Johnson's type of drive deeply entrenched in his men at Montford Point, life was very trying for many. When I asked Dad about another sergeant, Sergeant Major Edgar Huff, of course he remembered many days of his presence, and he said, "He was a ba-a-ad man," as he used an inflection to emphasize the words *bad man*, meaning that he in particular and the other drill instructors were single-minded of mission and not to be taken lightly. Dad recollects Sergeant Huff mighty well, but it was not on a personal level. "By the time I arrived at Montford Point Camp, Sergeant Huff was not always out in the open field, as his duties kept him located elsewhere on the camp most times. But I wasn't looking to see him either, moreover, because if you were called to see him, most likely you were in some sort of trouble. Sergeant Huff was a big man and looked even bigger because of what he represented and the authority he carried over you. A guy like Sergeant Huff didn't play with you. You didn't mess with guys like that. You steered clear of them. Both Johnson and Huff would inspect our barracks, though."[11]

Dad remembered both Sergeant Major Huff and Sergeant Major Johnson when they would come into the barracks for an inspection. "After spending time making sure that our footlockers were packed the way we were taught to pack them and our beds were made according to the Marine standards, where you had to crease them a certain way, we would check everything to make sure things were right. The men would be hustling around, and nobody would be saying much of anything.[12] We all took pride in what we were doing and how we were looking. Belt buckles were shined up and we were all shaved up. The next thing you knew we'd get the order to stand at attention. Ol' Sergeant Huff and Sergeant Johnson would march in and march out almost before you realized it. They would stand at the foot of the bed and ask you a few questions. Going down the barracks, you'd hear them. Everything was serious. There was no smiling or grinning going on with anyone. These guys were top-notch, and they were serious too."

"What is your fifth General Order, soldier?" Huff might say. Then you'd hear another one, "Soldier, do you know what your first General Order is?"

My dad shook his head at that. "On and on they went, right on down the line. It seemed to me as if they were generals or at least colonels. No matter how fast they seemed to be in and out, by the time they left, you found yourself in a heavy sweat with no doubt they had been there for a while."[13]

Sergeant Major Edgar R. Huff had his own version of recruit training at Montford Point. During an interview later in life he described some of his own experiences. He arrived at Montford Point Camp on September 24, 1942, under the 51st Defense Battalion and was in the 16th Platoon. By January 15, 1943, he was promoted to private first class. Edgar Huff was an imposing figure, as Dad described, and he was well aware of this fact himself. One of Huff's reasons for joining the Corps, he said, is because it was the toughest thing around, and since he was tough too, this was the place for him.[14]

The disarmament techniques shown by Corporal Arvin Arvin L. "Tony" Ghazlo and performed on his assistant, Private Ernest "Judo" Jones, no doubt saved many lives in hand-to-hand combat overseas. Almost every Marine from Montford Point remembers these two soldiers.

Huff said he had a gung-ho attitude, and eyes were watching him as one of the men who might make a good fit as a drill instructor (DI). Huff said there were two White DIs over his platoon at that time, and roughly forty to forty-five men in the 16th Platoon going through this rigorous training. Before long he was singled out and transferred to the Recruit Depot to be trained as a drill instructor—as White DIs were being transferred overseas.[15]

Once his training was complete, ironically he took over as the drill instructor over the same 16th Platoon. In addition, there was no second DI to share this post with, as there had been two initially. The responsibility was his alone, and Sergeant Huff was up to the challenge. There was no turning back for him. The same could not be said for many of the other new recruits. By the time the boot camp training was over, almost a third of the original forty to forty-five men would no longer be a part of the 16th. "Living up to its reputation, Montford Point Camp saw many new recruits that were not able to stand up to the rigors of the type of intense training they were subjected to."[16]

Every part of the training of these men was at maximum intensity. From the morning reveille to the roll call to the evening breather, all was at breakneck intensity. There were swimming lessons under the leadership of Private Paul Tolliver, training in swamps, hiking for miles, hand-to-hand combat training with Private Ernest "Judo" Jones, who was the assistant to Corporal Arvin L. "Tony" Ghazlo, and the main instructor of self-defense at the camp.

Not initially realizing that this was what they would be doing for the length of time boot camp would take, and then being shipped off to put their lives on the line overseas, many recruits realized they had had enough and now it was time to go "over the hill." According to Sergeant Huff, many of the men just went missing. For many of those who tried to endure this type of training in the brutal climate of North Carolina, be it the intense heat of the sun or the frigid cold blasts of Arctic air, it was much too much, and many wound up in the hospital from pure fatigue.

These types of incidents all point to the fact that these physically fit, strong men, by any normal standards, were not wanted by the Marine Corps, and this type of training in many cases was not warranted, especially if they were to be made to feel that they were a part of a unit or an organization that cared about their well-being. Sergeant Huff himself, in later speeches, declared that the program set up for the African American "boots" at Montford Point Camp was nearly impossible to survive.

Naturally, with the rigors of the day-to-day marching in the grueling heat of the day, in the sweltering temperatures of

Enjoying some music on the jukebox.

cotton-belt North Carolina, the grueling training in camp and through the woods and forests, not always in the heat but in the freezing temperatures of winter months, someone is bound to question the need for this amount of training.

Dad emphasized that rather quickly, and once again, the men in his platoon and throughout Montford Point realized that the officers and drill instructors were not going to lighten up when it came to obeying commands and working to achieve that high

Washing eating utensils at the temporary barracks.

level of discipline that had to be acquired by these men for their mission.

Any that thought it would lighten up were sadly mistaken. Sergeant Huff disclosed that pressure only intensified on him from the above command structure as more and more of the quota of men that were the goal arrived at the camp every day. The training would not be slowing down. Another factor that contributed to this barrage of intensities was that many of the commanding officers thought they would be able to make it all go away if they stalled by not being as cooperative as they needed to be in meeting the prescribed quotas that were set.

Dad conveyed a story regarding one of the men that wanted to test the theory regarding "hear and obey." "One of the guys decided to become the spokesman for the group, but of course the group, or platoon, was not looking for a spokesman as they had already yielded to whatever the commands would be. However, this one recruit decided to challenge one of the officers."[17]

For whatever the reason this may have occurred with this individual, it did not take very long for him to receive his reciprocity from a particular DI. "That night," said Dad, "this spokesman found a mattress full of rifles, from side to side and top to bottom, on his bunk. This was to be his cushion for the night, after a hard day like we had down there, and then to be ready to go by 5 the next morning." As Dad and I conversed, he exclaimed, "Can you imagine having to sleep on a bunk full of hard rifles? You're already whipped and tired, then having to get up early the next day and go after it again. What kind of rest do you think you're going to get on a bed full of rifles? All of that metal and wood! After that incident," Dad said, "the man acted like he wanted to go out again and challenge the officer." Dad said he and the rest of the men told him, "Man, you haven't learned anything yet? Don't let your pride get the best of you. Day in and day out you're going to have to go up against men like these drill instructors, and you think you can get a win?"[18]

Dad and the rest of the platoon knew solidly that the drill instructors were not to be challenged. Why this man chose to want to go after a drill instructor was beyond them. Dad also said some of these drill instructors would challenge you by themselves; they had no fear regarding a challenge by one of the recruits. He also said that a lot of these recruits had come from areas like Philadelphia and New York City and been involved in gangs and the street life and had been drafted. Many of them learned sooner rather than later, but some others were hard-pressed to learn. Still some accepted that they were not knowledgeable in the ways of military life and even had to learn the right foot from the left. Some had to put something on their boot to distinguish which was which. Times were still hard in civilian life for many African Americans, and many men at Montford Point Camp could not read or write. Obviously, this was not the case for all, but it did exist. While continuing to talk, it was obvious that Dad was working on a

Thomas Mosley, 1944.

name to go with the face of the individual that had challenged the DI. "Raymond, oh, what was his name? I can't think of it right now," he said, not realizing he just had disclosed it. But one can see the indelible impression that was left in his mind about those circumstances from so many years ago.[19]

Dad said, "I will guarantee you he didn't do that again. That was the last time this man had an incident, and he relinquished his role as spokesman."[20] Dad said he learned his own lesson well, and one that was not nearly as harsh, long before this incident ever occurred. He remembered the time he was nineteen years old and had gone down to enlist while in his hometown. He ended up enlisting in the Marines. However, after second thoughts, as he recalled, he remembered a relative that had been in the Navy, and he thought he might want to be in the Navy as well. Unfortunately, he had already enlisted in the Corps as opposed to the Navy.

He expressed himself to the recruiting officer a little later. "Sir, I would like to be exchanged into the Navy instead of the Marines."

At that point he said the recruiter looked at him with a perplexed stare and countered back, in Marine Corps fashion, "Get back over there and sit down. What do you think this is, an exchange store?"

"That was my first order from a Marine Corps Officer," Dad said.[21]

During this conversation with Dad, and through conversations with other Montford Pointers, I have found that some of the memories expressed are extremely crystal clear. Some of the events that have been spoken by these men are as detailed as if they were expounding on a mathematical problem in calculus, step by step. Also, at the time of this conversation, Dad was full of energy as he detailed the ramifications of disobeying a drill instructor.

One of his favorite lines has always been, "Can you *imagine* that?" Here it was again, and I knew that a discourse, however short or long it may have been, was about to take place again.

He asserted that all of the men had realized by this time that you did not disobey your DIs or other officers in any way. It was always "Yes, sir," or "No, sir," and that was that. Dad's words were, "What one would do, all would be accounted for." There was none of that "Let the officer or drill instructor find out on his own." No, there was another code among these men. "If a person did something he was not going to get away with, you had to tell who did it, and most of the men were on the same page."

"Our primary focus while we were at Montford Point was on what the training was for us. We didn't concern ourselves very much about what other companies were doing, only about our main focus. You didn't even get to talk to guys from other platoons, let alone other companies. You got a war going on; you better learn all that you can learn while it is being taught to you because there might be something you miss that might save your life someday. I used to hear some of the other fellows talk about different things and how bad their hardships were; you might not like it, but what could you do about it? I knew early on even from when I tried to switch into the Navy that things were not going to be easy."[22]

Truman Boone remembered some of the commanding officers who were on post at the time as well. There was Colonel Woods, who was the commanding officer of all training at Montford Point, and then there was Lieutenant Joseph White, Boone's commander. Boone's intuition at the time was that these officers had already been overseas in battle. "I think Lieutenant White had been in combat because he went for bad. It was like he wanted you to know that no matter how tough you thought you were, he didn't care, and was waiting for you to try him so that he could put you in your place. He was a small man, and we called him Little Joe White," Mr. Boone recalled while laughing. "Huff was the same

Relaxing in the newer barracks, including Sergeant Edgar Huff, at center, with three stripes up and three stripes (or rockers, as Dad called them) down.

way. He tried to be bad too, and he made you straighten up."[23]

Colonel Samuel A. Woods was the commanding officer who designed the training program for the men at Montford Point, although the primary plans were from the top brass. He was the one in charge of implementing the formation of the plan. Originally the Marine Corps brass thought that since Southerners knew best how to command Blacks and knew the temperament of Blacks as well, they thought it best to use a commanding officer who was from the South, and Colonel Woods fit the mold. He had also graduated from the Citadel, South Carolina's military college. In addition, he was a well-seasoned veteran of the U.S. Marine Corps, having received a commission in 1906.[24]

Although the Corps was designed at the time to be segregated, and to remain as such, many soldiers at Montford Point Camp, after a time, felt that Colonel Woods was a fair and just commander. Colonel Woods had served time overseas in Haiti, Cuba, and France as well as the Dominican Republic and China. With the types of environments and circumstances Colonel Woods had been exposed to, and the discipline and experience that he had, it was no wonder that his proficiency and temperament shined through.

Truman Boone pointed out that coming from a small town such as Sedalia, North Carolina, he did not want to go into any large branch of service. He was drafted, and somehow, after contacting the draft board, he was able to get a deferment for a while. During this period, he said, "I left Sedalia to go work at the Naval

Sergeant Major Edgar R. Huff (front row, at center) and his platoon.

Yard in Portsmouth, Virginia. I was working there, but I kept the Draft Board informed as to my whereabouts. They let me go for a year, and then my time ran out. At that time, I had to report to Fort Bragg for examination, and then to Raleigh, North Carolina, where I was sworn in."

While at Fort Bragg, he had an encounter with a Navy recruiter. "Hey there, feller," said the recruiter, "the Army's full, but you'd make a good sailor for the Navy."

Boone's reply was, "No, thank you. Too much water." They gave me a fourteen-day furlough, and then I had to report back to Montford Point Camp. Shortly after I got there, the 51st got shipped out, and they put me in the 5th Ammo Company. I didn't have any choice in the matter, and there I was. My drill instructor's name was Sergeant Van Hook, and he was a Black drill instructor. It wasn't very long, it seemed, that we were at Montford Point because we were just so focused on our training, and before you knew it, we ourselves were on the ship heading out on our way to the Pacific."[25]

Joseph Ginyard was born in Philadelphia. He joined the Marine Corps in 1943. He was only seventeen years old, and little did he know what was in store for him at Montford Point Camp. His story of the treatment that he and his fellow soldiers received at Montford Point is similar to the stories the other recruits talked about. Pastor Ginyard, as he is now known, shared the following:

> From the time Montford Point Camp opened until it closed, the stories are eerily the same, but unique and different all the same. That's why, when you spoke to these gentlemen, the stories they told were of proudness. They are absolutely proud to have represented the United States Marine Corps. Why? It is because they stood the test of time. They knew they were mistreated, degraded, and insulted, but they never gave up. They never gave up and, in the end, they were appreciative of the way in which they saw themselves beginning to be honored. These were very grateful men.
>
> They went through the harshest of training with little or no support from the drill instructors on up to those in command of the United States Marine Corps. That's why there

Thomas Mosley in 1944: a brief moment to smile before embarking on the USS *Lamar* for the South Pacific.

> was no choice but to accept all that you went through because there was absolutely nothing that you could do to change anything. All you could do was to put out the best that was in you, hope that you met the unreachable goals that were announced daily, and learned all that you could with the hopes that it would save your life in combat if it ever came down to that.[26]

Joseph Ginyard said he spent a lot of time studying his necessary manuals and remembering and rehashing what had been taught to him by his drill instructors. He also talked about his rifle range experience and recounted the times that he was a part of that. "I shot fifty rounds a day down in the rifle range," he said. "I had such a consistent interval in the way I fired my weapon that my body would just start rocking back and forth, back and forth. Also, when I was done, because I had fired the weapon that amount of times, my face would be puffed up because of the way the rifle rested against my cheek and took a large part of the recoil of the weapon."[27]

Every now and then there were more relaxing activities that went on at the camp. There were movies and shows, intramural sports, and music. There was plenty of music because there were men from the bands of Count Basie, Cab Calloway, Duke Ellington, and Erskine Hawkins who were in the ranks of the 51st Battalion Band, which ended up being the camp band.[28]

Of course, the band was top-notch and was capable of producing dance orchestras, jazz combos, and concert groups of the highest caliber. One of the young White officers at Montford Point was Lieutenant Robert W. Troup Jr., who was an accomplished musician and composer.

Montford Point Marines in dress blues.

It is ironic that Troup was born and raised in Harrisburg, Pennsylvania. Although my father was born in Steelton, Pennsylvania, he eventually moved to Harrisburg as a young man, and most of his children, including me, were born in Harrisburg and lived there for many years. As a matter of fact, many, many of our relatives live there to this day. Troup was also a graduate of the Wharton School, University of Pennsylvania, located in Philadelphia. Lieutenant Troup was the composer and writer of the classic hit "Route 66." He also wrote a song that, although it did not hit the charts like "Route 66," was certainly a huge hit to the men at camp, who would sing it all over Jacksonville. They could certainly feel and understand its content. Troup was the first White officer who had command of an all-Black unit at Montford Point. His song went something like this:

> Take me away from Jacksonville, 'cause I've had my fill
> and that's no lie,
> Take me away from Jacksonville, keep me away from
> Jacksonville till I die,
> Jacksonville stood still while the rest of the world
> passed by.[29]

It is said that this song could be heard all over Jacksonville, North Carolina. You could hear it being sung on the buses, on the trains, and in the streets. It took a strong hold on a lot of the soldiers there.

I also seemed to get a solid meaning and an unbelievable feel of this song because Dad had sung it for me on many occasions. As he sang it, I could feel Jacksonville come alive and feel the spirits of the soldiers and the pride one can only imagine they had coming out of their souls. Dad sang it with the same meaning, the same intensity as long ago, and probably even more so, because he was sharing it with his son and wanted me to feel those moments, no doubt, as he sang it years ago. I am sure of this, although he sang it in a softer voice while singing it to me. However, it was full of meaning, recollection, and conviction, not only for Dad, but with a newfound understanding for me of what these men went through. What was so riveting is that he was so in the moment, and I relished and basked in the glory of his beautiful voice while I vicariously imagined myself in Jacksonville, North Carolina, in 1943.

I know that I had overwhelmed him with my many calls, questions, and statements regarding Montford Point. Not only me, but his other children and grandchildren as well. He even had a presence on Facebook. I also know that my youngest sister, Sandra, had been right there at Dad's side as this large wave of victory was cascading him. I don't know all of the memories he shared with her, but I know she is full of pride and happiness over the "ol' boy," as she sometimes jokingly referred to him as the excitement built over the exciting news of the gold medal. The full meaning had not sunk in for him at the time, because although there was a tremendous amount of information on the computer and websites regarding the possibilities of these men receiving a Congressional Gold Medal, he was not a computer geek, and the information had yet to filter down to him. Besides, there was not very much local public or national news regarding these men and their story up until now, although that is rapidly changing. You can feel the electricity and the buzz. It is almost inevitable for this to happen, and one can only imagine what life will feel like then, for these men.

After all, the summary regarding what these men achieved is never-ending and is still being developed. One thing is certain, however, and that is that these men rightfully deserved these honors because of what they went through both at Montford Point and other outlying areas, and for the duties they performed overseas.

One stated fact that Sergeant Major Huff disclosed is best put in his own words: "'cause it was a very rigid type of training. It was almost impossible to survive. If you could get through training at Montford Point Camp, you could go through hell and sing a song."[30]

CHAPTER 8

Camp Lejeune: Part Training, Part Resort

The question becomes why was there so much distinction between Camp Lejeune and Montford Point Camp? Camp Lejeune was designated from the outset to become the best-equipped Marine station in the nation for any type of training for a Marine. Not only a home base for the Marines, it also served the Seabees, the Navy Construction Battalions, and for training in amphibious warfare. Camp Lejeune was massive at 173.68 square miles, of which 85,155 acres were on land and the balance, 26,000 acres, underwater. Eleven miles of Camp Lejeune were directly parallel to the Atlantic Ocean and could be used for any type of tactical training exercises necessary for training the 22,000 or more Marines who would be stationed there.[1]

Before delving into details of what would later become mainstays at Camp Lejeune, we need to start from the inception of the proposed plans for the camp. Since Quantico Base and Parris Island, two other bases used for Marine training, had become too small for the Marines, this new site of Camp Lejeune had been requested, decided upon, and negotiated to become the new home of Marine Corps training. On February 15, 1941, the request was granted and approved.[2]

The new location was perfect in that there was a tremendous amount of land that could be used for any type of purpose that the Corps could have imagined, and plenty of water and woods for recreation as well as training, and set well enough apart so that the two would never interfere with the other. This new location sat between two large rivers, the Neuse River and the New River. The Neuse River location was to be used for the new air station while the New River location was to be used for the ground base.

Camp Lejeune, as we now know it, was originally called Marine Barracks New River, North Carolina, but was changed to Camp Lejeune near the end of 1942. This honor was bestowed upon the Commanding General of the 2nd Army Division in World War I and the 13th Commandant Major General John A. Lejeune.[3]

On April 22, 1942, there were three firms that were awarded the initial contracts in the amount of $14,575,000 for building this Marine base. For the South this was an unheard-of amount. It was the largest ever that had been awarded for a military facility in Dixie.[4]

As stated by Gertrude S. Carraway, author of *Camp Lejeune Leathernecks,* written in 1946, "All work and no play makes Jack a dull boy"[5] was certainly true in this feature story.

Not known by me are the exact time frames for all of the facilities that were completed within this contract, but history records that in 1943, within Camp Lejeune, there were some extensive programs, including recreation and athletic facilities. There were theaters, gymnasiums, post exchanges, and facilities for women Marines. On Hadnot Point, within Camp Lejeune, there was the Hostess House, which was a sort of bed-and-breakfast for guests of the enlisted men and NCOs. Within a short time, in August 1943, there came to be a two-thousand-seat theater, and even more impressive was the fact that this was the ninth theater on the base, which also held movie productions and radio shows. On October 16, 1943, the first football team for the camps played in a ten-thousand-seat arena that was dedicated.[6]

On Wallace Creek, within the camp, there were a hundred rowboats, a hundred sailboats, and a hundred canoes for free use of the personnel on New River and its creeks. Along with boating, boat races and regattas were held frequently.[7]

Colonel Samuel A. Woods, who became well-known while at Montford Point among the Black Marines, established Montford Point Camp, and early in 1944 served as acting commanding officer at Camp Lejeune until Major General John Marston took over command until his retirement on July 2, 1946. Major General Marston had served thirty-eight years in the Marine Corps. Adjacent to Wallace Creek was the Marston Pavilion, named after the major general. The Marston Pavilion cost $168,000 to build and was befitting to the type of dance hall it was intended to be. It boasted two huge dance floors with more than 11,000 square feet of space. The grand opening of Marston Pavilion happened in November 1945, and after opening it was used by thousands of Marines and their guest while serving and on duty at Camp Lejeune. Louis Armstrong even played there once to a crowd of over four thousand people.[8]

Meanwhile, at another location on Onslow Beach within Camp Lejeune on the Atlantic Ocean, as many as ten thousand Marines visited on Sundays, it was reported, and for their use were a $100,000 officers club and a $200,000 beach house for enlisted Marines that contained a thousand lockers, snack bars, and a theater. There was, however, a $50,000 pavilion set aside for the Black Marines.[9]

Whatever the reasons, and for however long it was to last, Camp Lejeune continued to be designed and developed as a segregated facility. The segregation continued for some time until the men from Montford Point began to be exposed through the valor of the wars that they'd become a part of. It was then, and especially toward the end of World War II, that the Corps began to change the segregationist philosophy.

The Marines from Camp Lejeune, not Montford Point, were also allowed to hunt on the reservation, as the camp was referred to. The Marine Corps had the woods stocked with hundreds of quail at any given time. There were deer, foxes, weasels, and additional animals for the sport of hunting. For others who may have wanted to divert their attention to a different type of gamesmanship, there was a thirty-six-hole golf course. At the time it was one of the most heavily played courses in the nation. It was tremendously popular and in 1944 and 1945 was used by 58,000 people in one year.[10]

Toward my goal, the original purpose is to highlight the achievements of the Montford Point Marines and not necessarily propel the most negative regards to the positive things that existed in and around Camp Lejeune. Unfortunately, at the same time, the information that has been recorded by other authors and writers does expose the hypocrisy at its highest level that existed during this awful period of U.S. Marine Corps history. As a son of a Montford Point Marine, after learning of the types of treatment that existed in Montford Point Camp some time ago, and then recently discovered the "beauty, warmth, and provisions" that were a part of Camp Lejeune "proper" for White Marines, I find it very appalling, as I think anyone faced with the same information would be, knowing that their family member was unjustly mistreated. After all, each member was willing to give up their lives and was about to ship out for that very cause.

The description given by Carraway regarding the Montford

Pointers being "content" while being restricted to Montford Point Camp, and not being allowed to enjoy the facilities at Camp Lejeune, only furthers the inaccurate information that was spread regarding the so-called gratified nature of enlisted Blacks at the time of segregation in the military:

> Many times, the men declined liberty, preferring to remain in camp to sing. At their camp they had a moving picture theater, library, chapel, hostess house, post exchange, and superb dance orchestras. Frequently they staged amateur shows. On the nearby river and creeks, they enjoyed swimming, boating, and fishing.[11]

The truth of the matter is that most of the Montford Pointers had no idea of the facilities or the types of recreational avenues that were available to the White Marines at Camp Lejeune. Had they known about them or had the possibilities of taking advantage of them, as they may have wanted to at least see what was there for those possibilities for themselves. Nonetheless, the facilities were not developed for the African Americans to see or to enjoy or for their families to partake in those luxuries. At the same time, these men were in training and their focus was truly on preparing themselves for war. If those facilities had been available for these men, however, many of these avenues could have been used to possibly lessen the strain of the mistreatment against them and the strain of knowing, once shipped out, that they might never return.

Dad, when discharged from the Corps, was discharged as a corporal. He did not receive his second stripe as a corporal until he had finished his duties and tour, even though it had been promised to him nearly two years prior. On a personal note, knowing that my dad bordered on a genius IQ, and after learning about Camp Lejeune and all that was afforded the men there, it makes me wonder just how far the men of Montford Point might have gone had it not been for all the planned negative forces intentionally holding them back. In addition, as time unfolds, it has also made me and others wonder how Montford Pointer families may have fared after their distinguished service if they had been given fair, true, and proper recognition during their service and thereafter.

It seems implausible that the author Gertrude Carraway, who was well noted and established for her time, could accept and write about these two different groups of men, with the level of inequality that was out in the open, and not display the slightest hint of discord in her writing at what was happening between the two in the different camps.

Also, as we revere the outstanding commanders in the forefront that are now a legacy of the "chosen few," such as Sergeant Huff and Sergeant Hashmark Johnson, it makes one wonder how many other Huffs and Johnsons there might have been if these same opportunities had been afforded them, to feel part of a major system without the doors being closed on them at every turn. No doubt there would have been a lot more because many of these recruits were cloned, in a loose way of saying, it would seem, to act like, think like, and disciplined to respond like the Sergeants Johnson, Huff, and Carter. These men of Montford Point reached the highest levels possible because of the extreme discipline they were forced to endure. Many of us are just learning about the fantastic reputations of these men, while many have already known about them, nd how long these reputations have lasted, not seeming to go away even after over sixty-plus years. As a matter of fact, many realize their stories are just beginning to surface. Alas, with the Congressional Gold Medal now a part of them, they will always be a significant part of history and continue to grace the pages of American history.

These and other thoughts reverberate in my mind as I think back over the course of my dad's work history and the acceleration with which he performed his duties as a civilian. For most of his life Dad was ahead in his performance, wise in his duties, and was always a leader in his tasks while serving as an employee with the United States government. For thirty-eight years after World War II and a total of forty-two years including Marine Corps duties along with the federal government work time, Dad had always performed his duties at the top of his class. He maintained a secret clearance, and for many years worked with responsibilities initially involving the installation of sheet metal onto aircraft or on the body of planes. Later, and with many additional classes and teachings, he became involved in certain areas regarding the performance of aircraft, the workloads thereof, and management related to them. Surely, he was ahead of his time. Had he been treated fairly from Montford Point on, it makes one wonder how high up in the ranks he may have gone. Had he been treated fairly, I'm sure certain additional assets could have had a more pivotal role with his family and other relatives in the direction of growth and development.

As of July 1, 1946, $75 million had been spent or was authorized to be spent at Camp Lejeune.[12] The numbers were staggering, and so were the disparities.

CHAPTER 9

The USS *Lamar* Heading to the Pacific Islands

While some Black Marines were engaged in the tumultuous struggles at Montford Point Camp, there were Marines, Black Marines in particular, engaged in a life-and-death struggle overseas in the South Pacific. With urgency, it was time for Advanced Training at Montford Point for the wave of Marines to head overseas to join or replace some of the men there. There was plenty of room for all that were prepared to go because the war was fierce and deadly.

Realizing that new inductees were arriving faster than excuses could be derived, Lieutenant Blackett told his Special Enlisted Service personnel to treat the men according to the standards of the Marines, like Marines, and in turn they would be Marines. They were now in the Corps, and they were going to be treated like Marines. The Marine Corps has long-standing standards derived from the earliest Marines, and these new men would have to follow these standards. There would be no excuses and no shortcuts with any part of their training.

Entrance to Camp Wiley, Oahu, Hawaii, 1944.

Lieutenant Blackett's primary interest regarding these

new Black recruits was that now that they were here, they would go through the hard-core training that all other Marines would go through, although most times the training was much more severe, so that in the end no one could say they were given the uniform of the U.S. Marine Corps for free. In the Corps, from the earliest tradition, it is well documented that one must earn all that they are given and that nothing is given free. These standards were to be met by the end of advanced training. These new recruits would have to earn the title, and they would represent the tradition of the Marines to the greatest extent.

As a front note, Thomas Mosley was at Montford Point Camp at this time. I want to make it clear to my family and friends, or others that may read this history, that this memoire may seem old and irrelevant, but it is new to us. Not only is it new to us, it is new to the entire United States of America and the world. This is a part of our history as a people, and a major part of our own private family history that was hidden from us, yet it is critically important. Make no mistake about it, the majority of what is being written here from the time of Dad's enlistment, November 29, 1943, until the end of this writing, involved Thomas Mosley as a Marine in every step. From the time he woke until the time he went to sleep with the familiar "lights out," every movement he made was a movement under the watchful eyes of every officer that has been written about here and some who have not been noted. He is one of the men here at Montford Point Camp. He is your son, your brother, your uncle, your cousin, your father, your friend, your hero. He is a Montford Point Marine, one that is *Semper Fi,* "Always Faithful."

Again, Dad was in the 5th Marine Division, 5th Ammunition Company, and 365th platoon. He was later assigned to Camp Catlin in Hawaii.

From North Carolina, the men would be departing for Camp Catlin. Although this was a welcome area for these Marines to go to, with no COLORED OF WHITES ONLY signs, Camp Catlin was still under the jurisdiction of the United States, and with that being said, there was still racism that these Black Marines would be subjected to because the White Marines were initiating it and also spreading it around to the locals there. The ship that many of these Marines boarded for their destination to the South Pacific was called the USS *Lamar* (APA-47). Although the ship was a mixture of black and white soldiers, for the most part, they were kept separated.

The USS *Lamar* was an attack transport that was "laid down" or begun to be built on March 31, 1943, by Ingalls Shipbuilding Corporation in Pascagoula, Mississippi, under a maritime commission contract and launched on August 28, 1943. It was acquired by the Navy on November 9, 1943. It was first placed under ferry commission on November 10 for fitting out to Brooklyn, New York. Lieutenant Commander J. H. Budd was in command. It was decommissioned on November 22, 1943, for conversion at Todd-Erie Basin in Brooklyn and re-commissioned on April 6, 1944, with Captain Bruce K. Culver in command.[1]

The USS *Lamar* was tested by running to Norfolk, Virginia, on April 16 and 17. The *Lamar* had a very important stop to make. "Shakedown" is a term that is used to mean the testing out of a ship and its equipment, or to make sure it is functioning at top efficiency. This was completed, and needed to be, because the journey at hand was just the beginning of many that this ship needed

The USS *Lamar* (APA-47) in port in 1945.

to be in service for. The stop made at Norfolk was a stop for embarking 1,621 Marines. These were not just any Marines; they were Marines from Camp Lejeune, the White Marines, and there were also the Montford Pointers, including Dad, and the company of which he was a part, the 5th Marine Ammunition Company. These men had now become Master Ammo Technicians and their services could not wait a moment more, nor could they. On May 13, 1944, the attack transport departed for the Pacific. The *Lamar* reached Pearl Harbor on June 1, and total time on board was twenty days. Dad and other members of his company debarked and headed to Camp Catlin in Oahu, Hawaii, to begin the arduous task of structuring and receiving, organizing, stacking, and delivering the badly needed ammunition to the frontline Marines throughout the South Pacific.[2]

Truman Boone, a Montford Pointer, who was aboard the *Lamar*, commented that once aboard the ship, segregation was not the policy, and all were permitted to move about freely, but once you got to Hawaii, it was segregation time again. Boone said, "It was very unique and enjoyable going through the locks in the Panama Canal. That was one of a few bright moments for me."[3]

One of the things Boone learned while traveling aboard the ship over the ocean was that there were two types of water that they encountered. "On the other side of the Panama, the water was fresh water. However, in the Pacific water, when you showered, you'd be covered with a salt sheen, so we had to use a special type of soap."[4]

Montford Point Marines in combat gear on the deck of a troop transport ship in the South Pacific.

Once again the *Lamar*, on June 5, 1944, was back in the deep blue sea returning again to the mainland USA for yet another load of soldiers, this time for deployment to the Marianas. The *Lamar* was once again performing her assigned duty, transporting amphibious troops into the Asian Pacific. Sailing from San Diego, she then reached Seattle and began another journey to Pearl Harbor, arriving on June 26, ready to continue the journey to its next destination, the Marianas. As part of a convoy, the *Lamar* next departed on July 1 en route to Guam, where it unloaded 1,445 more troops on July 21, and then on August 10 again returned to Pearl Harbor. This time it was for landing rehearsals in preparations for the invasion of the Philippines. Under the Supreme Commander, Southwest Pacific area, General Douglas Macarthur, the people of the Philippines were told by General MacArthur that he would return. This time, however, he was returning with enough force to free the Philippines from the grip of the occupying force of the Japanese Army, and the *Lamar* was a part of this convoy of the 7th Fleet.[5]

The *Lamar* was amply fitted for its journeys and requirements. It was 492 feet long and its width, or "beam," technically speaking, at its widest point was 69 feet, 6 inches. The *Lamar*'s "draft," or the vertical distance between the waterline and the bottom of the hull (the keel), with the thickness of the hull included, was 26 feet, 6 inches. This is the part that is below water, and it was almost two stories high.[6]

Thomas Mosley in uniform, 1944.

The *Lamar* was well equipped for the high seas and for battle. The armament consisted of two five-inch, 38-caliber dual purpose gun mounts, one fore and one aft. It had four twin 40-millimeter antiaircraft gun mounts and eighteen single 20-millimeter antiaircraft gun mounts.[7]

Not only was the *Lamar* part of this convoy en route to the 7th Fleet, from September 15 to October 3, when she reached the 7th Fleet, the *Lamar* was the flagship of Transport Division (TransDiv) 38. The *Lamar* saw a tremendous amount of action in the South Pacific. There were intermittent enemy attacks while moving American engineers, troops, and supplies. It traveled to New Guinea, the Solomons, Luzon, and all through the South Pacific.[8]

The USS *Lamar* needed to be ready for the invasion of Okinawa, which was scheduled in due time. To be nearby, so to speak, although the distance was 1,080 miles from the Leyte Gulf in the Philippines, the *Lamar* operated out of the Leyte Gulf for the next two months, from February 1 until March 27. On March 27, 1945, she left the Philippines with another 1,366 assault troops on board and reached Okinawa on April 1 to unload the men and cargo, completing the operation in one day. The *Lamar* then began loading up the battle-wounded and transported those casualties to Guam. Thereafter, she sailed out of Okinawa with the destination this time to the mainland United States, and arrived in San Francisco on April 29.[9]

The *Lamar* left San Francisco once again on May 22, departing for Pearl Harbor and Ulithi atoll to deploy passengers and cargo, and then on to Guiuan, Samar, in the Philippines, where it arrived on June 23, 1945.

For a few weeks the *Lamar* was a receiving ship for ServRon 10. "ServRon" refers to a service squadron that supports fleet combat units. During World War II they allowed the U.S. Navy to operate away from the main bases, which were at great distances across the ocean. In essence they created a major forward base at a location near the area of operation.[10]

Ulithi atoll played a major role in the South Pacific for Americans in World War II. Being well prepared with strategic planning was the name of this battle. Admiral William Halsey Jr. felt that

The platoon. **Front row,** left to right: Sergeant Carter, Company Commander; Raymond Slater, N.Y.; unidentified; Maxie Williamson, Bucksport, S.C.; John Smith, Cincinnati; Corporal Denham, Drill Instructor.
Second row: Herbert Hughes; William Childs, Middletown, Ohio; Walter Stover, Winston-Salem, N.C.; Thomas Mosley, Steelton, Pa.; Herman Buchannan, Chattanooga, Tenn.; Bob Jackson, Dayton, Ohio; Robert Bradley, N.Y.; Leonard Mayo, Morton, Pa.; Ernest Coleman, Arlington, Va.
Third row: Simpson Sylvester, Corpus Christi, Tex.; James W. Smith, N.Y.; Randall Nelson, Doylestown, Pa; Jerome Briggs, Providence, R.I.; Frank Jones Jr., Saluda, S.C.; J. H. Adams, Columbia, S.C.; Frederick Alonzo Lee, Bronx, N.Y.; William Martin, Philadelphia; Nathaniel Peppers, Avenger, Tex.
Back row: Johnnie B. Alford, Memphis, Tenn.; unidentified; Jethro Robinson, St. Augustine, Tex.; Robert Delaney, Dayton, Ohio; Walter Studevent, Bethlehem, Pa.; Claudia Hewitt, Dallas, Tex.; Eugene Fields, Dayton, Ohio; Louie Brown, Ohio; Charles Robinson, Dayton, Ohio.

the only way to have the victories necessary to winning the war was "to seek out every opportunity for engaging the Japanese major naval forces in a decisive sea battle."[11] Admiral Halsey along with Vice Admiral Marc A. Mitscher's Fast Carrier Task Force (TF 38) struck out of Eniwetok atoll on August 28, 1944, for strikes against the Bonins, Palaus, Yap, and Mindanao. Chichi Jima and Iwo Jima were struck by carrier-launched aircraft August 31 to September 2, the Palaus on September 6–8, and Mindanao on September 9–10. Halsey reported to his superior that the "Enemy's nonaggressive attitude [was] unbelievable and fantastic."[12] So smooth were the operations being completed by Admiral Halsey that he suggested to Admiral Chester W. Nimitz that Palau and Yap-Ulithi were not necessary as a steppingstone in the support of commandeering the Philippines. His recommendation to Nimitz was to invade Leyte-Samar instead. Nimitz passed on the suggestions to the Joint Chiefs of Staff but also indicated that too many commitments had already been made and that the operation regarding the seizure of Ulithi had to be carried out.

The plan turned out perfectly, as Ulithi became a major base for the United States. In their war strategy, Japan had actually counted on the United States having to travel great distances for resupply or repairs of ships and planes or whatever else may have been necessary after sustaining heavy damage or problems en route. Occupying Ulithi changed the course of all these actions.

Capturing Ulithi turned out to be one of the greatest plans for the United States but also a dagger to the heart of the Japanese naval fleet in the Leyte Gulf. Emperor Hirohito, between the ages of thirteen and fifteen, while continuing his education during his final years of school, began learning military instruction. He and only five of his classmates began getting an additional education in the military and liberal arts. The other students did not receive military education. Within Hirohito's spectrum of study, starting in 1919 and presented by Navy theorist Captain Sato Tetsutaro, was the study of American Admiral Alfred Thayer Mahan and his theories of sea power. The other lecturer, Hirohito's own uncle, Admiral Prince Fushimi Hiroyasu, was an expert on German military theory.[13]

In the battle of Leyte Gulf, and other locations leading to Japan, it was theorized by the Japanese naval leaders that the important and most critical aspect of Navy battle was to follow the dictates of Alfred Thayer Mahan. His concept, and one that was required reading at the Imperial Japanese Naval Academy and the

Naval Staff College, indicated that in order to dominate a war on the high seas, one had to control the commerce on the seas. This theory, called Decisive Battle Doctrine or Kantai (Fleet) Kessen, taught that after the enemy depleted their resources, the Japanese navy could pounce, and in one major attack, destroy the enemy. In this case, with the Pacific Ocean being so vast and dangerous in and of itself, along with being so far from home, the United States would deplete its fuel, food, and other supplies, thus limiting the time they could remain in the area and be completely vulnerable.[14] This doctrine proved to be obsolete in the long run, but the belief dominated the senior Japanese decision makers.

Once again, after the mission was accomplished at Guiuan, the *Lamar* was called upon to deliver supplies to Pearl Harbor, the trip being from July 19 until August 1. It discharged its valuable cargo, and the very next day departed for San Francisco, arriving on August 9.[15] On September 8, it was on to the Marianas, where the *Lamar* arrived on September 24 in Guam. Here it discharged 1,517 military personnel and left after receiving 1,829 veterans of the great battle of the Marianas, debarking at San Diego on October 12.

The USS *Lamar* had transported many Marines in general and Montford Pointers in particular on the many trips across the Pacific Ocean. As the war wound down, the *Lamar* was still seaworthy, ready to do battle if necessary, and continuing to do her duty. The next trip would take her directly to Japan, where she would embark at Yokosuka on November 28. This was part of Operation Magic Carpet duty. Magic Carpet was that postwar phase designed to bring home those troops who had served in the war around the world. In this case, the *Lamar* was one of the ships used to transport Navy and Marine soldiers back to the States from the Pacific Theater. The *Lamar* picked up 1,810 passengers, then departed on December 1, heading to Seattle, where it arrived on December 14. Slowly it was moving toward the end of its service in the U.S. military. On January 14 it departed on its way to the Gulf Coast, stopping at New Orleans, then onward to Beaumont, Texas, on February 24. The *Lamar* was decommissioned on March 7 and turned over to the Maritime Commission on July 3.[16]

Although some transport ships do not receive much notoriety, this was one ship that also played a major role in the deployment of Montford Pointers and other troops as well as supplies into the South Pacific and other areas. The *Lamar*, along with its passengers, will go down in history because of the decisive role they all played. The USS *Lamar* received five awards for her service as a United States Ship:

- The American Campaign Medal
- The Asiatic Pacific Campaign Medal
- The World War II Victory Medal
- The Navy Occupation Service Medal
- The Philippines Liberation Medal[17]

CHAPTER 10

The Military and Tales of "Black Tails" on Hawaii

Pearl Harbor was attacked on December 7, 1941. Hawaii was under martial law until late 1944. Hawaii was besieged with war and became a war state. This was no longer a civilian area; it was dictated strictly by what the military needed and determined. It was only a few hours after the attack on Pearl Harbor that military law was dictated, and the military would be in control—with a few modifications—for the next three years.

Every resident of the Territory of Hawaii, including citizens and noncitizens as well, would now be under martial law. Once military rule was enacted, it also became crystal clear who were the primary targets of the new hundreds of general orders that were now part of the new rules, and why they became the primary targets. Although the Hawaiian legislature passed the Hawaiian Defense Act in 1941, giving the governor extraordinary and almost dictatorial powers in times such as these, the governor allowed the Commanding General Walter Short to convince him that there was an imminent invasion. As a result, even though Governor Joseph Poindexter had all the powers he needed to continue his own control of his territories in this time of war, he allowed the general to usurp his entire rule. The general then declared himself military governor of the territory.[1]

After the attack, there were over a million personnel brought to Hawaii to serve the war effort. These personnel included over thirty thousand people of African descent, both men and women who were now on the shores of Hawaii.[2]

Until this time there were no problems regarding Blacks in Hawaii, because according to a 1940s unofficial census, there were approximately two hundred "Negroes" of American birth living on the islands.[3] There were some variables regarding race in Hawaii prior to the war, but never were there any of pronounced importance, at least not until this point. As a matter of fact, in Hawaii, as opposed to in the United States, there was unprecedented racial equality. There was not the whiteness that existed as a rule of standard among the people in Hawaii. Of course, some people could not leave well enough alone and decided to bring some evil and negative discord with them to precede the arrival of these new Black Marines and other Black war personnel.

Up until the war broke out, Hawaii had a totally different system regarding people of various ethnic backgrounds and makeup. When Whites came to Hawaii, they could not believe that Blacks in Hawaii were not treated with the same negative discord that they were being treated with on the mainland. Black Americans also could not believe the fairness and the respect that they initially were being treated with. It was as if life had turned around 180 degrees.

The breakdown of ethnicity was totally different than on the mainland of the United States. In Hawaii, for example, there was no racial group that claimed a majority, although the Japanese did make up a substantial amount of the population. Caucasians also

Ammunition crew at Camp Catlin, Hawaii, 1944. Thomas Mosley (left) and Walter Studevent (right); two others are unidentified.

made up about a quarter of the population, but the ironic thing about "Caucasian" is that it meant something different here.[4]

The so-called "Negro population" in Hawaii was the Puerto Ricans, and they, right along with the Caucasian Portuguese, were classified as Caucasian.[5] There were also Chinese, mixed Hawaiians, Japanese, Filipinos, Koreans, and many other mixed people from various islands in and around Hawaii. Although there were prejudices in Hawaii prior to the war, they were not as clear-cut and as divisive with the hatred that existed on the mainland.

For Black soldiers and war workers coming to Hawaii, the treatment received was that for the first time in their lives, such as they had never received before, they felt an unprecedented racial equality.[6] To feel the respect and courtesies extended to them on such a mass scale was totally beyond words. The standards that Jim Crow laws had set for the racial divide on the mainland had not yet reached Hawaii. Black men who were exposed to this newfound way of life were able to absorb these new feelings, know that they were genuine, and letters abounded to the mainland to family and friends expressing what this new way of life felt like for them and their fellow workers. Up to this point the Hawaiians had never been exposed to the fictitious lies, misconceptions, and stereotypes that had been created for one group of people to cause them to be outcast in society.[7]

Of course, all were not pleased to see the treatment expressed toward these soldiers and workers. White men and women from the mainland were appalled to see and hear such sights after coming from a place where institutional racism was the norm and no one could see an end in sight of Black people living under such negative standards. So their correspondence back home was of a totally different nature. Of primary importance was keeping this newfound treatment toward Blacks from such dignified people from making its way to mainland Blacks, which in turn would upset the status quo on the mainland. After all, it was the early 1940s, and such thoughts had to be changed and had to be changed immediately. The days of relaxing in paradise in the tropical breeze under palm trees had to come to an end.

There were many sailors in Hawaii at this time, and many of them were from Texas and other parts of the South. Upon the initial arrival of Army soldiers, these men, with their hatred toward African Americans, had begun to spread poisonous lies about Black men throughout the area. In Hawaii, because of the multiracial nature of its inhabitants, Black troops were able to mingle in public places and areas and were not looked upon as being "below" White soldiers, and therefore did not have to "keep their place" as on the mainland.

This did not bode well at all with the racial mind-set of many of the White soldiers, and they needed to take action to correct it. Almost anything of dread was attributed to the Black war workers and soldiers.[8] Malicious lies that they were thieves, had diseases, and were murderers were also included in the lot. One of the most prominent tales that enveloped the islands was the tale that Blacks had tails. It was with a fury that this information was spread among the locals, and in virtually no time at all it was taking its toll. At the same time, military authorities mostly ignored the violations

Left to right: R. Brown, J. Ratcliff, R. McCall.

and may have likely pushed the same negatives as well.[9]

This became evident when American soldiers from the 369th Coast AA (Antiaircraft Artillery) Regiment, "the Harlem Hell Fighters," arrived. There were 1,800 of these men that were in an elite New York National Guard unit that had been federalized for the war effort. In 1941 it was one of the few all-Black regiments—officers as well as enlisted men. During World War I, the 369th, then also known as the 15th, under command of William Hayward, was assigned to the 161st Division of the French Army and helped to repel a major German offensive on the Western Front.

According to the National Archives, the 369th, along with the French, fought at Château-Thierry and Belleau Wood. Under the command of Colonel William Hayward, they spent 191 days in combat, 5 days longer than any other American unit in the War.[10] They earned fame in Europe and in America. Called "The Men of Bronze," these men fought so hard and courageously against the Germans that eventually 171 of its officers and men received individual medals, and the unit received a Croix de Guerre for taking Sechault in the northeast of France.[11] The Croix de Guerre—meaning "cross of war"—is a medal bestowed upon recipients for heroic deeds and bravery while in battle.

In view of the above, however, there were many twists and turns along the way. In 1917, World War I was already underway when America joined. Initially, Blacks were clearly not wanted in the war and especially not as soldiers. It then became clear that troops were badly needed, and they soon became a great part of the war effort. However, in the spring of 1917, there was a large fanfare at a gathering in front of the Union League Club in New York City where Governor Whitman presented the regimental colors of the 369th Infantry Regiment.

As Gail Buckley describes in *American Patriots,* "The crowd roared as the colors were marched up Fifth Avenue to Jim Europe's syncopated rendition of "Onward Christian Soldiers.""[12]

It was in April 1917 when America joined what was known as the "world war." At this time, the United States was trying to get 27,000 troops to France quickly. The idea was to deploy troops of that magnitude from a cross-section around the country. Major Douglas MacArthur, who was later to be five-star General Douglas MacArthur during World War II and the Korean War, had a good idea. Take National Guard units from across the country and combine them into one division. That division could then be deployed to France without slighting any particular state or region.[13]

Walter Studevent, 1944. Studevent and Thomas Mosley were close "ammo buddies" during the war.

After chow on Camp Sandy, Maui, Hawaii.

Montford Point tank crew on Camp Sandy.

After a lecture.

The "barracks" on Camp Sandy.

Some of the men of the 4th Platoon.

J. C. McGill.

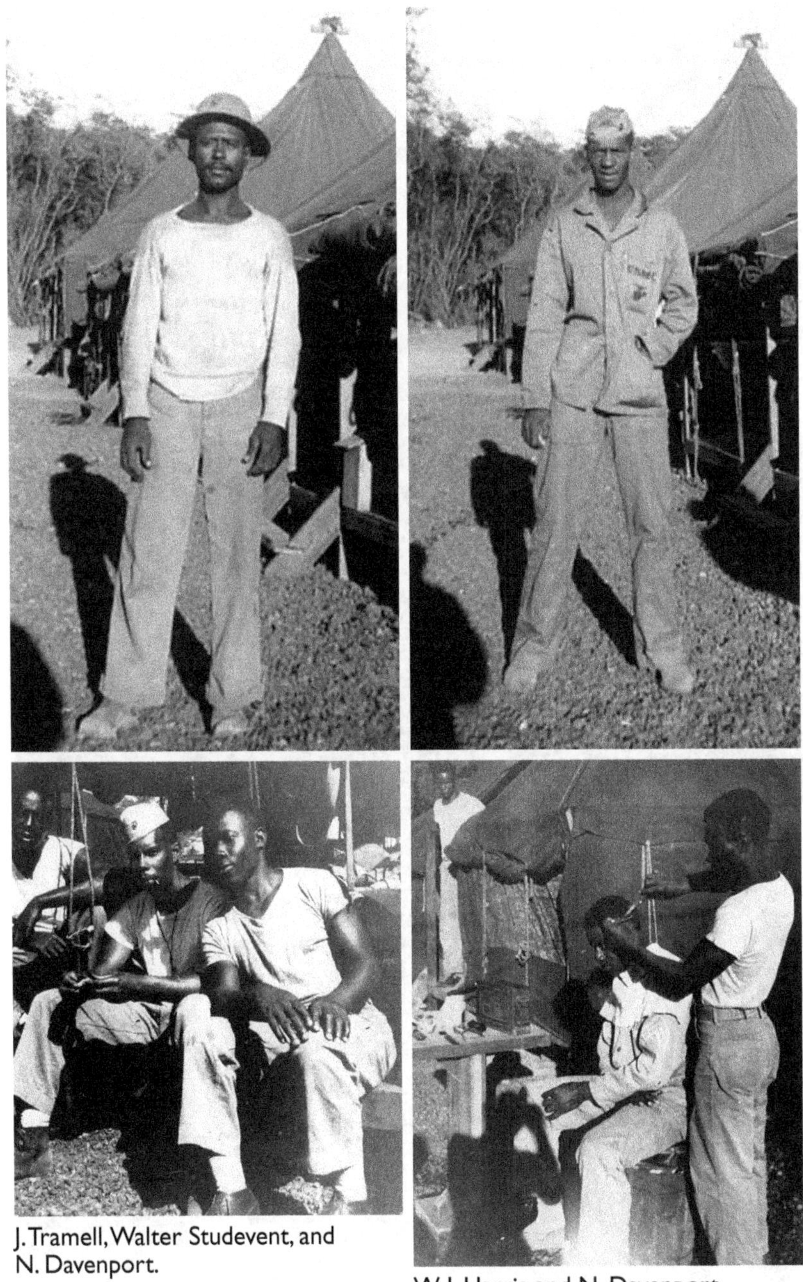

J. Tramell, Walter Studevent, and N. Davenport.

W. J. Harris and N. Davenport.

Thomas Mosley (left, no shirt), J. Tramell, Frank Jones Jr.

In the South Pacific.

Various types of training: resting, scouting, and on guard.

Weight training.

In Honolulu for a short break.

Front: W. Parker and R. Minor. Back: Walter Studevent and Thomas Mosley.

Corporal Otto Roach.

Liberty day on Maui with Thomas Mosley, William Martin, and C. Odoms.

"The Lodge" at Camp Sandy.

MacArthur, who at the time was the acting War Department's press person, described this operation as one that would look "like a rainbow" because the division would stretch across the United States. This division also became known as "The Rainbow Division." Eventually there would be twenty-six states and the District of Columbia that would have designated troops that would be a part of the Rainbow Division. Although there was much fanfare when the colors of the 15th, or later to be the 369th Artillery Regiment, were presented, when Colonel William Hayward, the commander of the 15th, asked to join the 369th Infantry and other 42nd Infantry Division units in a farewell parade through New York City that winter, he was told no. The reason given was that Black was not a color of the rainbow.[14]

Following the war, however, in 1919, the men were rewarded with a victory parade on New York City's Fifth Avenue to the music of their now famous regimental jazz band leader, James Reese Europe.

In early 1941, the 369th began training for antiartillery combat in Oswego, New York. It was the type of training that was designed to keep the men satisfied but still segregated from the large-scale combat operations with White soldiers. The 369th became masters at handling artillery weapons through training at Camp Ontario and were acknowledged overtly by White antiartillery officers. Then, while in Oswego, assault charges were brought against a black man. The entire unit was lined up and inspected for "evidence."[15] The men felt that the charges were brought only because the woman had been caught indulging in interracial sex, and this final act was her only way out, one that would preserve her "dignity."

These troops were very aware of the mistreatment of other Black troops serving in the military, and the mistreatment they received in World War I, and they were determined to be treated with respect. They knew the 369th was a legendary group and a special combat unit and felt wholeheartedly that their rights had been violated by the blanket lineup that they were forced to undergo. The men decided to use a strategy to counter the mistreatment by uniting together, with backing by their officers, of no longer shopping where they were not wanted or could not work. Some of the men recounted this strategy used by Reverend Adam Clayton Powell in Harlem in the mid-1930s. Before long, all charges were dropped.

Now nearing the end of their yearlong stint of training, the

369th were preparing to return home, but just prior to the end of the stint, Pearl Harbor was attacked, and the men received orders to protect the coast of Southern California. Ironically, the men were ordered to set up their antiartillery equipment in the backyards of some of the wealthiest people in America, including the yards of some famous movie stars, including Humphrey Bogart and Rosalind Russell. While there, they were visited by Lena Horne, Hattie McDaniel, and others. This method seemed to work for a while, until some residents began to oppose the heavy artillery and Black troops making use of and traversing across their manicured lawns. Before long, the 369th were ordered to Hawaii, and another chapter for the 369th would unfold.

In Hawaii, during World War II, while these men were being transported to their base camp on the sugarcane railroad, people would run away. The sugarcane railroad, officially named the Oahu Railroad and Land Company (OR&L), was developed initially in March 1889 by Benjamin Dillingham on the island of Oahu.[16] He initially arrived in Hawaii in 1865 as the first mate of the ship *Whistler.* Although scheduled to depart, an injury from a fall prevented that from taking place, as he needed to recuperate.

Over the next few years Mr. Dillingham worked in various businesses and was always one to think of expansion and possibilities. After assessing that the land was excellent for growing sugarcane, but not having the proper means to get the cane to various parts of Oahu, he decided to venture into the railroad business for hauling that cane. Hence the Oahu Railway and Land Company was born.

The railroad seemed to gel with other people's ideas in that, although slow at first, sales began to grow in land purchases and new agricultural ideas. Pineapple and sugar plantations began growing more and more, and his railroad began to be a major source of moving many of those crops.

During World War II, the OR&L became more than a sugarcane railroad. It also carried freight, passengers, mail, equipment, and workers and began to serve the major military bases. Included were Pearl Harbor, Hickam Field, Barber's Point Naval Air Station, Schofield Barracks and Wheeler Army Airfield. Declining in traffic by the beginning of the war because of competition from automobiles and better road systems throughout the area, they focused mostly on freight. OR&L became the main transporter of civilian workers and soldiers including Army, Navy, Airmen, and

Marines, shuffling from Honolulu to their respective bases and then back to Honolulu for needed R&R.

It was from this line, the main mode of transportation, that the men from the 369th found themselves face-to-face with the inquisitive people from this part of the island and began to see the reactions that they were causing. These people were extremely frightened because of the trains full of these Black men. The reac-

Thomas Mosley (middle) with two unidentified Marines, Camp Catlin, Oahu, Hawaii, 1944.

tion was quick to evaluate. The locals had been bombarded with the lies of the White sailors and Southern recruits that somehow Blacks were like animals. By that time, they had been repeatedly warned and the lies had taken a firm hold. In spite of the lack of support, these men were determined to combat the negative circumstances in any way they could. They would not run, and they would not turn their backs. When confronted with negative comments and outright calls for brawls, they had no reservations of going toe-to-toe with the White sailors or whoever the perpetrators were.

While many of the locals continued to uphold the lies and misconceptions they had been fed, many of them, after seeing another side of these men, began to side with these men of color. Eventually, beginning in November 1942, after many skirmishes and even deaths as a result, the military Governor of Hawaii, Lieutenant General Delos Carleton Emmons, who early in 1942 stated that the stationing of Black troops in Hawaii was "very undesirable," but who also at times seemed to be an ally on some issues, dispensed a memorandum declaring that racism in Hawaii was inefficient in maintaining the order necessary and critical to the war effort.[17]

On November 6, 1942, he issued another confidential memo to all commanders of every post indicating how vitally important it was for them to stop all incidents of racial disharmony, and then went farther still by declaring that he blamed the officers for creating the atmosphere that allowed this discord to continue to exist. The issuance of these memorandums did much to curtail the violence and discord that went on, but of course much of it continued.

Thomas Mosley on weekend-pass leave in Hawaii, 1944.

By the time Dad arrived in Hawaii on June 1, 1944, tales were still rampant. He disclosed to me firsthand these rumors. "When we would get leave and go to clubs to dance, the women would not dance with us. If you got on a bus and sat next to a local woman, she would get up, and in many cases, get off the bus."[18]

Truman Boone said, "Most of the people were scared of you, and in the villages those people were extremely scared of you and would run at the first sight of a Black Marine."[19] Opinions varied as to the reaction of the locals, but some Marines couldn't help but notice that people kept peering behind them, looking for their tails. For a long time, the various rumors persisted, and local women steered clear of the Black soldiers. The dances held by the USO were segregated between Black and White troops during the first part of the war, until the USO opened the Rainbow Club. Still, it was difficult to round up enough women volunteers for dances for the "colored" servicemen.

In a later attempt to reconcile these hostilities, Black troops were allowed to attend "regular" dances but with women that were USO-supplied. These racial practices continued to exist, although not on the same order as they were on the mainland American soil. However, the military knew that racist practices were profound and created extreme hostility and was incompatible with military procedures. This was the reason that they continued to keep African American troops segregated from the White troops or kept them completely in the lowest ranks of the service.

Another variation of this rumor is recalled by Marine Benjamin H. Patterson who was from Baltimore, Maryland and joined the Marines in 1942. He was in the 51st Battalion 90-millimeter group and was eventually deployed to an island called Funafuti. Funafuti is one of a group of islands about 2,600 miles southwest of Hawaii. At this time, it was a part of the British-owned Ellice Islands and was a major strategic location for both the allies of America and also for the Japanese, who planned to occupy this island group. As a result of this information, the Marine Corps sent a contingent of men and weapons to secure the island.

On October 2, 1942, the 5th Marine Defense Battalion, the Battalion of which Dad and many other Montford Pointers would later be in support of, made an amphibious landing at Funafuti and began setting up antiaircraft guns and searchlights amid the sand, palm trees, and four hundred natives of the atoll.

Benjamin H. Patterson imparted, "The first thing that happened to me, the natives walked up to me and said, 'Let me see your tail.' I said, 'We don't have tails. Feel back there.' And then he feels. 'Oh, that's not what we hear.' I said, 'No, we don't have tails.'"[20]

Included in this mind-set of spreading untrue rumors of the highest order was one officer who was a general in the Marine Corps. In *The Right to Fight,* Bernard C. Nalty states:

> Marine Major General Charles F. B. Price, in command of American forces in Samoa, had already warned against sending the African

> Americans there. He based his opinion on his interpretation of the science of genetics. The light-skinned Polynesians, whom he considered "primitively romantic" by nature, had mingled freely with whites to produce "a very high-class half caste," and liaisons with Chinese had resulted in "a very desirable type" of offspring. The arrival of a battalion of black Marines, however, would "infuse enough Negro blood into the population to make the island predominately Negro" and produce what Price considered "a very undesirable citizen." Better, the general suggested, to send the 51st Defense Battalion to a region populated by Melanesians, where the "higher type of intelligence" among the African Americans would not only "cause no racial strain" but also "actually raise the level of physical and mental standards" among the black islanders. After the general forwarded his recommendation to Marine Corps headquarters, though not necessarily because of his reasoning, two black depot companies that arrived in Samoa during October 1943, were promptly sent elsewhere.[21]

While discussing this negativity that began to circulate in Hawaii regarding black Marines, we must also look back at another aspect of fear and prejudice that began to take its toll back in the United States regarding Japanese and Chinese Americans.

In California, the climate of hostility against Japanese Americans was at an all-time high. For the United States to be attacked by any foreign power was a no-no. For the United States to be attacked by a power that just a few days ago it was in negotiations with, with seeming progress, and having tens of thousands of people living in this country that were originally from that country, was an even bigger no-no. Something had to be done with the Japanese that were living here, and it had to be done immediately for this act of betrayal.

Up until this point in 1941, the United States had had an ongoing relationship with Japan, and there were already over a hundred thousand Japanese living in California for many years prior to the bombing of Pearl Harbor. Sure, at times the relationship had been somewhat rocky, but nevertheless the relationship seemed to have smoothed over as the years passed.

However, in order to give a more accurate portrayal of this relationship, let's take a look back and get a brief idea of the interactions between the Japanese government and the United States.

The immigration of Japanese citizens did not begin in the United States until 1868.[22] Up until that time the Japanese government wanted to remain isolated from the rest of the world and therefore kept rigid containment on the Japanese population. With this perspective in mind, we must also look at the climate in America and the experience that preceded Japanese immigration and the important factors that had an impact on the thinking of many Americans regarding Asians.

Also, at this time, with the California gold rush of 1852, Chinese immigrants were becoming thickly ingrained in the United States and were striking out to the West Coast to partake in the riches that were certainly there.

This did not sit well with many of the citizens of the United States, and they had begun to harbor hostilities toward the Chinese. The Chinese had begun to get a foothold in many things that were taking place here, including the building of irrigation systems, which were sorely needed for farming and food production. They were extremely active in the building of the railroads that were an integral part of the movements of all types of agriculture and products that were being shipped all over the United States. As a matter of fact, they participated in the building of the first transcontinental railroad.[23]

These were not the best of times for American workers, and as resentment grew and gold as well as jobs for American workers became harder to find, racial tensions mounted. Actually, the Chinese workers were forced from the mines as competition became stiffer, and many of them went to San Francisco, where they began to work in low-paying jobs such as restaurants, factories, and laundries.

As the 1870s rolled around, Anti-Chinese sentiments became politicized, especially by labor leader Dennis Kearney and his Workingman's Party,[24] as well as governor of California John Bigler, who blamed the Chinese "coolies" for lower wage levels.[25] As anti-Chinese sentiment steamrolled across California, another group known as the Supreme Order of Caucasians was really beating their drums, as they had more than sixty chapters statewide.[26] The purpose of their movement was to run the Chinese out of the United States. All of these inclinations prompted the U.S. government to enact a major law called the Chinese Exclusion Act.[27]

Because of the issues of employment, or lack thereof, there were no questions as to who the Chinese Exclusion Act was singling out. It was strictly a racial determination because, as a minister named Otis Gibson in San Francisco reported in 1877, there was a constant demand for Chinese labor all over the Pacific Coast because White labor was available at wages capital couldn't afford to pay. Another California farmer stated that he could not get White labor to do stoop labor in the fields. "I must employ Chinamen or give up."[28]

This was one of the most significant restrictions on free immigration in the history of the United States. This law on Chinese exclusion went into effect May 6, 1882, and it suspended immigration for ten years against the Chinese and at the same time barred them from becoming U.S. citizens. Through the Geary Act of 1892, this law was extended for another ten years until it became permanent in 1902.[29]

Regarding the repeal of this law, it was not until the Magnuson Act in 1943, also known as the Chinese Repeal Act or the Chinese Exclusion Act of 1943, during World War II, when China was an ally in the war against Japan, was this law lifted. Even then, this act only allowed 105 Chinese to enter the United States per year.[30] Not until the Immigration Act of 1965 did this status change, which allowed large-scale Chinese immigration to begin again.[31]

Now we begin with the influx of Japanese into America. Entrepreneurs from the United States decided to recruit Japanese laborers into the mainland after anti-Chinese sentiment grew to the level that it did, thinking they would be a better fit than the Chinese. This did not start until six years after the Chinese Exclusion Act of 1882.

One of the main entities that recruited the Japanese immigrants for their labor was the railroads. Many Japanese had already landed in Hawaii, and many were still in Japan when the migration to the United States began. The location that these immigrants landed in was the Pacific Northwest. Here construction was underway for the railroads in the Columbia River Basin. Because the sugar beet industry was vying for the labor of these Japanese as well, they were receiving a very nice wage from the railroads.[32]

The Japanese were moving into the larger cities in Oregon and began setting up businesses to accommodate and help out newer arrivals that were coming daily. Portland especially was a major hub of Japanese activity, and they were able to accommodate new arrivals, as well as those already there, with contacts in fishing canneries, sawmills, farms, and especially in the railroad industry. Not only were they setting up businesses, they were also setting up cultural life and establishing churches and Buddhist temples.

The first wave of Japanese were called *issei*.[33] The great Northwest was expanding rapidly and employment was at an all-time high. Many of these workers worked for a time in one industry and would then work in other industries. Naturally, the season of harvesting beets and other summer products would only last for a while, and by then the other industries would be waiting for the return of workers or put out a call for new immigrants to come. Many Japanese had been involved in farming in Japan and many had come directly from farming backgrounds. Once in America, many hoped to own their own farms. However, when not able to materialize this dream, they would then rent as many acres as they possibly could. They realized that this was a way to move up the economic ladder.

As with any new life and many new opportunities, the *issei* were hard-working, but because of the same prejudices and racial discrimination that had proceeded them on the West Coast with the Chinese immigrants, many of the Japanese that lived and worked in this region were driven out by angry White mobs. With this came the controversial issues of immigration and racial segregation, just as it had with the Chinese immigrants.

The Japanese government, realizing the type of image they had in the eyes of the world, wanted to sustain that image, and therefore set about negotiating with the U.S. government on behalf of the *issei* and the *nissei* or second-generation Japanese. At the same time, the primary reason they wanted to expedite these terms was so that no legislation would be enacted barring any and all Japanese from entering the United States. The United States, after all, had had an agreement and a treaty with Japan in 1894 that assured free immigration from Japan.[34]

Thomas Mosley decorating the Christmas tree at Camp Catlin, in between stacking ammunition.

The Japanese who were established in the United States knew full well the ramifications that could result from the hostilities and envy that they were receiving from the White population in their region, and also as word spread across America. More and more Japanese immigrants were pouring into the United States, not just directly from Japan but from Hawaii, which was an intermediary stop for many Japanese coming from Japan.

More than anything else, the Japanese did not want the Chinese Exclusion Act to fall upon them. They realized the opportunities that lie here and those that had already materialized for them in many forms. It was the Chinese Exclusion Act that had given more opportunities to the Japanese when the act prevented Chinese laborers from coming into the United States, and the Japanese were rewarded with those same jobs. Also, this was for unskilled labor, which allowed even more Japanese to take advantage of these positions; only a strong back necessary.

Nevertheless, as the jobs and opportunities grew, so did the hostilities. Not only did hostility grow from individuals who felt their opportunities for employment had waned, it came especially from the labor unions. They were "stealing jobs and causing crime" was the cry. By the time 1905 arrived, the Japanese were the main topics in San Francisco–area newspapers. There was also the Asiatic Exclusion League.[35] This was a major organization whose primary goal was to stop Japanese immigration, but it included all types of Asians, including Koreans and East Indians as well, especially Hindus. Most of the supporters were from union groups who opposed the Asians because of the negative impact on wages that the Asians caused.

In San Francisco, which was ground zero for Chinese agitation, the Japanese were feeling the wrath of the exclusion swell. The most threatening aspects of the Japanese being shouted about were that they did not share with the White workers "God" and their "hopes, their ambitions, their love of this country."[36] Even more frightening was the fact that the Japanese, unlike the Chinese, were partially adopting American customs, and this made them even "more dangerous than the Chinese had been as competitors."[37]

On and on this negative spiral went until the Japanese succeeded in having at least an informal agreement with the U.S. government. This agreement occurred between late 1907 and early 1908 and was called the Gentlemen's Agreement.[38]

In this Gentlemen's Agreement, Japan agreed that they would not issue any new passports for Japanese workers that wished to come to the United States to work. The United States in the agreement said that they would recognize those Japanese already in America and also to allow the wives, parents, and children to immigrate here, and at the same time avoid legal discrimination against Japanese children in California schools. The school issue was extremely important as well because the Japanese culture always highly valued education and did not want their children to receive any type of inferior education.

When the San Francisco Earthquake struck in 1906, the city was in flames for three days. Afterward, when the Chinese Primary School, which had been destroyed, was reopened, many of the Chinese students that had previously occupied the classes did not return. The superintendent of the schools at that time, Alfred Roncovieri, dictated that the Japanese students would be included in enrolling into the Chinese Primary School as well as Koreans and Chinese. To add insult to injury as far as the Japanese were concerned, a policy was adopted in October 1906 that renamed the Chinese Primary School as The Oriental Public School for Chinese, Japanese, and Koreans.[39]

The earthquake and the subsequent fires devastated San Francisco. Afterward it was time for rebuilding and rebirth. The hostilities for a time against the Japanese had subsided but resumed when a wave of crime and violence occurred after the fires. The Japanese were being blamed, but this was for more than the crime and violence that was occurring. There was mass construction taking place in and around San Francisco, and the Japanese were included as recipients in the wealth as it was being spread around. Their shops began to grow, they began to purchase homes, and their businesses tripled in number compared to before the earthquake.

No matter how hard the Japanese were willing to work, no matter how much they tried to assimilate themselves, there was always a chasm between the Japanese and the American people, or the government trying to appease the American people with regard to the Japanese. In other words, there was always tension, and usually this tension could be found, according to the labor unions, with "them" taking land or taking money that should be in the hands of "Americans."

With tensions incessantly mounting, by the time World War II began, both the *issei* and the *nissei* were beleaguered in the anti-Japanese mass hysteria that was sweeping the country. According to the Columbia River Basic Ethnic History Archive:

> West Coast agricultural interests, which had long sought to undercut Japanese immigrants' success in farming through state exclusion laws, pressured the national government and local media to remove Japanese Americans because of their ostensible threat to national security. The military and federal government initially called for Japanese Americans to voluntarily relocate to the interior, but politicians such as Governor Chase Clark of Idaho vigorously opposed such a plan. Clark blocked California Japanese families from purchasing

> land in Idaho, and actively discouraged others from relocating. Yet Idaho would soon become "home" for 10,000 West Coast Japanese Americans removed from their real homes and sent to its Minidoka internment camp.[40]

When President Franklin D. Roosevelt issued Executive Order 9066 on February 19, 1942, it was to relocate 120,000 Japanese Americans from the West Coast inland. Governor Chase Clark, who initially vigorously opposed Japanese purchasing land or even coming to Idaho, now faced having to accommodate 10,000 at once.[41]

CHAPTER 11

The Depot and Ammo Companies

With the issuance of Executive Order 8802 by President Franklin D. Roosevelt, the influx of Black Marine inductees was at an all-time high. As was stated earlier, the Marine Corps did not know what to do with so many new Black recruits and had to find and create areas for these men to be absorbed into.

The ammunition and depot companies were being shaped and formed at Montford Point. Through the rigors of the toughest Marines ever and anywhere, these men were working through basic training and boot camp. Early in 1943, the Marine Corps realized that the logistics system was not working properly and was in dire need of repair. The need for stevedores was at an all-time high. The stevedores were needed specifically for hauling supplies and ammunition in movement stretched from the factories and warehouses in the United States to the front lines of the battles, almost to Tokyo.[1] This linkage was through the Asian Pacific through some of the most remote areas in the South Pacific.

According to Sergeant Huff, at that time, in evaluating what the requirements would be to perform this duty, "all that was needed was a strong back from these men ... to load and unload ships and haul ammunition to the line for the fighting troops."[2]

When there are thousands of fighting men thousands of miles away from their homeland and in the most hostile and remote locations, and these men need supplies of all sorts, including medical supplies, food, clothing, ammunition, and other essential supplies, they have to be delivered and maneuvered by specialists. Despite minimizing, as anyone may want to or tried to do, it is obvious that the system of maneuvering and channeling had to be done by masters. The operation of loading and unloading thousands of ships with thousands of boxes and crates and pallets and other essential items was enormous. The items had to be unloaded from the ships, stockpiled, sorted, moved to different locations, and then the same procedure used over and over again for as many times and locations as were necessary until that part of the operation was completed. With that in mind, these items then had to be put into the hands of those fighting men who were on the front lines fighting the Japanese.

When put in those terms, that task seems workable, but that summation ended up being so far from the reality of what takes place in that type of movement or maneuvering that it must be correctly spelled out to negate the minimization of that type of report. And so, with the perspective from Sergeant Huff in mind as a starting point, one needs more details for another outlook.

Stacks of ammunition in Hawaii, 1944, waiting to be shipped by the Montford Point Marines.

World War II was the deadliest war ever and at the time involved all the great powers in the world.[3] The men of Montford Point needed a "strong back" indeed, and the training these men went through was rigorous to say the least, but to indicate a more realistic aspect of what these men had to encounter puts another spin on what else was required in these maneuvers.

The story of these men with the strong backs also had other issues that were an integral part of loading and unloading. On almost all the islands that the men from Montfort Point encountered, with names such as Tarawa, Kwajalein, Eniwetok, Saipan, Iwo Jima, and Okinawa, to name a few, and they were on all of these islands, they were met with enemy gunfire. From the moment they were in sight of the Japanese, in all but a few cases, they were being fired upon, but they still had to perform their operations. From the moment they disembarked from the ships with armloads of ammunition and supplies, gunfire was all around them.

In one major case, Iwo Jima, for example, in order to inflict even more severe casualties, the enemy allowed the men to come ashore, as if the island were almost deserted, and when the American soldiers thought all was clear and were mostly stuck in soft volcanic ash on the beaches, the doors of hell opened up with all its fury in the form of machine-gun fire, rifles, and grenades.

Prior to the landing, beginning on December 8, 1944, carrier planes first hit the island through the rest of the year and pounded the island with a seventy-four-day continuous bombing campaign by both the Navy and Army Air Forces.[4] Then immediately before D-Day, for three days again, the Island was pounded. On February 19, 1945, the first armored amphibious tractors made their way ashore, and shortly thereafter the tractors carrying troops landed and came ashore and made their way through the ankle-deep sea of volcanic ash.[5]

Initially there was no enemy fire, and so the Marines thought the mission would be swift. After all, the island had been bombed all those days with no letup. The commanding officer in this case, General Tadamichi Kuribayashi, commanding officer of all Japanese forces on Iwo Jima, knew that it was best to stay underground until the bombardment slowed. Iwo Jima was very small, measuring only 4½ by 2½ miles, and so the Marines thought the objective would be easy to accomplish. At the southern tip of the island lay Mount Suribachi, an extinct volcano. Nevertheless, it too was on the list to capture along with two airfields.

While the Marines walked along the base of the volcano, all at once machine-gun fire and rifle fire blasted them, followed by artillery and mortar fire alongside that. From out of the extinct volcano, the concealed positions revealed themselves as part of the 642 blockhouses, pillboxes, and other gun positions that were placed prior to the attack.[6]

This was just the beginning days of Iwo Jima. Supplies still had to be brought in under intense enemy fire. Anything moving, including tanks, tractors, and soldiers, was getting trapped in the soft ash, which was much softer than sand. There was hardly anything moving except bullets and artillery fire.

However, these Montford Point Marines were there on Iwo Jima until the end. There were over six thousand Marines killed and more than eighteen thousand Marines wounded in a two- by four-mile area. These Montford Point men were also there on that eight-square-mile island when twenty thousand Japanese soldiers were killed as well. And not only were they still unloading ships and hauling ammo to the lines, they were also moving dead and wounded American soldiers back to the hospital ships waiting off shore. It was not an easy task indeed.[7]

According to Dr. Steven E. Anders, the Quartermaster Corps Historian of the U.S. Army, in "Quartermaster Supply in the Pacific during World War II":

> The Japanese attack on Pearl Harbor in December 1941, suddenly and without warning, put our nation at war for the second time in just over two decades. Only this time it really was a *world* war. Fighting spread to the far reaches of the globe and included multiple theaters of operation. But no area proved more challenging for the U.S. Quartermaster Corps than the war in the Pacific.[8]

This war was monstrous in its size. It was a multifaceted operation, but each operation related to another in some form. As this war began to approach the United States, in no way were we prepared. We were still in the Great Depression and not prepared to battle in a war of epic proportions.

> General MacArthur said afterward that the magnitude of the Corps' assignment in the Pacific Theater and its performance in carrying it out was "without parallel in the history of warfare." They had to generate unheard-of levels of supplies and maintain a steady flow of goods across thousands of miles of ocean. And support varied actions on widely separated islands in what can only be described as a "new kind of war"—all the while overcoming hurdles never before encountered.[9]

Although the Corps for 167 years wanted no part of African Americans, they now had realized in more ways than one that it was imperative for them to be a part of the establishment. Bernard C. Nalty, in his *African American Marines in World War II Commemorative Series,* states:

> By the spring of 1943, the Marine Corps discovered a need for full-time stevedores within the logistics system that channeled supplies from factories and warehouses in the United States, through rear area and forward support bases, over the beaches, to the Marines fighting their way inland. To provide the missing segment of the supply line, the Marine Corps organized two kinds of units, depot companies and ammunition companies. Their comparatively compact size—companies rather than battalions—meant that the new organizations could be formed and trained rapidly and deployed in numbers that corresponded to the size of the amphibious forces being supported.[10]

Once it was determined that these new recruits from Montford

Point would fit the bill for the labor necessary to make this operation successful, the Marine Corps brass got on it right away. Instead of trying to develop battalions or larger structures, the Marine Corps formed these men into company-size units—smaller units that could be almost instantaneously deployed just as soon as these ranks were filled and as soon as boot camp was completed.

Additional history here may help to tie in what was happening in the context of the shaping and forming of these depot and ammunition companies as well as the defense battalions. Once the Marine Corps was forced to use the draft, it meant that these African American men would be coming into the Corps faster than expected. As a result of this rapid influx, the Corps wanted to adopt some of the Navy's prior tactics of a separate Stewards Branch and the Army's method of creating large numbers of small Black units, most of them for rapid deployment for service overseas.

On May 25, 1942, the Commandant of the Marines Corps, Lieutenant General Thomas Holcomb, issued a communications letter to the "District Commanders of the Marine Corps, All Reserve Districts except the 10th, 14th, 15th, 16th." The subject was "Enlistment of colored personnel into the Marine Corps." This letter, by direction of the General Board, Navy Department, stated, without going into all of the details, that:

> 1. By reference (a) the Marine Corps Recruiting Service has been directed to begin on June 1, 1942, the enlistment of colored male citizens of the United States, between the ages of 17 and 29 years, inclusive, for service in a combat organization. Accepted colored applicants will be enlisted as privates in Class III(c), Volunteer Marine Corps Reserve, and transferred to an inactive status in the General Service Unit of the Reserve District in which they reside on the day of enlistment. All enlistments of colored personnel will be for general service, although quotas call for the enlistment of a number of occupational specialists, such as cooks, bakers, barbers, and truck drivers, will be ordered to the training center beginning about July 15, 1942.
> 2. Present plans call for the formation of a Composite Defense Battalion, to be assembled in the vicinity of New River, North Carolina. It is necessary to place colored men on inactive status until the training center now under construction is completed.
> 3. District Commanders will not order colored reservists to active duty until specifically directed to do so by this headquarters. Recruiting officers have been instructed to stamp on the front cover of the service-record book the word "COLORED" to identify staff-returns of men enlisted under this authority."

This document was signed "P. H. Torrey, By direction."[11]

Although exclusive of any Blacks in the Marine Corps since 1798, only a few at that time, it did not take very long for a response to be given to the Secretary of the Navy by Lieutenant General Holcomb, apparently stalling and giving a negative report. In the letter dated June 23, 1942, Holcomb states:

Subject: Enlistment of Negroes

1. Upon initiating the enlistment of Negroes on June 1, 1942, for the composition of a battalion for general service in the Marine Corps, a fair interest was shown throughout the Eastern, Southern and Central Recruiting Divisions and there were a considerable number of applicants who applied for enlistment. The general type that applied was not at all representative and physical and mental examinations quickly deleted most of the original applicants. Negro Colleges, high schools, and institutions have assured our recruiting officers that there would be no difficulty in securing or in filling our requirement, but to date, that prediction has not been borne out, and to include June 18, a total of only sixty-three (63) had been enlisted in the Marine Corps Reserve.
2. Unofficial advice from various recruiting offices indicates that there will be a considerable acceleration in the number of enlistees in the immediate future.

T. Holcomb[12]

The very first depot company was activated at Montford Point Camp on March 8,1943, and was called the 1st Marine Depot Company. There would be ten more depot companies formed before the next type of company was formed, the 1st Ammunition Company. During the process of developing the depot companies, it was not the intention of the brass to have them turned into "screaming eagles" but rather men who were in excellent shape, could move quickly, obey orders, and most of all, have an excellent understanding of orders and carry out those orders. Without question they had to have a strong back, but as long as the back was strong, anything else would be the least of worries. Most did not have a tremendous amount of training, and almost as soon as boot camp was over for the depot companies, they were being shipped out. The ammunition companies had to have more training, as handling any type of ammunition required them to be briefed in some of the technical components of those items. This is not to diminish or to undermine the extreme importance of the role that the depot company man was saddled with. Absolutely it was on the grandest of scales.

Outside the 51st and the 52nd Defense Battalions, all the other companies that were a part of Montford Point Camp were either depot or ammunition companies. There was over sixty ammunition or depot companies out of Montford Point Camp. The very first company formed there was the 51st Composite Defense Battalion.

Although the plans called for the Marines to enlist 1,200 colored troops for duty as the 51st Composite Defense Battalion, with 900 being enlisted prior to August 1, 1942, and the remaining in October 1942, it did not materialize. In an explanation as to why it did not occur, K. E. Rockey, at the time the Director of the Division of Plans and Policies, in a letter dated Oct 29, 1942, to the Commandant of the Marines, indicated that in essence, although the first 647 men were enlisted, and 428 had been called to duty, the remaining 219 were still inactive. Rockey insisted that the first 900 were not procured because of the qualifications of the remaining 300. He also replied that, "It is doubtful if even White recruits could be procured with the qualifications listed in the enclosure."[13]

He further specified that instead of sending these remaining men to the specialist schools that were already in existence, these men should be ordered to inactive duty status until such time as facilities were available at the Training Center in New River, North Carolina, at a rate of two hundred men monthly. This information and planning were in conjunction with the Division of Recruiting, the Division of Personnel, as well as the Division of Reserve. In keeping with that line, Rockey, who at this time had had a long-standing career in the U.S. Marine Corps, suggested that the Marine Corps, instead of sending the Negro recruits to the specialist schools, unless there was a colored school available, "to send instructors to the Negro camp to conduct the special schools required."[14]

Particular to the ammunition companies, these men would have to receive additional training as occupational specialists, as did those in the defense battalions, because of the care needed in the handling of ammunition for all types of weapons, and also to receive the training necessary for handling the actual weapons that were needed for the maneuvers that these men were to be involved in, such as the heavy antiartillery weapons and other heavy-caliber weapons. Upon my questioning of such intricate training, Dad remembered, "There were only a few men from each ammunition company, as I recall, that were sent to specialized schools for ammunition handling and camouflage training. We were told that with this extra training, and because we would be specialists at the end of training, that it would earn us another stripe. This never happened as we were told, and for me it didn't happen until the end of my service period. We learned to handle the ammunition, though. And we handled it day and night too when we got to the South Pacific. When nighttime fell, we were taking ammunition out to the ships. We hauled it down by flatbeds, backhoes, and trucks of all types. We already had designated which ammunition we were ordered to send out at any given time, and we were ready to go. You had to move that stuff, but you had to be careful too. It was a mechanized system, and everybody did what they were supposed to do. We worked all night long, fighting the heat and other creepy crawlers, although the heat was not nearly as bad as in the daytime. But those mosquitoes were rough all night long. It was hard to get away from those little buggers. Lots of guys got sick from those terrible bites. You had to keep that kerosene nearby and rub your body with it to keep those mosquitoes off you. We all smelled like tubs of kerosene."[15]

CHAPTER 12

The 5th at Work: The Spearhead

Montford Point Marines in the Battle for Iwo Jima

Dad's time in the Marines continued in Oahu, Hawaii, as a Marine and as an ammunition technician in support of the 5th Marine Division. Duties of the ammunition technician included, but were not limited to, procurement, storage, issuing, handling, salvage, and renovation of ammunition.

Dad, in recalling his duties, stated, "My days, along with other members of our unit, were spent lifting and moving large hundred-pound metal-encased wooden crates filled with high explosives, missiles, and all other types of ammunition. These crates were about eighteen by twelve by six inches or so, or a variation of these measures. Sometimes we had to make the ammunition for certain weapons with black powder ourselves. We had to stack the ammunition and keep it sorted, based on lot numbers. If any reports came back that any ammunition had misfired or that it was just too old, the ammunition had to be disposed of. There was to be no chance that this ammunition would result in any casualties because of its uncertainty or failure. Some of these same ammunition guys were sent to some of the other islands such as Maui, Hilo, Hawaii, and other locations in support of the 5th Marine Division. But I have to say again, you're talking about some big mosquitoes on these islands; hoo-wee. We had to keep that kerosene on us at all times. And it seemed like they multiplied at night. They were rough all night

Insignia of the 5th Marine Division: The Spearhead.

long. You could hardly sleep. If it weren't for the kerosene and the netting that we used, I don't know what we would have done. You darn sure would not have slept. A lot of people over there ended up with malaria and other diseases related to those darned mosquitoes."[1]

Dad's words were completely true in every sense. According to Eric Bergerud in his book *Touched with Fire: The Land War in the South Pacific:*

> The worse medical problem throughout the South Pacific was malaria.... Most people living in tropical regions have developed genetic defenses against malaria. Others from temperate climates generally fall victim to it. Once bitten by a female *Anopheles* mosquito, a tiny parasite is transmitted to the liver, and other processes begin having devastating effects. As such, malaria usually recurs several times. Malaria can kill, but generally an intense and high fever is most common.[2]

As Donald Fall, describing malaria in the same book, said:

> I had malaria. You get a fever. You shake like you're going to rattle the teeth right out of your head. You're freezing. Then you're roasting. All of a sudden, bingo, it's gone. And you're hungry. But the minute you look at the food, you're not hungry anymore. You feel like you have to defecate. You try, but all you do is dribble some water. It took seven years for that bug to burn out entirely.[3]

Another soldier, Bill Crooks, said, "I had it about six years, three to four attacks per year. One just lays in bed and regorged or sweated it out because it left one like a wet dishcloth with the gussy threads gone out of it."[4]

To give a brief history of the 5th Marine Division, called the Spearhead, whom many of the Montford Pointers were attached to, they began at Camp Pendleton in California. This was one of the companies that Dad's outfit was in support of and that helped them to become noted as the outstanding group they became. "In support of" meant that they were to provide support in various forms, be it ammunition, other supplies, work details, carrying out the dead and wounded, and more.

They were officially activated at Camp Pendleton on January 21, 1944. However, the activation actually happened prior, on Armistice Day, November 11, 1943. Major General Keller E. Rockey was the commander. Under his leadership the division was brought up to its authorized strength and trained in every aspect needed in order to become the type of division that the Marine

Corps wanted them to be. General Rockey had seen action in Château-Thierry in 1918. Although the 5th was just being developed, it was being built with top-flight Marine veterans who had fought with other outfits previously and were well versed in the art of war. It was General Rockey's duty to overtake the island of enemy-held Iwo Jima.

In conjunction with other operations taking place, it was thought that Iwo Jima would be extremely easy to crumble. Not only that, but the intelligence also indicated that it was only lightly defended and that it could be taken inside of a week.[5]

Men of the 3rd Ammo Company taking time out on Saipan. Left to right: Corporal Willis T. Anthony, Private Emmitt Schackelford, Private Eugene Purdy, Private Horace Boykin.

Taking Iwo Jima within a short period of time was just what General Tadamichi Kuribayashi wanted the United States to believe was possible, and he even projected this misconception. Kuribayashi was an aristocrat who was educated in Canada and had also toured the United States. Highly regarded by Emperor Hirohito, he was one of few soldiers to ever be granted an audience with the emperor. After being selected to defend Iwo Jima, the General had started working to build an elaborate system of bunkers, tunnels, and corridors on Iwo Jima. This operation had begun the previous year, in June 1944. Japan, with the island under the direction of General Kuribayashi, had no intention of giving such a strategic location such as Iwo Jima up to anyone. It would definitely be death to the last man.

By that time, Kuribayashi was aware that the Imperial Japanese Navy was crippled and could not offer any support whatsoever whenever the United States would decide to attack Iwo Jima. Obviously it was coming, because this island was in the direct line to Japan—the ultimate mission—from the movement of battles, by the United States, which had taken place, and directly in line of where fierce battles were currently underway. Iwo Jima was the early warning station for Allied bombing raids and was also the base for Japanese fighter pilots to intercept approaching bomber planes. Iwo Jima, without question, was one of the most important staging grounds for the country of the Rising Sun.

According to Colonel Joseph H. Alexander, U.S. Marine Corps (Ret.), in the article "Closing in: Marines in the Seizure of Iwo Jima," the island is within a thousand miles of the homeland of Japan. As the B-29 long-range bombers were either en route to Japan or coming away from Japan, they were met with antiaircraft resistance from Japanese defenders on Iwo Jima. Iwo Jima needed to be taken, as had Saipan and Tinian, to further the strategic bombing of the Japanese home islands. The reason they were so easily picked off was because the radar on Iwo Jima gave the Japanese defenders a two-hour notice of every strike headed their way by the B-29s.[6]

To prevent having to fly either higher or circuitously, and also with a reduced payload, Iwo Jima needed to be a part of America's arsenal. It would also provide a friendly emergency stop for damaged or crippled B-29s returning from Tokyo. The planning of the seizure of Iwo Jima was known as Operation Detachment.[7]

Lieutenant General Tadamichi Kuribayashi, Imperial Japanese Army, Commanding General, 109th Division and Commander, Ogasawara Army Group, was one of the toughest opponents the U.S. Marines would ever face. As indicated earlier, General Kuribayashi knew he would be on his own when the Marines arrived. He would have to depend on all his earlier planning for defending the island as best he could. General Kuribayashi had even gone as far as using the best mining engineers and fortification specialists in the empire to assist in his planning to utilize Mount Suribachi to its maximum defense. He was an outside-the-box thinker, which was one of the reasons he did not set up his immediate line of defense on the beachfronts as other defenders had on the other islands of battle. He also knew the volcanic ash was perfect for superior strength for mixing concrete for installations. One other aspect that he was aware of was that the soft rock on the island lent itself to rapid digging, which "provided interlocking fields of fire, miles of tunnels linked key defensive positions, and every cave featured multiple outlets and ventilation tubes. One installation inside Mount Suribachi ran seven stories deep."[8]

General Kuribayashi knew that he would never leave Iwo Jima. As Herbert P. Bix highlights in his book *Hirohito and the Making of Modern Japan,* Kuribayashi's mission while defending Iwo Jima "was to make the enemy bleed as much as possible." The Japanese Navy could offer no help, and General Kuribayashi and his twenty thousand troops would give it their all.[9]

Negative rumors had also spread about the White soldiers, as they had been spread previously about the Black Marines, although with regard to another critical matter. The shoe was on the other foot now. It was that as Japanese, civilian or soldier, you did not, under any circumstance, surrender to these White savage and barbaric American soldiers. The things they would do to you under capture were just too insane for words. Although not true, the Japanese believed these thoughts with every fiber of their being and were confronted with these very thoughts as they began to be captured or forced to surrender.

In an article written by Steve Rabson, he describes the accounts of several writers in which one describes the horrors of capture by American forces. Rabson quotes Jo Nobuko Martin's 1984 *A Princess Lily of the Ryukyus:*

> Later, much later, some of us learned a Japanese officer named Akamatsu had ordered the inhabitants of [Kerama] Island to commit mass suicide to avoid being captured.... Hand grenades were distributed. There was one grenade for twenty to thirty people—Not nearly enough for a clean, instant death for everybody. Those who did not die immediately used clubs, axes, grubbing hoes, razors, or rocks to finish each other off. In ordering their suicides, the Japanese military had told Okinawans that if they were captured, the Americans would torture them for information, then rape the women before killing all of them.[10]

Even though the Marines, through B-24s, pounded Iwo Jima for seventy-four days prior to the landing of the Allied forces, it had little effect on the Japanese defenders. There was a combination of Naval artillery shelling and also aerial bombing. The inefficiency of this, however, would not be found out until later. There was also another three-day heavy shelling before the combat assault took place. Placements of the rounds from each of the ships were in designated areas so that overall, the entire island would be bombarded. This of course had some bearing on the assault, but not as much as originally thought by the Americans. Whether it had cleared the island or not, the combat team going in would find out for certain what damage had been done, what else needed to be done, and what would take care of the balance of the job once they were on the Island.[11]

At 8:59 a.m. on February 19, 1945, the troop assault was underway. The first of an eventual thirty thousand or more of the new 5th Marine Division were to begin going ashore on the southeastern beaches and to capture Mount Suribachi and the southern airfield, Moto Yama, on the first day. The 5th Marine Division was given a part of the monumental task of invading Iwo Jima. The Spearhead saw their first battle at Iwo Jima, the largest all-Marine amphibious operation in the South Pacific, and Black Marines were well accounted for. Included in this attack force were the Stewards Branch personnel, who always served in all combat operations that the ammunition and depot companies took part in. "At Iwo Jima, the 8th Marine Ammunition Company and the 33d, 34th, and 36th Marine Depot Companies served as part of the shore party of the V Amphibious Corps. Elements of the 8th Ammunition Company and the 36th Depot Company landed on D-Day, February 19, 1945, and within three days all the units were ashore."[12]

Some were going ashore, but also the majority of the Montford Point Marines, as combat service support, had their work cut out for them unloading the ships and bringing all the necessary supplies on shore. It got even worse on February 22, when the Japanese Army let loose with a nonstop barrage of almost constant enemy fire. Part of the largest struggle was making it through the soft ash beaches. At least ten enlistees, possibly eleven, and one White officer were wounded, two of them fatally.

J. David Rogers, author of "Iwo Jima: The Costliest Battle in American History," states, "Eventually there would be a total of approximately sixty thousand U.S. Marines and ten thousand Sailors and U.S. Navy Seabees in battle on Iwo Jima. The Iwo Jima battle droned on for six weeks and sixty thousand Marines and ten thousand Sailors and Seabees were deployed before the island was declared secure on March 21."[13]

The Montford Point Marines were imperative to be there as well because ammunition and supplies had to be brought ashore, and it was their duty to handle these logistics, especially for the 5th Marine Division. Needless to say, with the ammunition and supplies that were necessary to sustain this frontline assault, Marines on Iwo Jima kept the Montford Pointers back at the ammunition and dump sites busy beyond imagination. Not only at the dump and ammunition sites were they busy, but with some of the storage locations, and unloading the ships, and the establishment of the dump sites in Iwo Jima, all while working in extremely dangerous conditions.

Ammunition and supplies for sixty thousand or more troops in a battle that lasted less than month is almost unfathomable. The total number of Marines on Iwo Jima has been recorded as high as seventy thousand.[14] Furthermore, they did not know that the number of dead and wounded would be colossal because of what the Japanese had in store for these American troops, and therefore thousands of bodies, both wounded and dead, would have to be removed from this hellhole by Montford Pointers.

Bringing supplies ashore in these choppy waters was a formidable task no matter what the circumstances were or with whatever help was there to assist you. The men of Montford Point knew from experience, either firsthand or through some form of correspondence, some of the things to expect, but they also knew that each island was different and each had its own set of unique circumstances. Another aspect of life in the South Pacific that became abundantly clear, no matter which of these islands they were on, is that pictures of the lush tropical breezes and palm trees swaying in the breeze were nothing more than nightmares.

For starters, the heat did not change, and it was still blistering. The lava rock that had formed this island was sharp and jagged underwater in many places, and it was difficult to get a foothold because the sand was so soft underfoot. It was actually not sand but a much softer ash.

Whereas on some of the other islands in the South Pacific, the surging troops were met with immediate resistance even before they hit the beaches, Iwo Jima would be different. General Kuribayashi went with the plan that had been used on Peleliu: to hold the line until the Americans were well grounded on the island, and only then open up with a massive assault against them. When the divisions first landed on the island, many of the troops, including officers, speculated that most of the Japanese had been killed in the nine-month-long bombing campaign that had taken place from June the previous year until now.

On Iwo Jima, the Japanese had an elaborate system of concealed bunkers and tunnels interconnected so that they could move about freely from one to another. Once the Marines were at close range, the Japanese soldiers would open the heavy steel doors and commence firing with heavy machines guns and heavy artillery, and then close the doors to prevent counterattack, and then move to another bunker and repeat the process for some time. On those bunkers that were exposed, the American troops would clear them with flamethrowers, but then they were reoccupied sometime later. This was a system designed and planned by Kuribayashi because he expected heavy American naval and air bombardment. To make matters worse for American soldiers, it was impossible to dig foxholes to evade the onslaught of artillery because the soil was made up of volcanic ash that would not sustain a foxhole. It was also difficult to get a good foothold for advancing because the soil was so loose. What's more, the Marines, thinking that those bunkers that had been previously battered with flamethrowers were cleared, suddenly found themselves being ambushed by fresh fire from these same ports when the Japanese reoccupied those bunkers easily through the interconnected tunnel systems. Within the catacombs of Mount Suribachi the tunnels were not made up of loose soil. It was hardened lava rock and stone. The defenders had no problems traversing the system underground and had prepared for a substantial period of time in creating a honeycomb of tunnels throughout the mountain.

In their planning on Iwo Jima, the Japanese at first were going to dig in at or near the locations that the Americans would later become bogged down in, but then changed their tactics. As it turned out, it was at these locations where the Marines' supporting vehicles became backed up because they could not ascend the soft cliffs. In the few areas that did provide some access to ascend the slopes, they similarly became bottlenecked with tanks and amphibious tractors, many of which got blown up by mines, which then created even more jams.

It was because of these problems that the Americans were in the precise locations where the Japanese soldiers wanted them to be. With no place to hide and no place to escape to, the American soldiers began to receive what they initially thought they had wiped out: hell in its full fury.

Heavy naval artillery and aerial bombing support on Mount

Suribachi, along with armored tanks, helped the advancing troops to begin to make progress and to advance past the beaches. By this time they had taken many losses. By the evening, Mount Suribachi was severed from the rest of the island, and by this time there were thirty thousand Marines on the ground, with about forty thousand more to follow.

The fighting raged on day after day with the Japanese defenders of the island. There were hundreds of hidden artillery and mortar positions along with landmines all over the Island. Because General Kuribayashi had been able to gain some time to prepare for this anticipated battle, he was able to reinforce it with defense preparations so that they could be used more effectively. To this end he placed Japanese snipers in the best possible positions and had machine-gun operators camouflaged more efficiently because of the extra time that had been available.

Ironically, Black Marines were not initially a part of the plan to be on Iwo Jima, or the Marine Corps at all, for that matter. Word was spreading throughout the Pacific, and in the higher offices, that the Montford Pointers were doing an excellent job of handling of ammunition and supplies. This type of operation had required the hands of specialists all along because of the terrain, which was unbearable. The ocean waves were paroxysmal, and the labor required the experience of knowing how to strategically handle the ammunition, supplies, and rations from the ships to the shore, which came from continuous experience alone. It was an operation that required foot-by-foot movement, with wreckage and debris everywhere making any kind of progress next to impossible. However, the men were able to get the supplies in to where they needed to be. One vitally important factor to note here is that initially it may not have seemed, under the intense analysis they had originally received, that the Montford Point Marines would have been able to do an effective job of an operation of this type. Conversely, when tested under fire and then scrutinized by the military, it was shown without a doubt that no one else, without exception, could have done a more outstanding job. There was also another mystery situation and test that took place at Montford Point Camp that solidified their place in the Corps and on Iwo Jima.

Quoted in an article titled "Montford Point Marines Worked and Fought on Iwo Jima," Sergeant Jim Rundles of the Montford Point Marines tells his story of being on Iwo Jima. Sergeant Rundles was chosen by the top-ranking African American Marine at the time, Master Sergeant Gilbert H. Johnson, while at Montford

Point Camp, to shout out the commands while only six feet from General A. A. Vandegrift, Commandant of the Marine Corps, to the Montford Point Marines, to commence the "pass in review." There were twelve hundred African American Marines on the field that day, no doubt looking as sharp as humanly possible, in full dress with shouldered rifles, waiting to impress the Commandant so that their days in the Marine Corps could be long. Sergeant Rundles states:

> General A. A. Vandegrift was a veteran of the Solomon Islands and Guadalcanal Campaigns, the heroic struggles that Marines first engaged in against the Japanese in World War II. Vandegrift was a tough and seasoned veteran. Originally the plan for the Marine Corps was to enlist only 1,200 black Marines, one Battalion, and it would be a defense battalion, originally named the 51st Defense Battalion.
>
> And we were supposed to "defend" some lonely island that the white Marines had already taken. It was a cold, calculating plot, designed to keep "Negro Marines" away from any part of any battle. We knew of the plot, and we also knew that General Vandegrift's visit was designed as an inspection that would make or break the future of Negroes in the Marine Corps.... One mistake and the whole thing would be fouled up.
>
> When the last man passed, I followed the orders given me before that day, did an about face, and saluted General Vandegrift. He returned my salute, smiling broadly, and said, "Good show sergeant ... good show."
>
> The other sergeants almost mobbed me when we got back to our area. Sergeant Johnson said, "You did it. By God, I knew you would."
>
> I told him no, you all did it, you were great. Indeed, they were. I later discovered that following his visit to Montford Point, General Vandegrift lifted all restraints on enlisting African American Marines, and more than 20,000 served before the war ended.
>
> A year later a general order came down from Marine Corps Headquarters in Washington, stating, "There are only two kinds of Marines. Those who have been in combat and those who are going ..." A month later I was informed that I would be leading three platoons of African American Marines into a battle area "somewhere in the Pacific. That "somewhere" was a place that wrote a powerful chapter in American history, and the history of the Marine Corps. That somewhere was Iwo Jima.[15]

On February 19, 1945, the United States invaded Iwo Jima, located between Japan and the Mariana Islands. During World War II, Iwo Jima "had only one function": as an early detection warning base for the Japanese inner empire, which could signal warnings of incoming bombers. It was perfect as a vantage point for the Japanese soldiers, the reason being is that Mount Suribachi was a dormant volcano, 546 feet high, giving an excellent aerial view in all directions. Not only was it a perfect lookout post, but it was also perfect for the Japanese Army to set the heaviest possible artillery fire onto the United States assault teams when the time arose. Besides these reasons, of the utmost importance in their own right, there was another major reason: "because she could support several large airfields, which nearby islands could not."[16]

Iwo Jima was a prefecture, or territory, of Tokyo, meaning that it was in that city's jurisdiction. This island was heavily fortified with Japanese soldiers, but it seemed liked "easy pickings," as it was described by the U.S. military command, since it had previously been bombed for seventy-four days in a preinvasion bombardment, beginning the previous year and for several days before D-Day. The frontline Marines thought what they had previously heard was true. When they touched down on the beaches, all was quiet as they made their movement inland. For a short period of time gains seemed to be being made by the Marines to the open areas away from the coast, which were about five hundred yards beyond the beaches. At that point, hell's fury was unfurled, just as General Kuribayashi had strategized, on the American soldiers. Machine gunners and riflemen unleashed all that they could. They had the Americans just where it was planned for them to be.[17]

At the same time, the softer-than-sand ash would not hold long enough to create foxholes because the ash was not rigid enough to stay put when shoveled to form a proper foxhole. Down on the beaches the heavy equipment could not make any movement because the wheels would sink into the soft ash. Even the tanks could not get enough traction to make any forward progress. As Eric Hammel indicates in *Iwo Jima: Portrait of a Battle,* "anything with wheels sank to its axles in the volcanic ash. Even the treads on tanks and amtracs slipped and dug into the bottomless ash."[18]

It was a matter of honor for the Japanese to prevent its capture, and the Americans would realize just how much this land meant to Japan. In four days, the American flag was raised, and if there had not been so much action and movement above ground by the American forces, they may have easily heard the Japanese, by the thousands, underfoot in the tunnels below. The Japanese finally emerged and came back ferociously. It would take thirty-one more days of intense fighting, loss of life, and much injury to finally secure the Island. The capture of this location weakened the early warning system for the Japanese government.

The Marines were told that "the whole operation wouldn't take but about a week" to topple Iwo Jima, and then "we'd head back to the beautiful Hawaiian Islands,"[19] but that did not turn out to be the case. For most every Marine on the island, including the Montford Point depot companies and the Montford Point ammunition handlers, it was time to use their weapons in addition to the other duties previously described.

Sergeant Rundles recollected that no matter where they hunkered down, they seemed to be in the wrong location: "The shells from the Japanese continued to rain down." The Japanese fighters were training their weapons on the 75-millimeter Howitzers that Sergeant Rundles's men were using. Also, he stated that only after a few minutes of landing, two of his men were killed. "As indicated earlier, it was the responsibility of Black Marines to work and fight, and on Iwo, for the first few days, you couldn't see anybody to fight, but somebody kept pouring hell's fire of shelling all around us."[20]

Archibald Mosley, in a transcript of an interview conducted by the University of North Carolina Wilmington, William M. Randall Library, on December 11, 2004, described Iwo Jima:

> One of the methods of attack used by the Japanese was to advance at night from the caves and tunnels. Sometimes it was for food and sometimes it was for battle. This time, and especially on Iwo Jima, with twenty-two thousand Japanese soldiers, it was strictly for battle as the American Marines were wreaking havoc on the enemy troops. There was only life or death. There was no in-between, and any method that may have possibly worked was employed by both sides.[21]

One of the things Archibald remembers vividly was the night of the Great Banzai Attack. "Because at night, you would have to put a bayonet on the end of your rifle." Apparently, this Banzai Attack, at least to the Japanese, would work to their advantage because they could not be as easily picked off with a weapon, and could hardly be seen. "You could not shoot because everybody was around fighting, and you wouldn't know who you'd be shooting at," Archibald said.[22]

The Marines continued to move forward, inch by inch, gaining ground, but matters only got worse. On March 1, for example, Japanese mortar shells started a fire in the ammunition dump operated by the company, but Second Lieutenant John D'Angelo and several black Marines, among them Corporal Ralph Balara, shoveled sand onto the flames and extinguished them.[23] The next morning, still in darkness, another barrage of the Japanese struck the ammo dump, but this time they hit a bunker that contained high explosives and white phosphorous shells. As the ammunition exploded, fires were started all over the dump. The heat was so intense that it warped the steel barrel of a carbine that was inadvertently left behind.[24]

As Archibald Mosley continued to describe another memory, he told of a time that stories were being told, and one of the stories was that a cave of Japanese soldiers had a Marine outfit pinned down, and orders were given for a squad of the men to go knock it out. They went in, threw grenades into the tunnel, came back, and reported that it was knocked out. The officer asked the men if they had gone in to make sure that it was knocked out, or that the mission was accomplished. Archibald, totally perplexed, and about to learn a lesson that sticks with him to this day about Marine Corps battle, protocol, and sacrifice, had a question of his own. "You mean to tell me," he asked his captain, Captain Harvey, "that you would send a squad of nine men up to a place like that, knowing they wouldn't come back? You would order them to death?"

The captain's reply was, "I am not required to explain anything to you, just give you an order. But since you are my boys and you have been so faithful, let me ask you: which would you rather do?"

And with those words, Archibald Mosley would receive one of his greatest lessons in life. Captain Harvey, imparting one of the lessons that he himself had already learned somewhere along the lines of battle, stated to Archibald, "Would you rather sacrifice a few to save many?"[25] Those words would reverberate in Archibald's mind for dozens of years to come.

Archibald witnessed the sacrifices and deaths that were a part of Iwo Jima. The prayers that he learned from his mother were used many times on this island. He prayed not only for himself but for others as well:

> When I first arrived at Montford Point, others would laugh at me when they discovered I was saying prayers. Now under the watchful eye of death, many others were begging me to say prayers. One of my friends, whom we called 'Baby-Face,' because he was only sixteen when he found his way into the camp, was wounded severely in the Banzai Attack. Screams were coming in for me to say prayers for Baby-Face, but all I could do was to put my hands on him. It was to no avail, and Baby-Face died on Iwo Jima.[26]

Archibald said he was so glad that he learned how to pray. "Because those bullets were coming, not just for Blacks, not just for Whites.

Those bullets—you know what was on those bullets? 'To whom it may concern.' And those bullets were just as much as a concern to us as they were to everybody else."[27]

Henry I. Shaw and Ralph W. Donnelly also describe how, "in early March, the ammunition company suffered several more casualties." On March 2, Private First Class Melvin L. Thomas died of his wounds, while Private J. B. Saunders was wounded.[28]

Almost down to the last man, General Kuribayashi's men kept their promise of fighting to the death on Iwo Jima. It is what he wanted, and this was their promise to Emperor Hirohito. There is no true way to describe the carnage that the battle on Iwo Jima was. The numbers of those killed and wounded on both sides reflect the toll that was paid.

There were many African American soldiers who died in World War II. Many were wounded. Many of the brave men, and later women, risked and gave their lives for America. Some of the very ones that knew that these brave people were laying their lives down in defense of their honor and country were the very ones determined that these men would not receive any credit for their actions, or very little.[29]

Marine Corps brass did not want anyone to know what these men of Montford Point were doing and what they in fact did during this period. They certainly did not want anyone to know how courageous and magnanimous these men were. So, for the most part, many in the upper ranks, charged with recording the bravery and achievements of the Montford Pointers, decided to hide them from the world. How selfish some people are![30]

According to Eric Hammel in his book *Iwo Jima,* a total of 6,821 American casualties were sustained in the battle for the island. Out of that total, 5,931 were Marines, 197 were Navy medical personnel, 633 were Navy nonmedical personnel and airmen, 51 were Seabees, and 9 were soldiers.[31]

Another epic number was the astronomical tally of the wounded: 19,217 in all, of whom 17,272 were Marines, 541 Navy medical personnel, 1,158 Navy nonmedical personnel and airmen, 218 Seabees, and 2,647 soldiers who were combat fatigued. The Japanese had 1,083 captured, and those killed were estimated at 20,000 to 22,000.[32]

Although there were many good reasons speculated about why the need for taking Iwo Jima was so important, it seems that there was a more prevalent reason that prevailed. Iwo Jima was a required location, in case it was needed, for an emergency landing for one or both of the two aircraft scheduled to transport the nuclear bombs to Japan. Had one or both of the planes been lost at sea, with multimillion-dollar weapons aboard, it would have taken at least two more years, it was felt, while replacements were remanufactured, and thousands more lives would have been lost. Hence, the famous battle of Iwo Jima.

CHAPTER 13

Montford Point Ammunition Specialists

The South Pacific Theater Needed the Montford Point Ammunition Specialists

One can clearly see the importance of one's weapon while in battle and how critical it is, and how seriously it must be taken. It is absolutely a must to know how it all fits together; otherwise it won't function properly when needed. As with the ammunition needed for this weapon, it was absolutely essential that the correct ammunition be used, otherwise it would malfunction.

Just as we talked about one weapon for each Montford Point Camp Marine, there were dozens of types of weapons used by Marines of Camp Lejeune and from the other bases as well. The ammunition companies from Montford Point, when deployed abroad to the various staging locations in the South Pacific, were responsible for the ammunition being received, moved to the proper location for storage, stacked in the proper manner, then retrieved when needed to ship in rapid form.

What people who are not aware of this process must realize is that it was not a simple formula to accomplish these goals. It's one thing to know where your ammunition is for your own weapon, but imagine having to know where ammunition is for the dozens of various types of weapons that would serve hundreds of thousands of men, and also having to deliver that ammunition to those Marines on the front lines.

Back at Montford Point Camp, according to Morris J. MacGregor Jr., in *Integration of the Armed Forces 1940–1965*, "Each of the ammunition companies sent sixty of its men to special ammunition and camouflage schools where they were told specifically that they would be promoted to corporal when they completed the course."[1]

However, that did not happen for most of those the promise was made to, that I know of, as reflected on the original Muster Roll that I possess from my father, who at that time was one of the clerical typists. Had he received his stripe as promised at that time he finally reached his end of service in 1945, he would have had three stripes, as many of the others would have as well.

This was a story that Dad told me many times while he recounted his story as an ammunition specialist. I think he was taken aback that this was a lie told to him and others as incentive. As the stories unfolded, countless men from Montford Point said that even though they were maltreated (though not all were), they would go through the same thing again. The lie was superfluous.

The sincerity that these Montford Point soldiers showed in doing whatever was asked of them at the camp by their DIs was out in the open. Not very many substantial problems did these DIs encounter from these men. In one of my many conversations in 2012 with Major Joseph R. Giesel, who served as a warrant officer at Montford Point, I asked him, "What was it about the enlistees of Montford Point that made them stand out to you at that time?"

His reply was, "No matter how grueling boot camp was, or any other training the men were going through, they were always willing to go above and beyond what they were asked. They always seemed to want to do more when you asked anything of them."[2] So, the fact that they were lied to outright when not necessary was the thorn in the side.

Thomas Mosley was always *Semper Fi,* as most others were, as the proof was that these men were gallant and patriotic heroes. The truth of the matter is that if these men had been awarded this extra stripe at that time, making them corporals, then as they progressed through the war and rose up through the ranks, they would eventually be of the same rank as the White officer, that is, the staff sergeants. This could not happen, as they would remain ordinance specialists throughout the war, supposedly justified on the grounds that such units required experienced supervisors to emphasize and enforce safety regulations. And, of course, Blacks could not have the same rank as White officers. If that were the case, the White officers were always moved out.[3]

In the meantime, however, the war was hot and heavy.

Hundreds of thousands of Marines were being deployed to the South Pacific to places never heard of before. One thing was for certain: although so many other items were crucial, such as medical supplies, food, medicine, and water, ammunition was one of the most important items of all. There was not just a small array; there were countless types of ammunition that had to be shipped for the types of weapons that were used.

For most every Montford Point Camp Marine of World War II, there was a weapon that he had to learn about because it was going to be his personal sidekick or companion. He had to know every detail of his weapon and spend many, many hours inspecting it, cleaning it, oiling it, firing it, and thinking of it. It was not something that could be taken lightly. As a matter of fact, it was one of the most important things in any Marine's life because it was a lifesaver. The main weapon that would be used by an Infantry Marine would be the M1 service rifle.[4] For the Montford Point Marine ammunition technicians, such as Thomas Mosley and others, not only did they have to know their weapon, but they also had to have a working understanding—to some degree—of other weapons they would be supplying ammo for. There were also other peripheral items related to those weapons that needed to be distributed along with the ammo as well. One of the other aspects that weighed heavily on the men is that they had to know, at all times, where the locations of all such items were. They became specialists.

Some of the ammunition was needed, of course, for the M1 service rifle. The M1 rifle was a gas-operated clip-fed but air-cooled and semiautomatic. The M1 weighed 9.5 pounds and without the bayonet was 43.6 inches long. The average rate of fire was thirty rounds per minute and with a maximum effective range of five hundred yards. It also had an eight-round clip.

Prior to the M1 rifle being used in World War II, starting in 1941 with the Marine Corps (the Army switched over in 1936), the weapon used to this point was the M1903, nicknamed the "Springfield," or the "03." The 03 continued to be used throughout the war, although there were many M1s in use.[5]

Another weapon these men had to be aware of and know the type of ammo used by it was the M1918 Browning automatic rifle. Also called the "B-A-R," this weapon has accompanied the Marines in infantry since World War I. It was also used in the Pacific and was maneuverable in the rugged terrain in some of these areas. For these weapons, there was a tremendous amount of ammunition that had to be at the ready. The BAR was an air-cooled, gas-operated, magazine-fed shoulder weapon. The BAR was also a heavy weapon that weighed 20 pounds with the attached bipod legs. It had a 20-round magazine clip and could fire up to 120 to 150 rounds of ammunition in a single minute. Its maximum effective range was six hundred yards.[6]

Ammunition was also supplied on a mass scale for the U.S. carbine 30-caliber M1. This was also a gas-operated, magazine-fed, air-cooled, self-loading shoulder weapon. Dad said he also remembers these being the weapon that was used by many officers, such as sergeants. They had a stronger wallop than did a sidearm, yet they were lighter than a traditional M1 rifle. These rifles weighed only 5.75 pounds, including a full clip. Their maximum effective range was three hundred yards, and they had a fifteen-round magazine. Mark Flowers, who has supplied extensive information on this subject and who has supplied most of this detailed information regarding the weapons I am describing, says this rifle was created especially for officers, heavy weapons crewmen, and communicators.[7]

Another weapon these ammunition technicians had to be aware of was the Thompson machine gun. Although not used as readily as other weapons, it was still popular and therefore had to have its supplies of ammunition. Known as the "tommy gun," it weighed 11 pounds and used .45 ACP caliber shells. Its range was fifty yards. Most either liked it or hated it. Its most effective use was in close quarters, and therefore if one needed long-range assignments, the tommy gun was not for them. Liking it or not liking it was not a choice for the Montford Point ammunition specialist; he had to know where the ammo was for these weapons at all times.[8]

Additional ammunition that was stockpiled and distributed by the ammo men was used for the M7 rifle grenade launcher. Widely in use during World War II, the ammunition men no doubt were stockpiling and loading this type of ammo on a daily basis. It was used against enemy tanks, pillboxes, and troops. The grenade launcher itself was a device that could simply be attached directly to the muzzle of the M1 rifle. It had an effective range of three to four hundred yards.[9]

Up this point, the information supplied regarding the types of ammunition used was for what is typically called small arms weapons. In and of itself we can see what Dad and his team were faced with during the period these Montford Pointers were at the

Montford Point Camp trying to learn this information. When one thinks about how much these Montford Pointers had to learn about ammunition, and how quickly they had to learn it, it is astonishing that they were able to master it the way they did. Under the hardship of segregation, especially, it was amazing they were able to focus on all the other tasks that they were required to learn and to be abreast of.

Let us not forget, these Montford Pointers started at a base camp whose facilities were nothing to speak of, at least in comparison to what was at Camp Lejeune or Parris Island. They were also the ones who were told they could leave the camp at any time and that no one would miss them, who were degraded not only by the Marine Corps but also in and around the towns in which they sought recreation, or maybe to purchase something as simple as a sandwich, and now, quite ironically, they were being asked to master distribution responsibilities and to distinguish by category the various types of ammo that were to be used by the fighting men of the Marines throughout the South Pacific. It is amazing that that they were able to accomplish this feat.

It was not a small feat, for these men eventually distributed a vast number of Marines with these supplies in and around the South Pacific, and there were thousands of these Marines that needed these supplies twenty-four hours a day. How difficult it must have been for these men to rise to the occasion for what was asked of them. Without a doubt, in spite of this, they did. Every Montford Pointer that I have asked about their experience under these most trying and difficult conditions has told me that they would have done it again.

Dad also said he would have done the same thing and gone where he was asked to serve, wherever that may have been. He said, "I felt certain that I was contributing to the service of my country and that I was capable of being counted upon as a citizen of America."[10]

What is most striking is that whether these men were in a depot company, ammunition company, or any other company, all that I heard when speaking with any one of them—whether in a formal tone or casually—is that "I would do it all again." These men were beyond proud. While my wife, Soonai, my sister Sandra, and I were at the Congressional Gold Medal ceremonies, which took place June 27–28, 2012, in the nation's capital of Washington, D.C., they and I both spoke with dozens of Montford Pointers. In fact, the two hotels in which Dad and Sandra stayed while we were there for the ceremonies were adjoining one another and were full of Montford Pointers; there had to be at least two hundred in all. From my knowledge, there were four hotels in and around the nation's capital where these men were staying for this event. Rooms were blocked off, with reservations, for a certain number of these men and their caretakers, friends, families, or wives. Needless to say, we all verbally congratulated as many as we could and shook hands with as many as we could under the circumstances.

It was the greatest moment of my life, and it sure seemed to be the greatest of both Sandra's and my wife's. On June 26, the evening before the ceremonies, I went to meet Sandra and Dad at their hotel. Upon arrival I began to see some of these Montford Pointers. Some were in suits, some in casual outfits by this time, after long trips from Georgia, Florida, New Jersey, Illinois, and as far away as California.

One Montford Pointer, Theodore Peters, from Chicago, who was in the 90th Platoon of the 51st Defense Battalion, A Battery, told me that I wouldn't believe how they were treated. I'm only guessing his size at this point, but Theodore Peters appeared to be about 5-foot-9 and was somewhat stocky. When I first spotted him outside the hotel, my dad, sister, and I were going to find an outside restaurant to get a small bite, and he was walking behind us. Mr. Peters and I looked into each other's eyes when he began talking, and if I hadn't known the truth about the treatment these men received at Montford Point Camp, I would have been shocked when he revealed his "secret," that "we were treated like sh__ while we were there."[11]

It was as if he made sure he would be around to enact his revenge by receiving "his" Congressional Gold Medal. But Theodore Peters does not live his current life seeking revenge, and does all he can in his current hometown to help those in need through a program of which he is a participant.

We now come to the M1919A4 light machine gun. It was called "light" but in no way was the firepower light, nor the number of men designed to accompany these pieces. Its effective rate was 150 rounds per minute, but it could get up 450 rounds per minute on the cyclic rate. It used .30 caliber ammunition, and it also had a cloth belt that carried 250 rounds of ammo per belt. In the Marine Corps, this weapon was one of the primary anchors of the company's fire support.[12]

The M2 heavy barrel machine gun, called the M2HB-50 caliber machine gun, weighed 128 pounds and could fire 450 to 550 rounds per minute. Another primary weapon was the 2.36 rocket launcher (bazooka). This was a single manned operation but was needed for armor-piercing capabilities. Then there was the M2 60-millimeter mortar, which was perfect for shooting into ravines, gullies, or obstructed areas where one had to fire above and then have the artillery fall into an area where needed. Also, there was the M1 81-millimeter mortar, for heavier firepower and longer range, up to 3,290 yards. It could also fire up to thirty-five rounds per minute. They used shells called M43 and M56. Another heavy-weight weapon was the Oerlikon 20-millimeter antiaircraft gun that was armor-piercing and capable of 450 rounds per minute with a range of 4,800 yards or 2.72 miles. This antiaircraft gun was credited with downing 32 percent of the enemy aircraft.[13]

In addition, there was the M3A1 37-millimeter antitank gun. Its weight was 912 pounds. Used for opposing tanks and for heavy-duty firepower when needed. The maximum range on this two-wheeled gun was 12,800 yards, which equals 38,400 feet, or over seven miles. How much ammo was called for with these? Speaking of ammo being called for, how about ammo for a weapon that would down over 50 percent of your enemy aircraft. We're talking about the 40-millimeter antiaircraft gun, called the M1 40-millimeter, that were the backbones of the teams, created in the United States. This weapon fired 1.96-pound shells at a rate of 120 per minute with a maximum range of over four miles. This piece could be set up in only twenty-five seconds and was ready at that point to do some serious damage. The ammunition and depot companies of the Fleet Marine Force were continuously pulling ammunition for these screamers.[14]

The 75-millimeter Pack Howitzer was one of the bigger guns, and that also meant larger ammunition. It weighed 1,440 pounds and had to be hauled around on the back of a jeep. The maximum range was 9,620 yards and it could fire up to five rounds per minute. The crew required for this power-packer was seven men plus a sergeant. That was a whole crew. The shells were monsters that were each 18 inches long. I know the ammunition companies will never forget these shells when they had to carry so many at one time.

The M3 75-millimeter gun motor carriage was bigger still. It was actually an armored truck and part tank in many ways. It weighed in at 27,000 pounds and used five Marines as a crew. Its maximum range was 9,200 yards, and it was used as an armor-piercing weapon that could pierce a steel plate that was 3.2 inches thick. Each piece of ammo weighed 18.8 pounds.[15]

Still there were many more weapons than I have not described here. Two that come to mind were the 90-millimeter antiaircraft guns and the popular 155-millimeter antiaircraft guns. Had I not listed these, I would have probably had Montford Pointers knocking on my door, asking how I could have left these two primary weapons out, with the many times they exhausted themselves carrying the shells for these two giants, not only for others to use, but for themselves as well. The Montford Point Marines specialized in the use of these big antiaircraft guns. In a ceremony by the Veterans of Foreign Wars (VFW) of the United States, which occurred in Reno Nevada, July 21–25, 2012, Commander-in-Chief DeNoyer presented the VFW Commander-in-Chief Gold Medal and Citation to the Montford Point Marines. He went on to state that day in his speech that:

> And each of these pioneering men proved through their performance both at home and abroad, despite the strictures placed on them by society, that they were true Marines. Adding insurance to this claim, they broke every antiaircraft gunnery record that had been set by white Marines, with records that remain unbroken to this day.... They paved the way for future generations, regardless of background, to serve in the finest military in the world, and each of us remain free today in large part due to their service.[16]

The 90-millimeter M1A1 antiaircraft weapon system was the primary training weapon for the 51st and the 52nd Defense Battalions at Montford Point. The weight of this weapon was 19,000 pounds, and it was also the primary antiaircraft weapon used in World War II by the United States. Its firing capacity was 15 to 25 rounds per minute.[17]

The primary purpose in providing the above list is to let people who may not understand the complexities of battle know the scale with which these Montford Pointers had to work in and around in handling the ammunition for these weapons. This was by no means a small operation. There had to be a system with the highest standards in its operation if this supply was to be maintained and distributed properly, from receiving to organizing to stockpiling. Also, when we say "distribute," we are talking about distributing all over the South Pacific.

And they were not just haphazardly distributing; they had to retrieve specifically those items being called for and label it as to where it had to go. There would be thousands of items at one time being shipped out. Then, as Dad said, "These items had to be loaded on the ships under the cover of darkness to begin heading to the various drop points."

At the same time, there was a massive operation getting these items to the ships. Trucks and other machinery were needed to pull items down from high levels where they were stacked. This was a massive operation, and these dedicated men from Montford Point, when one looks at the history, were some of the finest soldiers ever in American history.

While this type of operation was going on with the ammunition companies, the very same thing was going on with the depot companies and their responsibilities. Their operation was just as intense and critical with all of the supplies that they were in control of and the other duties they had to perform. These were some additional superb and outstanding soldiers.

With all of the weapons that were discussed, there were millions of rounds of ammunition that were stockpiled waiting to be called for and delivered for those weapons. These men of Montford Point were working around the clock to retrieve what was called for and to hand-deliver these items to the men on the front lines throughout the South Pacific. One can see the enormity of the amount of ammunition used by having an idea of the number of enemy combatants killed on the some of the various islands.

For example, in the battle that took place on the island of Leyte, in the southern Philippines, in October to December 1944, which lasted for eighty-two days, according to Herbert P. Bix in *Hirohito and the Making of Modern Japan,* there were "about 80,000 Japanese defenders" that lost their lives. From April 1 to mid-June 1945, tens of thousands of Japanese combatants were engaging Marines on the island of Okinawa, in which between "94,000 to 120,000 Japanese combatants" were killed in battle and "150,000 to 170,000 noncombatants," one way or another, were caught in the crossfire and died.[18]

Also, in a three-week period beginning in mid-June, the United States engaged the Japanese Army in the Marianas on the islands of Saipan, Guam, and Tinian, and as on the other islands, the body counts were high. In that short a period of time they lost the "entire garrison of 23,811."[19] Even getting onto many of the islands in the South Pacific where these battles were taking place required expending unbelievable amounts of ammo in gunfire exchanges with the defenders of these places. In these decisive battles on these outlying islands, in order to prevent American forces from reaching Japan, the Japanese government was using the Japanese Army and their civilian population as well. Even as

Emperor Hirohito sought to prevent an allied drive from recovering Burma, by having an offensive from Burma into Assam Province in India, also with the hope that this move would start "an uprising of Indian nationalists against British rule," and the Imphal campaign, which cost the lives of "approximately 72,000 troops either killed or wounded," he seemed unfazed.[20] Meanwhile, ammunition had to be delivered to this location as well, which required the movements of ships and ammo men to deliver the goods to the front lines.

From the Kwajalein atoll in the Marshall Islands to Saipan in the Marianas Islands, from Pearl Harbor to Peleliu, and into Tarawa and Makin in the Gilbert Islands, pallet after pallet and crate after crate had to be retrieved, moved in back loaders and trucks onto ships, and hand-delivered by Montford Point Marines to the front lines of the United States Marines fighting these battles. These men worked round the clock to get the job done. And on all of these islands, the end results were the same: enormous amounts of killing and load after load of ammunition having to be dispensed.

Bernard C. Nalty, in *The Right to Fight*, describes the experience of one young soldier who happened to get a lift from a soldier on the battlefield:

> A young White Marine, Edward Andrusko of Company I, 7th Marines, saw his first Black leathernecks as he crossed the beach at Peleliu in September 1944, returning to the fight after having his wounds treated at a hospital ship off shore. The African Americans were transferring ammunition from landing craft onto trucks and delivering it to the front lines. Handling ammunition struck him as "a dangerous task at any time," but with enemy shells churning the coral sands, "it was a heroic, thankless job that few of us wanted." The Black driver of one of the trucks offered a ride inland, and Andrusko accepted, taking his place in the cab, with a cargo of high explosives behind him. As the sound of battle drew nearer, he concluded that he had made "a stupid and dangerous choice of transportation," but he reached his unit safely.[21]

The job of an ammunition handler was the job of specialists. Mr. Carroll Reavis, who retired as a gunnery sergeant after reenlisting subsequent to his discharge in 1946, stated, "During the war, that's all I did, was handle ammunition. During the whole entire war, ammunition."[22]

When I met Gunnery Sergeant Reavis in the summer of 2012 in Jacksonville, North Carolina, I had the opportunity to sit at the breakfast table with him and several other Montford Pointers. I felt like I could listen to them for hours. Every now and then I'd have some questions I thought might be relevant. I didn't realize it at the time but later discovered that Dad and Sergeant Reavis were in the same 5th Marine Ammunition Company up until the company split up while on Camp Catlin. I discovered this while looking at the Company Muster Roll that Dad typed up as a clerk typist in 1946 when he was returned to the States and held over for "the convenience of the government."

It was like a roundtable, a sit-and-learn moment or discussion with several Montford Pointers there each morning for a few days. On these mornings, Sandra would come and meet many of these Montford Pointers as well and share in the experience of realizing just who we were in the presence of.

During a 2004 interview with Dr. Clarence Willie, Lieutenant Colonel, Retired, United States Marine Corps, Sergeant Reavis spoke candidly about himself being an ammunition handler:

> You load it. You unload it. You learn how to separate, or segregate, is what they called it at the time.... That went from small arms up through 1055 ammunition.... The thing about Ammunition Company is ... no matter what your background was, you could not rise above the rank of sergeant, but the platoon sergeant had to be a staff sergeant, and he was White. At that time, you could not make staff sergeant in the ammunition company. In Depot Company they could.
>
> I went to Oahu ... Camp Catlin, and then they split my company up.... I was over to the island of Maui. We attached to the 4th Marine Division ammunition and stayed there during the entire war, and when the war was over, we came back to Camp Catlin. During the war, though, just prior to the Iwo Jima operation, my company was together on Maui because we were supposed to go out with the 4th Marine Division after we had loaded all the ships.[23]

Dad had heard something similar in terms of moving out, specifically that his company, although split and in support of the 5th Marine Division, would be going to Japan. This gels somewhat with what Sergeant Reavis indicated. The following information gives a very clear picture of Dad's story, indicating moving out to Japan.

As recorded by Charles R. Smith, who wrote the article "Securing the Surrender: Marines in the Occupation of Japan":

> In the period immediately following the conclusion of the Luzon Campaign, the U.S. 6th Army, under the command of General Walter Krueger, was engaged in planning and preparing for the invasion

> of Kyushu, the southernmost Japanese home island. After more than three years, the major land, sea, and air components of the Central and Southwest Pacific forces were to merge in the initial ground assault against Japan itself.
>
> Although it looked as if an early surrender would take place … General MacArthur directed Krueger to also plan and prepare for the occupation of Kyushu and western Honshu should the Japanese government capitulate. General Krueger's initial plan for the occupation called for five amphibious corps, commanded by Major General Harry Schmidt, to land the 2d and 5th Marine Divisions in the Sasebo-Nagasaki area on 4 September.[24]

The islands listed above were just a few of the many desolate places that ammo and other supplies had to be taken to and where, once again, hundreds of millions of rounds of ammo were expended day after day, year after year for the duration of the war in the South Pacific.

CHAPTER 14

The Fleet Marine Force

"During World War II, the most primary tactic that was used by the United States against Japan was the amphibious assault."[1] Without a doubt, each time we see an amphibious landing and see soldiers emerging from the landing craft, we think of the Marines as the ones who are emerging. The U.S. Fleet Marine Forces (FMF) are contingencies within the Department of the Navy that come together and are designed for the engagement of offensive amphibious or expeditionary warfare and defensive warfare while at sea. The term *expeditionary warfare* is used to describe the organization of a state's military to fight abroad, especially when it has to be utilized or deployed in an area away from its established base, such as on foreign soil.[2]

FMF - PAC

Insignia of the Fleet Marine Force.

The Montford Point Marines, including Dad, were members of the Fleet Marine Forces that were engaged in the Asian Pacific Theater of the campaign. These Montford Pointers were part of the link of the great battalions and divisions that were used in the movement toward the defeat of the Japanese Army. These two components, that is, the U.S. Naval Fleets and the Marine Corps Forces, came together and made up the Fleet Marine Forces for the Pacific and the Atlantic coasts.[3] While it serves directly under the Marine Corps organization, the FMF personnel, Marines, and sailors are subject to the operational control of Naval fleet commanders. However, the Commandant of the Marine Corps (CMC) retains training and administrative control.

According to this Marine Corps Operation, the Fleet Marine

Forces began on December 7, 1933, when Secretary of the Navy Claude A. Swanson issued General Order 241 defining the Fleet Marine Force. Prior to that, the Fleet Marine Force was called the Advanced Base Force. One of the characteristics of the Fleet Marine Force was the capability of rapid deployment and movement of its forces.

The forces that were now moving toward Japan in World War II were elite military personnel. The ongoing battles were vicious, and it was critical to have items being supplied that would help achieve those missions and goals at hand, and as quickly as possible. As elaborated earlier, it was absolutely critical to have all elements and supplies able to reach their target and destination in a timely fashion.

> The tradition of Marines serving on board ships and landing on foreign shores dates back to the Revolutionary War. Throughout the nineteenth century, as occasion demanded and as dictated by the expanding interests of the United States, Marines distinguished themselves in operations on the seas or on foreign soil. Their exploits became legendary at home and abroad; their existence and immediate availability in time of need became a factor in the foreign policy of the United States. To those viewing this country with unfriendly eyes, they became a force to be reckoned with.[4]
>
> In 1921, Major Earl H. Ellis foresaw that Japan may one day become an adversary and that the United States may have to one day seize bases from them in the Marshall, Caroline, and Palau islands.[5]

Thus, critical methods were needed in the development of amphibious operations. The development of the FMF with its headquarters in Quantico, Virginia, was one of the most significant developments in the Marine Corps. Once the three-thousand-man FMF was developed, there was an operations manual that was prepared that outlined the overall command relations, the techniques that were to be followed for controlled ship-to-shore movement, the possible means of ship-to-shore communications, and other detailed operations. Included were the relationships of air support and naval gunfire support. As important were the details of combat-troop loading and the loading of supplies and other such details. The finished guidelines were introduced as the Tentative Landing Operations Manual. Within four years, it was also adopted by the Navy as their official doctrine for all landing operations. Eventually the U.S. Army would also adopt a modified version called the Army Field Manual.[6]

In September 1935, the FMF headquarters moved out to San

Diego and organized into two brigades, one at Quantico and the other at the Marine Corps base in San Diego. A Marine Corps Equipment Board was established at Quantico for the purpose of testing equipment that could be used for amphibious warfare, and through this program the development of the amphibious tractor was developed.[7]

For some years, in the mid- to late 1930s, the Army continued to support and were a part of the amphibious operations that were being developed in the Pacific, off the Coast of California, in Hawaii, and at Midway. However, in 1939 they declined to continue being a part of the exercises, and it was at this point that the field of amphibious warfare became the U.S. Marine Corps' alone.[8]

There was no doubt that by this time the United States could clearly see war looming, and the vision of Major Earl H. Ellis was undoubtedly at the forefront of the command structure. World War II started in Europe in September 1939. Germany was having a field day with victory in Poland, Denmark, Norway, and France and was obviously moving toward Great Britain. With this headway, surely Great Britain was in the line of fire, and the United States would almost certainly become involved.

Meanwhile, however, the FMF continued to experiment and train with everything at their disposal to develop what was necessary to become the finest amphibious assault team possible. From the command structure to amphibious tractors, boats, barges, and landing craft of all types, the FMF was strategically experimenting with them all, including landing exercises and maneuvers in and out of the water.

Also during this period, the FMF was experimenting and testing the numbers of Marines within the Corps, and the FMF was also expanding. It was correspondingly obvious that because of the state of affairs in the Pacific Theater, the largest form of offense "would be based on large-scale amphibious warfare, all or most of which would be carried out by the Marine Corps."[9]

The organizational charts and components that were developed by the time the spring of 1944 arrived were staggering with the amount of support that had become a part of the Fleet Marine Force. The FMF was ready to do battle, and they were well equipped, as history will testify.[10]

CHAPTER 15

The Fleet Was Massive

To understand the scale and complexity of the number of Fleet Marine Force personnel that were a part of this operation is staggering. It is so staggering that it would take an amount of coverage that I am not capable of properly covering. Here is a partial listing, as indicated by "The Western Pacific Operations, the Development of FMFPac, etc.," of some of the elements that comprised the FMF, Pacific, of which Dad was a part:

- Headquarters, FMF, Pacific
- Headquarters, III Amphibious Corps, and Corps Troops
- Headquarters, V Amphibious Corps, and Corps Troops
- 1st Marine Division–6th Marine Division

Included was the Aircraft, Fleet Marine Force, Pacific, with 1st through 4th Marine Aircraft Wing, and the Marine Fleet Aircraft, West Coast. Additionally, there were the 1st through 5th 155-Millimeter Howitzer Battalion and the 7th through 12th 155mm-Millimeter Gun Battalion. Also, there were the 1st through 14th Antiaircraft Artillery Battalion and the 15th through 18th Antiaircraft Artillery Battalion, and the 52d Defense Battalion, with two detachments.

There were the 1st through 11th Amphibian Tractor Battalion and the 1st and 2nd Armored Amphibian Battalion, and the 3rd Armored Amphibian Battalion (Provisional). There were the 1st and 3rd Base Headquarters Battalion. Some others that made up a portion of the FMF were the 1st, 3rd, 4th, 5th, 6th, 7th, 8th, and 16th Field Depot, including Supply Service, Fleet Marine Force, Pacific, with the 1st, 2nd, 3rd, and 4th Service and Supply Battalions. And of course, there were some additional changes that took place with this structure.[1]

And yet, this was only a portion of the FMF. One has only to imagine the mammoth number of troops that needed to be sustained while these operations in the Asian Pacific were going on. These men needed supplies of all types, including shoes, boots, socks, medical supplies, shirts, helmets, weapons of all types, rations of various types of food, water, and ammo of all types. Initially, who would know that the men from Montford Point would fill an immense portion of this void, which they did? This was such an integral part of the operation. This was an extremely critical segment of the operation and so essential. One could easily argue that this part of handling supplies and ammo being filled by these men was just as important as any other portion of the war effort.

It is vital to understand just how important this effort was with supplies because all of the items mentioned above were needed at all times for this huge war effort. Supplies of this nature were constantly needed every minute of every day. So, for the men of Montford Point to emerge at this critical time was nothing short of a miracle for the other Marines on the front lines of the battles, as well as every other man that was engaged in duties in support of these courageous frontline soldiers.

Dad said most guys in the outfit had no idea where they would end up. In another of our conversations he said to me, "At one time, word among the group was that we were headed straight to Japan, but of course, wherever we were called to, we would serve."

It was so impressive to hear these words from him. In spite of the ill will and treatment that these men received, they were still willing to go anywhere to serve, as well and to lay their lives on the line. I also asked him, "Dad, how did you feel with all of the uncertainties that were going on at the time?"

With a deep breath, he stated, "I had a lot of anxiety then. There were so many things going on at the time. Many days now I still have a lot of anxiety related to that experience. I have dreams about those experiences even to this day. Many nights I just lay in bed but can't go to sleep."[2]

This is easy to imagine. Here you are, some of these youngsters at the age of seventeen, having misrepresented their age to get into the service. Most others were probably around age eighteen through twenty-four on average. You are no longer in the comfort of home, miles away from families and loved ones, and certainly not loved by the Marine Corps. You are either in boot camp, on a ship, or disembarking on some faraway island where people think you have a tail. So all of this is strange. There is a massive war going on, and you're tired, fatigued, and hungry, having to work twelve-hour days, six days a week, and also hearing that you may have to go into battle, just not knowing when, and many being forced into battle just by circumstance. So, yes, this is frightening, weary, and dreamlike, but when you pinch yourself, you find that it hurts, and you know you are not dreaming.

One only has to imagine the call for ammo and supplies are at an all-time high. There are calls like never before, and then those whispers again. *I hear we may have to go to Japan and get on the front lines. Who said it? I'm not sure, but that's what I've been hearing.* Then, of course, many mornings on the front lines, men had awakened and found others who were not able to wake up because the enemy had quietly, almost eerily slipped into the tents or foxholes that previous night and made sure that all would not awake the next morning. These Japanese had no fear whatsoever, and those actions happened may times during the war. Of course, these whispers found your ears too, no matter where in the war you were. This was another reason to pinch yourself, but again it hurt, and once again you know it's real. These experiences didn't always go away, or have a shutoff valve, or come with a guarantee that they'd ever go away. These experiences without a doubt have a serious long-term effect, many lasting a lifetime. What my dad was experiencing is now primarily known as post–traumatic stress disorder.

When you couple that with information that the Japanese pilots were flying their planes directly into battleships, it created another surreal experience that went even deeper into your battle-fatigued mind. This was especially true of the men that worked the ammunition dumps because these men were in the heart of nothing but ammo, and tons and tons of it. These ammo dumps were huge: blocks long and two stories high in some cases. There were thousands of tons of ammo of all types. Who knows if the ammo sites would be a target? They usually were, and were always high on the list. Who were these men who used these planes as missiles?

Many of the ammunition and depot men from Montford Point were stationed on the islands of Hawaii, which was a formidable staging location for supplies. However, many of the companies went far beyond Hawaii. In June 1944 some of the depot companies were entrenched on Saipan, and the action was fierce. The battle began on June 13, 1944. The depot and ammunition men had to unload the ship's cargo onto the landing craft and then continue fighting to get the supplies distributed to those fighting units on the front lines. There was the 18th and 20th Marine Depot Companies in support of the 4th Marine Division. The 19th was in in support of the 2nd Marine Division, and there were others including the 3rd Marine Ammunition Company. Here a squad of depot men had to arm themselves and exchange gunfire in battle in order to gain traction inland against an assault that was preventing them from moving ashore. Shortly thereafter, they had to continue fighting the enemy as they had penetrated the boundaries that had been set up between the 23rd Marines and the 8th Marines of the 2nd Marine Division.[3]

The supplies, which had been transported from the supply dumps on Hawaii or air dropped from elsewhere, were not an easy task for unloading. Obviously, the ships could only come so close to the beaches, and then they had to be unloaded onto landing craft, including DUKW amphibious trucks or LVT amphibious tractors for the last leg to shore. A large portion of these duties were being performed by the 3rd Marine Ammunition Company. There were also the pontoon barges that were strapped to the sides of landing ship tanks (LSTs) during the voyage from Hawaii or from elsewhere. These landing ship tanks were designed to move men, supplies, and ammunition right up to the shoreline. At this point, the front gate on the front of these tanks would open directly onto the beach.

Captain William C. Adams, company commander of the 20th Company, landed in the fourth wave in support of the 1st Battalion, 25th Marines, 4th Marine Division, as indicated by Bernard C. Nalty in *The Right to Fight:* "All hell was breaking loose when we came in. It was still touch-and-go when we hit shore, and it took some time to establish a foothold." The orderly for the captain, Private Kenneth J. Tibbs, was not fortunate after being struck and wounded, and became the first African American Marine killed in combat during the war.[4]

The Black Marines were not only unloading ships of their cargo and supplies of all types. They set up security that would keep snipers out as they removed the wounded and other casualties and made their way to the waiting hospital ships or other boats waiting for that purpose. Meanwhile, the Japanese were using the caves and would maneuver around at night to counterattack, but they received heavy tolls. The Japanese high command had mistakenly thought that the Americans would attack farther south on Saipan, and therefore did not have the number of men at one of the most critical locations necessary, which would have strengthened their support. But there were at least thirty thousand garrisons on the island, not including the civilians, who numbered around twenty-five thousand. The fighting never let up as the fighting men on the front lines fought over the hills and cliffs and muddy terrain. Many people lost their lives, including many Japanese civilians. While the fighting raged, the depot and ammo men had to continue working to bring in what was needed.

As briefly described, the primary method of moving supplies and troops from ship to land was the DUKW (pronounced "duck"). These machines looked like tanks but could also float, had the ability to move vital supplies directly from the ships and right up to the front lines as well as to the supply dumps that were set up behind the front lines. Many African American Army personnel were utilized in the driving of these DUKWs and were well-known for shouldering that responsibility on many of these islands in the South Pacific. These DUKWs were also used in hauling artillery pieces and ammunition directly to the troops.[5] Nonetheless, it was not an easy maneuver because of the terrain, the soft beaches, and other distresses. In many cases the surf was high. Some vehicles ran out of fuel while in route. Many were also overloaded with cargo and sank the moment they left the ships. The safe operating conditions of these DUKWs were about five thousand pounds, and many times they were loaded to seven thousand pounds. There were many problems that could foul up the transports, yet these Montford Pointers continued to work through the most difficult and trying moments.

And these moments were astonishing, to say the least. When possible, these men and assault troops heading to these Pacific island shores would be preceded by battleships and destroyers that were continuing with an onslaught of artillery, to open the way for the assault troops and supplies that needed to go ashore. There was firepower from every angle and every type of machine that was capable of helping pave the way for the movement of these items to get to the shore. These operations were not haphazard in the least. Every soldier had a duty to perform, and when not performed properly, stood out like a sore thumb. Fire support units, whose job it was to watch the flanks of the advancing troops, lashed out with a fury onto those areas where the enemy might unleash their firepower. With the firepower from battleships, destroyers, other support units, and the hollers and screams of the dying and wounded on both sides of the battle, the sounds and eeriness of all these activities were mind-boggling.

As the assault and replacement troops moved onto the beaches by the thousands, they knew that the bombardment of artillery onto the shore was to announce their arrival to the enemy. It was no secret surprise. In other words, "We are here, and we are here to do battle to take over this island." As these men moved toward the shorelines, the naval guns might let up their wrath for a brief period of time so that the fighter pilots could unleash their fury from overhead as well. The ammunition and depot companies of Montford Point were in the midst of some of the most intense fighting that anyone can even imagine.

This bombardment from sea and air was prior to the landings onto the beaches. The onslaught, when possible, was totally systematic. There were thousands of armed personnel waiting to go ashore with dozens of LVTs and armored amphibian tractors rearing to break from their gates. All of the movement and strategic penetration was only a testament to the military might, planning, and capabilities of the military of the United States.

As the sea and shore conditions at these areas became almost intolerable, it still did not cease the activities that had to go on. These Montford Pointers had to continue, just as everyone else did, performing their duties. Other details, aside from transporting ammunition and supplies, were gathering mail and making messenger runs in the midst of the furious fighting that was occurring.

The Montford Pointers were going at it feverishly, along with all the other soldiers making their way onto the beaches. They were working to unload ships that were being tossed around by the waves that were crashing into the boats and onto the shore. Not only were waves crashing onto the shore, but also gunfire was coming from all directions. Calls were coming in from all locations about what was needed. Many soldiers needed water badly, and many were hungry after traveling through almost impenetrable mud and wet sand. Many needed medical supplies for major injuries, while some needed bandages for scrapes and cuts or lacerations. Some had been shot or seriously wounded and needed to be evacuated. The Montford Pointers removed many of the injured soldiers from these areas through the unstable terrain, cliffs, sand, mud, and raging water to the waiting boats below. Of all the action and heavy fighting that was being done since the landing on Saipan, the first day saw only one depot man killed. However, the next day, another man, Private First Class Leroy

Seals, was injured and died the following day of his injuries.[6]

Nalty also describes some of the duties that were performed on the D-Day landing on Saipan: "While the depot companies underwent their baptism of fire, the 3rd Marine Ammunition Company performed three closely related functions." Sergeant Ernest W. Coney remembers that morning: "Some of the men helped move ammunition from ships into landing craft, and others worked on the pontoon barges, lashed to the sides of LSTs during the voyage from Hawaii and now moored on the ocean side of the reef, where they transferred the ammunition DUKW amphibious trucks or LVT amphibious tractors for the final trip to shore."[7]

After all of the resistance, impediments and maneuverings that had been part of General Holcomb's methods of impeding Blacks from entering the Marine Corps, and with him having served as Commandant of the Marines since 1936 until December 31, 1943, it was astonishing that the new commandant, General Alexander A. Vandegrift, who had just recently taken over the reins in January 1944, was almost immediately able to see these Montford Pointers in a totally different light than Holcomb. When the new commandant reviewed the actions and worthiness of these men in the killing fields, giving their lives and support, and continuing to work unloading supplies, aiding the wounded, hunting down the enemy, removing the wounded to receive first aid aboard hospital ships, and the actual fighting in combat, he was so impressed that he wanted every person in the Marine Corps and on the civilian side to know how he felt and what the new status would be that was to be inferred on these soldiers. Lieutenant General Vandergrift stated: "The Negro Marines are no longer on trial. They are Marines, period."[8] This was then followed by correspondent Robert Sherrod, who was working for *Time* magazine and covering the war in the Central Pacific, who wrote: "The Negro Marines, under fire for the first time, have rated a universal 4.0 on Saipan. There was no other higher rating for the Navy."[9]

On July 21, 1944, on the island of Guam, American forces embarked in order to recover American territory that had been taken by the imperial forces in 1941. Again, Japanese forces fought heavy and sadistically from high ground overlooking the oncoming Marines. The 4th Marine Ammunition Company set up an ammunition dump under intense enemy fire and secured it. Later that night, the enemy tried to blow up the dump with a squad of fourteen explosive-bearing infiltrators but were caught and paid the ultimate price. These Montford Pointers were able to kill the infiltrators while receiving no casualties of their own.[10] Onward through August 10, these Montford Pointers helped secure the island until success was gained. Along with the 4th Marine Ammunition Company, there was the 2nd Marine Ammunition Company in support of the 3rd Marine Division. The Navy Unit Commendation awarded the 1st Provisional Marine Brigade included the 4th Ammunition Company from Montford Point and the attached platoon from the 2nd Marine Ammo Company.[11]

Another example that illustrates the determination and fierceness of the fighting spirit of these men is shown while Montford Point Marines were still on the Island of Guam. In December 1944, one of the men, PFC Luther Woodard, from the 4th Ammunition Company, was on post guarding the ammo dump and saw what were obviously some fresh footprints that did not appear to be from his companions but from a Japanese patrol. Well aware of the many times Japanese soldiers tried to invade Marine Corps posts, Woodard immediately sprang into action, and on his own, followed the trail cautiously but decisively through the dense underbrush.

Holed up in a clearing where these tracks led, PFC Woodard spotted six Japanese soldiers apparently resting near an abandoned shed and immediately began to fire his service weapon, killing one and wounding another, as the others began to engage his fire. Woodward was determined to complete his mission and returned to base, where he gathered five of his comrades to accompany him in the search to rid the area of these infiltrators. After returning to the area, the enemy was hunted and two more would perish, one of them, once again, by Woodard's rifle.

For Woodard's "courage and initiative," he was awarded and decorated with a Bronze Star on January 11, 1945. This was eventually upgraded to the Silver Star. [12]

The soldiers from Montford Point were also engaged in all of the major battles that took place on the island chains of the South Pacific, including Iwo Jima, Saipan, Peleliu, Okinawa, and many other locations.

Bernard C. Nalty, one of the most prolific military historians of modern times, explained to me personally in one of my phone interviews that, "On many occasions, when the men from Montford Point would arrive with supplies and ammunition, some of the commanders commandeered them and put them right into the battle, on the front lines, preventing them from returning to their outfits." He emphatically stated that, "Most people don't know that."

Of course, I was astounded to hear this profound information from Mr. Nalty. "They laid their lives on the line and always worked feverishly, going above and beyond the call of duty, performing what they had been trained to do, and much more."[13] What I didn't realize at the time of our initial communications was that he was such a prolific historian.

According to George M. Watson, author of many books and articles and coauthor with Mr. Nalty, described Mr. Nalty in an excerpt as "the most prolific historian of the Office of Air Force History to date."[14] Therefore, as time went on since I first heard those words from Nalty in our personal conversations, it has taken on a tremendous amount of more understanding.

The island of Tinian was another stop closer to the goal of reaching mainland Japan. As Nalty describes in *The Right to Fight,* Montford Pointers that had been on the Island of Saipan boarded landing craft proceeding to Tinian. Here, beginning July 24, 1944, some of the 3rd Marine Ammunition Company members joined the assault troops of the 4th Division. The depot companies followed up in support of that organization and the 2nd Marine Division, which did not land until July 26. When the Presidential Unit Citation was awarded to the 4th Marine Division Black Marines and their outstanding performances on Saipan and Tinian, it also included members of the 3rd Marine Ammo Company and members from the 18th, 19th, and 20th Marine Depot Companies, which were components of the 7th Field Depot, for their outstanding services.[15]

Although there continued to be negativities thrown at the men from Montford Point by White officers as late as November 1944, some were obviously not aware of the significance and indelible impact that these men were having overseas. Not having deep concern nor human compassion, or having unjustified ulterior motives, of course, would tend to cloud one's vision.

Undoubtedly this would have been the case regarding the rant of the commanding officer of the 4th Marine Ammunition Company, 5th Field Depot, Service Fleet Marine Force in San Francisco, when he wrote to the Commandant of the Marine Corps on November 8, 1944, describing his black recruits. Russell S. LaPointe stated:

> In the greater percentage there is an outstanding lack of interest to better themselves. They just don't appear to care about getting somewhere in life. Respect for one another is unheard of among these men, because they steal from each other without any thought of the act whatsoever.... After close scrutiny of the physical fitness of the colored troops, it is the opinion that they do not have the stamina to endure tropical climates.[16]

Another of the comments made by LaPointe went on to indicate how he felt about the "colored personnel" under his command, which obviously did not gel with what was taking place on the battlefield: "The good points of colored personnel are few."[17]

With another critique in the letter, he goes on to describe how there had never been any racial discrimination in this organization, but described it this way

> There is a total of 110 years of service between the officers and staff noncommissioned officers of the company. The experience connected with those years of service has been put to use in every way possible in trying to teach these men how to be good Marines. There has never been an instance of racial discrimination in this organization.[18]

One of the other jaundiced points made by this officer was when he stated, "This report was compiled as a result of months of careful observation by the officers and staff noncommissioned officers of this company. During this period of observation, the character of the personnel concerned was under close scrutiny at all times and varied circumstances."[19]

In the meantime, the brave men of Montford Point ammunition companies, depot companies, and stewards were engaged in every major amphibious landing and battle made by the Marine Corps, beginning with Saipan, as recorded thoroughly by Nalty. It would seem that information regarding the heroic deeds would have filtered their way to LaPointe by this time, especially since it was crucial to have those facts and ideals that would add not only to the information of these commanding officers but also to the morale and confidence of the African American foot soldiers under his authority. This was vital information that these officers should have been on the lookout for so that they could have used these solid facts to help boost and embolden the soldiers under their own watch.

Some of the comments spoken by Major General William H. Rupertus, Commanding General, 1st Marine Division, were with regard to the 7th Ammunition Company and the 11th Depot

Company, which were on Peleliu, where they had attacked on September 15, 1944. Fighting was extremely fierce there, as on other islands where battles took place in the South Pacific. By some accounts, it was reported that Peleliu was one of the worst. The enemy fire was intense and heavy. It was reported by Henry I. Shaw Jr. and Ralph W. Donnelly, in the book *Blacks in the Marine Corps,* that for the first few days the Black Marines were occupied with unloading the supplies for getting them to the shore.

After getting the supplies to the shore under heavy fire, those supplies then had to be taken to the dumps, and once there, another operation had to be organized and carried out: strategically organizing all of those supplies. Under the most intense enemy fire one can imagine, the ammunition and supplies had to be gotten to the front lines and the frontline Marpines. From September 20 until October 19, many of the men of these two companies sustained the highest number of casualties on Peleliu. Actually, they sustained "the highest casualty rate of any black Marine unit in World War II." In addition, these men were charged with removing the dead and wounded to be carried back to the hospital ships waiting off shore.[20]

After delivering the ammunition to the front lines, the men then had to remove the wounded back to the ships while being picked off by snipers, and once again, through even more dangerous obstacle courses. After receiving the reports and performance of these men, Major General Rupertus, in an official letter of appreciation, declared:

> The performance of duty of the officers and men of your command has, throughout the landing on Peleliu and the assault phase, been such as to warrant the highest praise. Unit commanders have repeatedly brought to my attention the whole-hearted cooperation and untiring efforts exhibited by each individual.
>
> The Negro race can well be proud of the work performed by the 7th Ammunition Company [11th Depot Company] as they have demonstrated in every respect that they appreciate the privilege of wearing a Marine uniform and serving with Marines in combat. Please convey to your command these sentiments and inform them that in the eyes of the entire First Marine Division they have earned a "Well done."[21]

Also in support of the 1st Marine Division was the 16th Field Depot, which also did an outstanding job. The 16th Field Depot consisted of both the 11th Marine Depot Company and the 7th Marine Ammunition Company, both units being from Montford

Point Camp. The ammunition company had seventeen of their men wounded, the highest casualty rate of any company of African American Marines during the entire war.[22]

Information of this type was vital to receive, analyze, and pass on because men from the assault or frontline divisions were the ones that initially were assigned to carry out the task of handling the ammunition and supplies, and now with them no longer having to man this operation, it was easier for them to focus on the fighting alone. Therefore, it was a plus to have this added load shouldered by others, like the Montford Point Marines. Moreover, it would alleviate the replacement units having to focus their attention on manning this most crucial part of the operation as they were just coming in from the ships to a new position as well. The job of unloading supplies and ammunition was a job for the specialists, and the assault units on the front lines knew it, as well did the replacement units.[23]

The process of logistics was duplicated on Okinawa. Over two thousand Black Marines from Montford Point participated in this battle. It began on April 1, 1945. There was the 1st and 6th Marine Division along with the 2nd Army Division as well as the 2nd Marine Division. The 2nd Marine Division was supported by the 8th Field Depot who was in support of the III Marine Amphibious Corps, and they consisted of the 1st and 3rd Marine Ammunition Company and the 5th, 38th, and part of the 37th Marine Depot Company.[24]

The 1st Marine Division and the 6th Marine Division were supported by the 12th Marine Ammunition Company as well as the 18th Marine Depot Company and also a portion of the 37th Marine Depot Company. By the end of April, the 20th Marine Depot Company also reached Okinawa. They were arriving fresh from the battle of Saipan. As May rolled around, the 9th and 10th Depot Companies arrived from Guadalcanal along with the 19th Depot Company, who were also coming from Saipan to join the 7th Field Depot.[25]

These supply operations were unequivocally supported and expounded by the men of Montford Point. This is a vital factor that must be recognized. These men were working with logistics for twenty-four hours a day, seven days a week. Supply lines were in and of themselves an extremely complex logistics system. This is the historical information that must be imparted to all who served in World War II and to those who did not. Not only must it be imparted to those fellow soldiers that served in this war, but it must also serve as an historical fact and reminder to those African Americans who came along afterward and have reaped the benefits, however slow they came, of a "job well done."

These soldiers from Montford Point were the beginning crew of those that laid the foundation for the other African American Marines who followed. Their contributions were outstanding and set the pace for those that followed and raised the bar to a level that has been unsurpassed to this day. Therefore, credit must be given where credit is due and earned.

The frontline Marines who were in the thick of battle must also recognize that these men, their brethren Marines, although African Americans, were there for them and had their backs no matter what the odds may have been. There now was never any talk of these men shunning their duties, or being lazy, or being afraid to fight, because these assault-line Marines were counting on these men. These Montford Pointers, in many, many cases, were the difference between life and death. The supplies had to be delivered, and they were there. The rumors were laid to rest because it was now a known fact that these men were willing to sacrifice themselves and were also there in the thick of combat, maintaining a steady rhythm of carrying out their complex duties.

This information must be imparted because people must know the facts that these men were initially not wanted by the Marine Corps and received the worse treatment of any recruits ever, and *any* Marine or Marine recruit will tell you that the standard boot camp for any new inductee is already a "make you or break you" proposition in and of itself. There are no ifs, ands, or buts. These men of Montford Point Camp gave their all, as all Marines must do, in time of battle and service for America and the U.S. Marine Corps. Their motto was then, and has always been since then, *Semper Fidelis.*

Of course, these men were not alone in their movement of supply and the distribution thereof. There were millions of workers on the home front that played a major role in the process as well; however, these facts were never kept underground. As a matter of fact, this information was held up for the world to see, while at the same time these Montford Pointers, these African American Marines, were quietly slipped under the rug and hidden from sight.

These same men, however, when being shipped out to various locations in the South Pacific, were as willing as any men in history who had gone before them to lay their lives down and accept the challenges that for the service of their country. In most cases, they had no idea where they were headed. All this while being challenged at every turn and being hated, despised, and criticized. Nevertheless, in the overall aspect of these times, there are few cases shown where these men acted in an outright rebellious or contemptuous manner toward authority and the status quo of the Armed Forces, even though they were absolutely warranted to have done so. Of course, there are instances of these matters that have been cited, but in most cases, it has been clearly shown that most negativity has been projected and directed toward these Montford Pointers and not the opposite. Yet it is now revealed that these same men were fully woven into the fabric of most operations that was required by the U.S. Marine Corps in the Pacific Theater of war.

On most islands in the Pacific Theater, these men were involved in the movement of supplies, security, fighting, hand-to-hand combat, sentry duty, and the guarding of prisoners that had been captured. As Turner Blount, a Depot man from Montford Point, indicated through a series of transcripts taken by the Montford Point Marine Association, their job was, in many cases, that of a supporting unit to make sure that supplies got to the front lines and to keep the front lines supported with everything they needed:

> We lived in a foxhole everywhere we went. We had to dig in and stay. Never lived in a hut, a tent, or anything like that. We were just in foxholes as we moved.... I spent a lot of time doing guard of supplies. For instance, supplies have to go to the front. I don't care what time of night it was. You would have to be on the truck to guard the driver so the driver wouldn't get ambushed.... You would have to get on the truck, on the supplies, and sit on the outside, on the supplies.[26]

Saipan was another of the brutal battles in the Pacific. According to *History of World War II* by Francis Trevelyan Miller:

> Submarines littered the waters of the Pacific with the wrecks of a large part of Japan's prewar merchant fleet and served as eyes for American naval craft in paving the way for invasions.[27]
>
> Early in June Admiral Spruance assembled his 5th Fleet, the greatest invasion armada the world had yet seen, for an amphibious operation against the Marianas," and the Task Force 58's carriers mission was to wipe out the enemy's air opposition on the six-hundred-mile chain of islands.[28]

Overall, it was a combined effort of United States forces. In his historical work *Saipan,* Brian Blodgett describes the combination of forces going into Saipan:

> The invasion forces under General H. Smith were the 2nd Marine Division, commanded by Major General Thomas E. Watson (USMC), the 4th Marine Division, commanded by Major General Harry Schmidt (USMC), the 27th Infantry Division, commanded by Major General Ralph C. Smith (USA), and the XXIV Corps Artillery, commanded by Brigadier General Arthur M. Harper (USA). The 2nd Marine Division had already seen action on Guadalcanal (one regiment) and at Tarawa (over 3,000 casualties). The 4th Marine Division had participated in the invasion of the Kwajalein atoll. The 27th Infantry Division was a New York National Guard unit and was called into federal service in October of 1940. It was the first National Guard division to enter the Pacific War.[29]

The Japanese had been working to beef up the island's defenses since 1934, and by 1940 had spent well over the equivalent of $7 million. Even though the Japanese government said that the operation and development were for peace projects, it became clearer as war loomed over the Pacific that this was not the intended purpose. There were ammunition storage facilities, barracks in twelve lighthouses, additional lookout stations, as well as a torpedo storage facility.[30]

As the United States moved through the areas of Tarawa and Makin, of the Gilbert Islands, it was clear that Saipan was on the list for the next movement of attack. By all means Japan continued to increase its defense for the island with whatever else they had at their disposal. Saipan may have had a more defensive strategy had their command on the island not been split between the forces of the army and navy. Each was traditionally dependent on the other, but things were not fully working out because of the lack of mutual consent about who was in charge of the forces on the island. "Failure to establish clear-cut command relationships between the army and navy was characteristic of Japanese military organization in the Central Pacific."[31] Although eventually resolved, it was a costly major error in planning. Besides, additional units that would have added abundantly to the strength of Saipan had been sent elsewhere.[32]

Furthermore, as David A. Crowl states in his historical book *Campaign in the Marianas,* American forces were contesting Japanese forces going into the Marianas, specifically Saipan, where they were attempting to continue reinforcing the island. These were major blows being delivered on the movements of these

Japanese carriers and troops. For instance, the 29th Division was being transferred from Ujina, Japan, on February 26 aboard three transports. On February 29, the convoy was struck by American submarines, and the *Sakito Maru*, which had 3,080 troops aboard, was hit and completely sunk. From that ship there were 1,392 that drowned. The 1,688 survivors of the 18th regiment were rescued and taken to Saipan but had almost no type of equipment. As Crowl states, according to one report, "All their weapons were lost except seven rifles, one grenade thrower, two light machine guns, and 150 bayonets."[33]

In less than three weeks, on March 12, another large convoy from Yokohama, carrying the 1st, 5th, and 6th Expeditionary Units, was attacked, and although there no army troops lost, a naval transport, the *Kokuyo Maru*, headed for Guam, was torpedoed and sunk. In April there were more ships sunk and more men rescued, but many died. Over and over more survivors were rescued, taken to Saipan, again without any defense weapons.

A convoy carrying seven thousand men of Japan's 43rd Division was hit by submarine torpedoes, and five of the seven carriers were sunk. Although nearly six thousand of the men were rescued, their fighting and survival gear was not, and essentially, once again, they were incapable of being combat ready.[34]

Analyzing once again the strategy of Japan, it was clear why their forces lost to the military might of the United States. Although Japan had approximately thirty thousand men on Saipan, their preparations destroyed them from the beginning. The United States had the manpower, the assault power, and a strategy for taking Saipan and the other islands on the way to Japan. Heavy-duty air and sea power meant that any defense forces would have had to prepare in a decisive manner and not in a haphazard comportment in order to have a winning strategy against such might.

Because Japanese forces did not have the concrete, the steel, the barbed wire, and other defensive booby traps needed for reinforcements as well as other backups necessary for a solid defensive strategy, they were almost ruined from the onset. By not being prepared and not having the proper fortifications for this type of island, which was different than the atolls in that the atolls were protected with offshore obstacles and reefs, the Japanese had to use a "hold the line at the beach" tactic, which was not an effective stratagem.

Unfortunately, this plan did not work effectively, as the United States Task Force 58's carriers struck a day earlier with a four-day preinvasion battering. Task Force 58 was the long-range naval striking arm of the U.S. Pacific Fleet. These were the fast fleets. They were also designed to wipe out the enemy's air opposition. Then planes from far off bombed the islands of Saipan, Tinian, and Guam, which caught the Japanese by surprise. By the time planes and warships had done their preparatory job, which lasted three days, every coastal gun had been knocked out.[35] "There were no plans to offer opposition, and most of the Japanese shipping was at the bottom" of the Pacific.[36] Although the Japanese did muster an air attack, their calculations were off once again, and the skies lit up as the Japanese pilots had no chance whatsoever, and their planes fell like firecrackers from the sky.

On June 14, in the face of heavy artillery fire, the 2nd and 4th Marine Divisions went ashore on a two-mile stretch of beach at the southwest end of the island. With this movement, the men of Montford Point also went into action, as it was their duty to unload the necessary supplies needed onto the island. Equipment had to be moved that was loaded with every type of necessary item needed for operations. Heavy artillery, light artillery, and many other types of supplies had to be gotten onto the shore. The Japanese were now firing down on these men with everything at their disposal.

The Montford Point ammunition and depot company men, as has been noted, were responsible for unloading the ammo that was needed from their ammo ships at the same time that the assault troops were debarking. They worked around the clock in shifts, about eight hours at a time, until a crew was relieved. Not always were they relieved on schedule; it was dependent on the circumstances, and how much ammunition was being called for and being used on the battlefield. Also, if a crew were assigned to a ship for the specifics of unloading ammo, this is where they stayed until the necessary ammo was unloaded, and then and only then did they move onto the island to continue with distributing the ammo or setting up the dump sites. As the specialists, when the calls came in for certain types of ammo, these men had to know the location of what was being requested and be able to retrieve those items expeditiously. Those men assigned to ship duties, when relieved, found a rest area on board ship, and when it was time to begin again, they'd start their duties all over.

The depot companies of Montford Point Camp were just as important as any other company from Montford Point Camp. Their service was outstanding, and their role was just as significant as the role of any other outfit in the war in the Pacific. They played major roles in Noumea, New Caledonia, the Solomon and

Russell Islands, Iwo Jima, Saipan, and Okinawa. Anywhere there were Marine troops and Army troops as well, in some cases, the depot companies played a distinguished major role.

Hawaii was the primary staging location for the drive across the Central Pacific, and five depot companies were there with the two that had recently returned from Funafuti, loading supplies that were headed to the Gilbert and Marshall Islands. Those two companies had spent nine months there. As a matter fact, these companies would help the 2nd and 4th Marine Divisions that were headed to Saipan load the ships while they were in Hawaii, and then many would head to Saipan to help unload that precious cargo once they arrived at the destination.

Also called D-Day, this was June 15, 1944. The workload was immense for these depot companies. It was no easy task removing cargo from ships' holds into landing craft, moving from the ships through the beaches, and then distributing those supplies to the combat units. "The 18th and 20th Marine Depot Companies landed with the 4th Marine Division on D-Day, while the 19th was going ashore with the 2nd Marine Division. Attached to the 3rd Battalion, 23rd Marines, 4th Marine Division, one platoon of the 18th Company arrived at its assigned beach about two and one-half hours after the first wave."[37] Four of these men were wounded. One squad fought as infantry to reinforce a line. The next morning these men helped eliminate Japanese infiltrators who had penetrated some boundaries that had been breached.

Regardless of the dangers, these men had to work in the waist-high agitating water while bringing in supplies needed to sustain the troops. Food, water, and a host of other necessary items had to go ashore. Much of their time was also spent keeping an eye out for snipers as well as tracking down those that had been spotted infiltrating the perimeters. Of course, casualties also had to be removed and taken back to ship. Whatever was needed that could be handled by hand for support and assistance, these men were responsible for, including oil and gasoline for vehicles.

In order to bring the heavy equipment needed onto the shore, including sufficient troops and supplies, the Marines had to push hard. The first day the movement had landed on the beaches, but the men were still taking heavy fire, and it wasn't until three days later that the Americans were able to secure and expand to a 5.5- by 2-mile area. This island was needed desperately. The Navy felt that it was a location that would allow them to attack Japan's air-sea communications and also to be in striking distance to Palau, the Philippines, Formosa, as well as China. The Army Air Corps needed it as a base from which its new long-range bomber, the B-29, could make nonstop strikes on the homeland of Japan. Saipan was situated more than a thousand miles from any U.S. base. This was one of the largest amphibious operations ever in the Pacific, and Saipan could be used to shorten the distances for strikes on Japan. In addition, capturing the island of Saipan would effectively cut off any Japanese forces south of the island from reaching the mainland. The noose was ever tightening.

Nonetheless, the Japanese fought with everything they could muster. Time and again from unseen locations they would muster a charge, and many Marines would die or become wounded in battle. From June 14–15 through July 7, the Japanese gave it everything they had, from heavy artillery to hand-to-hand combat, though it was not enough. The Marines were tough and unstoppable. Meanwhile, knowing that there was no support that could be obtained for his soldiers, General Yoshitsugu Saito, the Japanese commander on Saipan, ordered his men to fight to the last man around the defensive line of Mount Tapotchau, the first place of attack, at the country's mountainous center. As on Iwo Jima this mountainous area was lined with tunnels and caves. From here the Japanese would execute nighttime raids against the American forces. The Americans could only clear out the caves or rout the enemy using flamethrowers in conjunction with the artillery.

At the same time, Saipan was so strategic that Japan sent Vice Admiral Chuichi Nagumo, Commander in Chief for the Central Pacific, to take charge. It was Commander Nagumo who had delivered the sneak attack on Pearl Harbor and was also in charge of the carriers at the Battle of Midway. However, it was not Vice Admiral's Nagumo's idea to attack Hawaii. He knew all too well the risks that were involved in sending carriers such a great distance on open waters. The risks were too dangerous for such a long distance, and so Vice Admiral Nagumo continued to verbally resist while expressing his ideas. His primary objections were that an attack on Hawaii "far too risky, coming after a six-thousand-mile voyage. His carriers were too vulnerable and bound to be spotted. But Admiral Yamamoto overruled him, and Nagumo finally conceded."[38] He would never leave the island; Admiral Nagumo was killed on Saipan.

General Saito also knew the end was at hand. On July 7, he ordered a mass attack by all of his able-bodied men under his command. Not only did his three thousand men push with all they had, but they were also joined by those that were wounded as well as the Japanese civilians that were on the island. General Saito made it clear to the civilians on the island that there was now no distinction between them and the troops. There was no longer any place to retreat for anyone, and even if they used bamboo spears, it would be best for them to join in the attack, for even in death there is life. Well over 4,300 of these civilians also died. Below are the words spoken to his men in their final charge called the Banzai Attack:

> I am addressing the officers and men to the Imperial Army on Saipan.
>
> For more than twenty days since the American devils attacked, the officers, men and civilian employees of the Imperial Army and Navy on this island have fought well and bravely. Everywhere they have demonstrated the honor and glory of the Imperial forces. I expected that every man would do his duty.
>
> Heaven has not given us an opportunity. We have not been able to utilize fully the terrain. We have fought in unison up to the present time but now we have no materials with which to fight and our artillery for attack has been completely destroyed. Our comrades have fallen one after another. Despite the bitterness of defeat, we pledge "seven lives to repay our country."
>
> The barbarous attack of the enemy is being continued even though the enemy has occupied only a corner of Saipan. We are dying without avail under the violent shelling and bombing. Whether we attack or whether we stay where we are, there is only death. However, in death there is life. We must utilize this opportunity to exalt true Japanese manhood. I will advance with those who remain to deliver still another blow to the American devils and leave my bones on Saipan as a bulwark of the Pacific.
>
> As it says in the Senjinkun battle ethics, "I will never suffer the disgrace of being taken alive and I will offer up the courage of my soul and calmly rejoice in living by the eternal principal."
>
> Here I pray with you for the eternal life of the emperor and the welfare of the country, and I advance to seek out the enemy. Follow me.[39]

Japan did try to garner more forces together initially, knowing that winning or losing the war hinged on winning the battle of the Marianas: Guam, Tinian, but primarily Saipan. Japan had added a "restored strike force of nine carriers and more than 460 aircraft to oppose the landings." Just a little too late, as the American forces sunk three carriers and an unbelievable 395 planes were shot down. "Saipan, Guam, and Tinian fell and quickly became forward U.S. bases for long-range B-29 Superfortress bombers." As Herbert P. Bix describes in *Hirohito and the Making of Modern*

Japan, "The capture of Saipan ... was a particularly heavy blow for the high command.... Japan had lost virtually the entire garrison of 23,811 as well as ten thousand noncombatants."[40]

Once secured, the American forces watched in horror as thousands of Saipan's civilians who lived on the island committed suicide either through the Japanese customary method or by jumping off a ridge called Suicide Cliff, over seven hundred feet high, onto the rocks on the side of the mountain.

Turner Blount is one Montford Pointer that was part of the operation on Saipan and stayed in Saipan until the end of the operation there. Many of the civilians that were on the Island, approaching twenty thousand, were contained in a two-square-mile camp called Susupe and then later moved to another site called Camp Chalan Konoa. Blount then moved onto another island, Tinian, which was also in the Marianas, and he performed the same type of operation and duties there. There was complete and utter destruction for the fighting Japanese on Saipan and Tinian, including all of their operations from airfields, airplanes, and coastal defenses. From there, this group of men from the 19th Marine Depot of Montford Point found themselves in Okinawa and again moving supplies onto the front lines of the operation, guarding prisoners, as well as performing guard duties and setting up dump sites. And, of course, they never knew when the fight would be coming their way.[41] Staff Sergeant Timberlate Kirven and Corporal Samuel J. Love certainly proved this point by each receiving Purple Hearts in the Saipan Campaign for injuries sustained in battle.

CHAPTER 16

The Kamikaze Pilots

It is also important to note another factor that was in play with regard to World War II and the type of fighters that were engaging the American soldiers. It is critical to document that the kamikaze pilots were a threat to all of the fighting soldiers, including the Marines, although they were primarily engaging warships. Background information is important in setting the stage for these unusual men.

> In the year 1281, Japan was under attack by a Mongol invasion—led by the powerful Kublai Khan. However, just as it appeared that the invading Mongols were about to overwhelm the Japanese, a catastrophic typhoon swept through the land, eliminating the entire Mongol army. From that point on, the typhoon that saved Japan became known as the Kamikaze, or Divine Wind.[1]

The "divine wind" later materialized as Kamikaze pilots in World War II. Once the commander of the First Air Fleet in the Philippines, Japanese Vice Admiral Takijiro Ohnishi realized the damage that could be done by one plane flying directly into a warship, he decided to use that strategy to its fullest potential. That would be to equip them to achieve maximum damage. It began during the Pearl Harbor attack when some pilots, as a spur-of-the-moment decision, began crashing their planes into the ships there.[2]

As a reinforcing consideration in his planning of the devastation that could occur with this method, it was shown again when the Royal Australian Navy heavy cruiser HMAS *Australia* sustained massive damage when hit by a Japanese plane off Leyte Island on October 21, 1944. Although the plane was carrying a 441-pound bomb, it never exploded, but the damage was so severe it was almost as if the bomb did explode, and at least thirty crew members were killed and dozens of others received severe wounds.[3]

Because the Japanese military, and Vice Admiral Takijiro Ohnishi in particular, were always looking for ways to do more and more damage to their Americans enemies and to take more lives in the process, he decided to expand his program into one that purposely included crashing planes into ships. This time, however, the attacking planes would be equipped with bombs specifically for the purpose of doing as much damage as possible to the ships and the crew members. Feeling assured that this plan would cause devastating and crippling blows to the Americans,[4] there were more than two thousand planes that staged these attacks during the next few months.[5] Not only were planes used in these attacks, but there were small manned torpedoes that the pilots were able to ride within torpedoes and direct them into large carriers, cruisers, or warships.[6]

These guided torpedoes were called *kaiten* which means "sky change," according to Yutaka Yokota, author of *The Kaiten Weapon*. "*Kaiten*, in our connotation, means to bring about a tremendous change in the way things are going, to make a radical reverse in affairs."[7]

Two men, who at the time of the Battle of Midway in June 1942, were pilots of midget submarines, knew of the value of these minisubs. They were Ensign Sekio Nishina and Lieutenant, Junior Grade, Hiroshi Kuroki. All of Japan, "thanks to the much publicized double-promotion of midget submarine men lost in the Pearl Harbor attack, felt that such craft played an important part on the war's opening day. They were considered very valuable weapons" and needed to continue to be used for maximum damage to American ships. These two men would help to continue with the development of these midget subs. They were able to find Hiroshi Suzukawa at the Kure Naval Arsenal and persuaded him to join their team for building one-man torpedoes "so designed as to be quickly released from the deck of a submerged submarine."[8]

The final design was constructed to be able to mount four, five, or six *kaiten* on each deck. Not only was the mounting crucial, but it was also designed to insert a pilot's compartment aft of the warhead. Within this chamber would be a periscope, a seat, and a set of controls.[9] By January 1943, everything these men had worked to develop was now complete. This torpedo, Model 93, was much larger and thicker, growing from thirty feet to fifty-four feet, and the main feature is that it would carry a monster charge—three thousand pounds—of high explosives, which was five times that of enemy torpedoes, right in its nose.[10]

These and other weapons were the types that kept American soldiers on edge at all times. Whether you were on land in ammunition dumps or on the seas in transport ships, carriers or otherwise, it was always in the forefront of one's mind about where the next attack would come from.

Well known was the spirit of loyalty to Japan and especially to Emperor Hirohito by all citizens of Japan. World War II was especially a time for citizens to express just what that loyalty meant, whether by choice or otherwise. For the kamikaze pilot, it meant a one-time final journey in a flying death trap.

Yuki Tanaka, in her article "Japan's Kamikaze Pilots and Contemporary Suicide Bombers," says that contrary to the major belief that "the major source of kamikaze suicide pilots was the Air Force Cadet Officer System in the Japanese Imperial Navy and Army Forces, which recruited university and college students on a voluntary basis," the fact is that the "the majority of kamikaze pilots were young noncommissioned or petty officers, that is, graduates of Navy and Army junior flight training schools," at least initially. The number of noncommissioned Army officers that died as kamikaze pilots was 621. There were 1,732 petty officers in the Navy that died as suicide pilots compared with 782 officers. There was a firm belief for many years and still today in many circles that many of the kamikaze pilots were college science students. The major reason for this is that their records "were compiled and published as books and pamphlets after the war." The records by the noncommissioned and petty officers are not available publicly.[11]

As more Japanese soldiers died exponentially, the call for healthy male university and college students, twenty years of age or older, was granted in October 1943. These younger pilots gained extreme notoriety as these battles continued.[12] These were the models chosen by Vice Admiral Takijiro Ohnishi for his expansion of his program of planes distinctly flying into ships to cause more damage and create more loss of life. It was also crystal clear that at this point in the war, Japanese air forces were not having the success needed to engage in air-to-air combat, so flying directly into allied ships could create more damage than engagement by air anyway, and at the same time create another element of psychological fear and surprise among the Allied Forces. It was also another way for a faster turnaround time for getting more pilots into the battle—faster because the kamikaze only needed to learn takeoff and direction. All the other typical elements needed to command an aircraft were not essential. There was also no need to learn to land the plane, because he would not be returning.[13]

There were rituals used by these "divine wind" men prior to their final engagement in battle. Some of these included writing poems and letters to loved ones, and also the ceremony of receiving a "thousand stitch" cloth belt.[14] Known as a *senninbari,* it was made in the form of a cap, a headband, a vest, or a belt and had one stitch sewn by a thousand different women. "This term literally means 'thousand-person-stitches.'[15] If a woman was born in the year of the tiger, she was able to include either twelve stitches or one stitch for each year of their age, rather than just one."[16] These pilots also thought they would be saved in their darkest hour by the divine wind, just as it had done in the thirteenth century. One of the final acts would be a drink of "spiritual concoction that'd ensure success in the mission" that would give him a spiritual lifting, just prior to strapping himself between two 550-pound bombs.[17]

In fact, on April 6, 1945, there were more than 350 kamikaze pilots that dove at the Allied Fleet at one time. The USS *Laffey* (DDE-724) was attacked by twenty Kamikaze planes and also by bombs from two other planes. It had fires, a jammed rudder, and big guns that would not work. It fought for eighty minutes against twenty-two kamikaze planes and other conventional aircraft but remained afloat despite the odds against it. This ship was hit more times in a single day by kamikaze pilots than any other ship. Captain F. Julian Becton and the crew beat the odds with their work of keeping it afloat and saving more lives of the crew members. Nonetheless, thirty-one or thirty-two men perished, and sixty to seventy were wounded.[18]

The kamikaze did much damage to the Allied Fleet, although they were the ones that fared the worst. By the end of the Battle of Okinawa twenty-three carriers were damaged and two escort carriers as well as three destroyers were sunk. Damaged also were five battleships, nine cruisers, twenty-three destroyers, and twenty-seven other ships and many lives.[19]

It was truly amazing that with all the ammunition being carried throughout the South Pacific by ship with soldiers from Montford Point aboard, and other ammunition laden ships, that they were fortunate to avoid devastating damage by these kamikaze pilots. Although the kamikaze had a substantial attack force, it was not enough to turn the tide of the battle, and it was later discovered that there were more than several thousand reserve kamikaze planes in wait for the invasion of the mainland of Japan, which never took place. The kamikaze strike played a pivotal role in the decision by President Harry S. Truman to drop the atomic bomb.[20] The Japanese surrender took place on August 15, 1945. The day after the Japanese surrender, the disgraced Takijiro Ohnishi ended his own life by *seppuku,* leaving a note of apology to his dead pilots: "Their sacrifice had been in vain."[21]

CHAPTER 17

Another Dazzling Chess Move: Navajo Code Talkers

The African American Marines were not the only soldiers who were initially in the background in the Marine Corps during World War II. Mention is given here to acknowledge the incredible services that were performed by the Navajo code talkers that also served in the South Pacific.

Philip Johnston was the son of a missionary couple. He was not a Navajo but spent years on the Navajo reservation as a child. He was familiar with the customs and was familiar with the Navajo language. Johnston was a veteran of World War I and knew the importance of communication in battle.[1] He knew that if the enemy could decipher your messages in battle, then your chances of success in war was greatly jeopardized.

He had also heard that during World War I there were eight Choctaw men that were communicating with each other in their native language near the end of the war, and that the Germans were not able to decipher their messages.[2] Because they were not able to pick up on what was being said, and also completely fooled by what they thought they were deciphering, crucial information was able to be communicated, and it helped the Americans to defeat the Germans.

Now in World War II, Johnston once again thought about how important it was to have a language that could not be deciphered by your enemy. He had also heard that the military was searching for a new secret code to use against the Japanese, and right away he thought of the Navajo language.[3] The Navajo language is extremely complex. There is a certain type of syntax and tonal quality, and it has several different dialects to it that make it completely unintelligible to anyone without intensive training and study, and even then it is nearly impossible. "Thus, it is difficult for a non-Navajo speaker to hear Navajo words properly, and virtually impossible to reproduce those words."[4]

The Navajo language had no alphabet or symbols, and then as now primarily spoken on the Navajo lands of the Southwestern United States. Prior to World War II, every code that the Americans utilized in war had been broken, and to this extent, the Japanese were experts at code deciphering.[5] During this period of time it was rumored that less than thirty non-Navajos could understand the language and speak it, and none of them were Japanese, so this seemed to be an excellent idea.[6]

According to Adam Jevec's writing on the code talkers, "Philip Johnston met with Major General Clayton B. Vogel, the commanding general of the Amphibious Corps, Pacific Fleet, and his staff, to convince them of the Navajo language's value as a code."[7]

"Johnston staged tests under simulated combat conditions, demonstrating that Navajos could encode, transmit, and decode a three-line English message in twenty seconds. Machines of the time required thirty minutes to perform the same job."[8] Thoroughly "convinced, General Vogel recommended to the Commandant of the Marine Corps that the Marines recruit two hundred Navajos."[9]

In May 1942, the first twenty-nine Navajos entered boot camp. It was at Camp Pendleton in Oceanside, California, that these men created the Navajo code. They had to create and develop a dictionary and words for military codes, and the dictionary and all code words had to be memorized during this process. It was also here that these men were formed into the 382nd Platoon, USMC. During this time, in order to test this new code, these recruits were asked to test the theory on some Navajos who were not code talkers, and they were not able to understand it. It was also at this time, at Camp Pendleton, that the USMC recruited and started training 200 code talkers.[10]

These men were then sent to the Pacific to join a Marine unit. On Iwo Jima, for example, there were six Navajo code talkers that worked around the clock during the first two days of battle. These six alone received and sent over eight hundred messages, and not one was deciphered. Even though the Japanese were skilled at breaking codes, they were never able to break the code of these men. Lieutenant General Seizo Arisue, the Japanese chief of intelligence, said later that while they were able to "decipher the codes used by the U.S. Army and Army Air Corps, they never cracked the code used by the Marines."[11]

Throughout World War II, according to these same stats, there were about 540 members of the Navajo Nation that served in the Marine Corps. Over 420 of these members served as code talkers.[12] It is a known fact and one without question that these code talkers were invaluable during this time. It is greatly acknowledged that these brave and courageous soldiers saved thousands of American lives.

CHAPTER 18

The End of the War

In the meantime, the Allies were engaged in every endeavor possible to get Japan to cease fighting and to give up. On July 26, 1945, in the Potsdam Declaration, President Harry S. Truman, the Chairman of the nationalist government of China Chiang Kai-shek, the Soviet Union, and Prime Minister Winston Churchill of Great Britain all appealed to Japan with a statement outlining the steps for Japan to surrender. Although thirteen major elements made up the declaration, it stated in short that if Japan did not surrender according to the terms outlined, which in fact would have allowed Japan a sense of peace and security after surrendering and abiding by the rules, it would face "prompt and utter destruction" if it did not comply.[1] The Potsdam Declaration would totally change the course of Japan's history for all time, with the details that were included within the context of the surrender agreement, but the most devastating part, "prompt and utter destruction," would no doubt have been avoided and would have saved hundreds of thousands of lives, and most importantly, innocent civilians.

During the many appeals to the Japan process, Japan was being devastated by a bombing campaign that was now striking at will. The United States and their Allies were able to strike much more strategically and effectively because of two major factors, the first being that they were now using B-29s, which carried a great payload. Second, they no longer had to fly planes from such long distances as originally. The bombing campaign had originally begun from Chinese airbases beginning June 15, 1944, which were some two thousand miles from Tokyo.[2] The bases in China were being supplied by air from India. This created lots of problems because the supply carriers had to fly over an area known as "the hump."[3] This was the eastern part of the Himalayas. At the time, charts and weather reports were unreliable for making this pass. Also, the distances from the airbase to Japan could only be reached if the B-29s replaced some of their bombs with fuel in tanks in the bomb-bays. Even then, it was a stretch for these Superfortresses to fly such long distances. After capturing the Marianas, the U.S. Forces were able to have airfields that could sustain hundreds of B-29s at one time.

Japan knew the importance of the loss of the Marianas and quickly assessed that the Allies would use this location for bombing raids against them. They were absolutely correct, as on July 21, 1944, three platoons of the 2nd Marine Ammunition Company were storming those northern beaches in support of the 3rd Marine Division, while at the same time the 4th Ammunition Company and one platoon of the 2nd assisted the 1st provisional Marine Brigade on the south beach.[4] There, the "4th Marine Ammunition Company set up the brigade ammunition dump and set in to protect it throughout the night of D-Day."[5]

As the night unfolded, Japanese soldiers snuck in to try to blow up the dump, but were unsuccessful in their attempt. The African American Marines killed fourteen infiltrators who were carrying explosives. On August 10, when the objective was declared secure, the ammo and depot companies were still supporting the assault forces.[6] Members of the 1st Provisional Marine Brigade, which included the African Americans of the 4th Marine Ammunition Company and the attached platoon from the 2nd Company, were awarded the Navy Unit Commendation.[7]

As Japan prepared with defenses against what they knew would be forthright in coming, the Allies were even busier planning on a multifold campaign for strikes that Japan could only imagine. Admiral Nimitz began to coordinate sea, land, and air forces that secured the southern Marianas along with Lieutenant General Millard Harmon, who on August 1, 1944, became commander of the Army Air Force, Pacific Ocean Areas. Included in this coordination was Major General Haywood S. Hansell Jr., former chief of staff of the 20th Air Force, and General Henry "Happy" Arnold. No one could even imagine the retribution that Japan was going to continue to absorb as the U.S. Forces acted on the Japanese homeland.[8]

In 1945, Major General Hansell was in charge of the XXI Bomber Command B-29s in the Marianas. There were many problems concerning the group and the lack of success they were having on bombing Japan, which in turn exacerbated pressure from Hansell's higher ups. The plan with the B-29 bombing campaign was initially not going as planned, with miscalculations, misplacements of the dropped bombs, searing jet-stream winds pushing the airplanes until they were beyond the target, and even engine malfunctions. One of the major factors was as these bombers were flying at 25,000 to 30,000 feet with a cloud cover at 6,000 feet, and only 6 percent of the bombs dropped were within 1,000 feet of the target.

One problem after another seemed to befall Hansell. "After the successful December 1944 fire raid by the India-based XX Bomber Command against Hankow, China, 20th Air Force Chief of Staff Brigadier General Lauris Norstad and General Arnold directed Hansell to launch similar fire raids against Japan from the Marianas."[9] Hansell reluctantly sent and incendiary raid against the city of Nagoya, but the raid did not reach the level of destruction his superiors had envisioned. It was time to replace Hansell.

Hansell was replaced by Major General Curtis E. LeMay. The advantages were on the side of LeMay because with the Marines having captured the island of Iwo Jima, it destroyed the ability of Japan's radar site "from which to warn the home islands of impending raids. Iwo Jima soon became a staging base, a fighter-escort base, and an air rescue station."[10] General LeMay began to use Iwo Jima for beginning his nighttime incendiary bombing as a supplement to his "high-altitude daylight bombing" of Japanese cities. This incendiary bombing campaign became hell on earth and possibly worse for hundreds of thousands of Japanese.

On February 25, 1945, LeMay struck Tokyo with 172 B-29s and left twenty-eight million square feet of urban properties burning.[11] On March 9–10, 1945, XXI Bomber Command passed over five of the largest Japanese cities, including Tokyo, Osaka, Nagoya, and Kobe and again delivered from 279 B-29s almost two thousand tons of firebombs. In this raid there were more than 83,000 people killed and more than 40,000 injured, while there were more than a million left homeless. Nagoya, on the night of March 11–12, was immediately struck again with 285 B-29s and incendiary bombs and was devastated again.[12] Just before dawn on March 14, Osaka had 274 B-29s deliver more bombs dropped on the city while Kobe on March 17 had 307 B-29s deliver the message in the form of more incendiary bombs.[13] In May and June 1945, the capital city Tokyo had no less than 520 B-29 incendiary bombing attacks, and then two nights later had 464 B-29s reinforce the attacks with three thousand tons of incendiary bombs.[14] City after city continued to be destroyed while their military leaders continued to think there was a way to continue the resistance.

Although nearly totally devastated, Japan continued their assault without the slightest hint of truce, not even for the innocent civilians who—by the hundreds of thousands—were now included in the destruction.

According to Mark Selden, in his article "American Fire Bombing and Atomic Bombing of Japan in History and Memory," the mission of the United States bombing campaign beginning with the March 9–10 raid was to unleash total devastation not upon military targets but on reducing the cities to complete rubble, killing the citizens that occupied them and forcing whomever was left to flee. If there was to be anyone left, the terror instilled in them would create zombie-like people. To avoid detection, these B-29s flew at an altitude of about 7,000 feet and carried 182 M47s, hundred-pound oil-gel bombs, per aircraft, each of which could start a major fire. Each aircraft also contained M69s, six-pound gelled-gasoline bombs, 1,520 per aircraft, and they reinforced those with high explosives to deter any firefighters that thought they had a chance to assist in fighting a fire. At night, because of Japan's weak defenses, the United States bombed almost with abandonment.[15]

There were high winds with terrific forces that propelled these firestorms with unbelievable speed and mercilessness. These winds thrust the temperatures up to "1,800 degrees Fahrenheit, creating superheated vapors that advanced ahead of the flames, killing or incapacitating their victims." The area of fire covered fifteen square miles in six hours, and nothing escaped the burn damage.[16]

After constant appeals and devastation to Japan, the Allies decided it was time to unleash the greatest firepower on their side, the atomic bomb. On August 6, 1945, the first of two atomic bombs would be unleashed. The first fell on Hiroshima, delivered from the *Enola-Gay*. Three days later, on August 9, the second bomb, delivered by the *Bockscar*, fell on Nagasaki.[17] Finally, on August 14–15, Japan surrendered.

Many of the Montford Pointers, after hearing of the news of Japan surrendering, hoped to be heading home. Enough was enough. It was now time to pack up. Unfortunately, that would not be the case. Members of the 5th Marine Division, which included many Montford Pointers, realized they would now be participating in the occupation of Japan. On August 27, many of them were headed for Japan.

Following the successful operations by the Montford Pointers in moving supplies, plans had been made to use almost all of these specialized units in the invasion of Kyushu, known as "Operation Olympic," which was supposed to take place in November 1945. However, it never materialized because the Japanese surrendered prior to the operation. However, many of these units shipped out to Japan and China anyway. In *The Right to Fight,* Nalty writes:

> Meanwhile, the V Amphibious Corps, which had conquered Iwo Jima, would participate in the occupation of Japan. Assigned to the 8th Service Regiment (formerly the 8th Field Depot) in support of the Marine V Amphibious Corps, the 6th, 8th, and 10th Ammunition Companies arrived in conquered Japan between 22 and 26 September, along with the 24th, 33d, 34th, 42nd, and 43rd Depot Companies. The 36th Marine Depot Company joined the earlier arrivals by the end of October.[18]

Then there were others who had arrived as well, including "men of the 1st and 12th Ammunition Companies and the 5th, 20th, 37th, and 38th Depot Companies."[19]

Sergeant Major Huff, of Montford Point fame, recalls the initial reaction from some Chinese. He indicated that a "Chinese might run up to a black Marine and touch his face to see if the color would rub off."[20] They kept a reserve about them regarding these Black Marines until they became familiar with them. Huff was quoted as saying, "as soon as they found that this paint wouldn't come off, or what they thought was paint, the Chinese "got to be very charming and very lovely."[21]

And so, after centuries of struggle and quagmire, fierce battles, lives given and thousands of questions regarding the validity and bravery of these African American soldiers and whether or not the colors would "come off when rubbed," the military establishment now knows that the colors are deeply embedded. Even after these decades of tests, the colors have shown that they are here to stay; they are going nowhere. People the world over, such as the Chinese, the Japanese, the Indians, the Germans, and others can verify this. Warriors who have come up against these fighters can rapidly attest to the bravery, fierceness, and preparedness of these men on the battlefield. The U.S. Marine Corps tested this concept as well. They rubbed hard, deep, and long, and they found the same to be true. The Marines are also the standard bearers, and no one can rub as deeply or test as thoroughly as the Corps. As a result, it quickly prompted Marine Corps General Alexander Vandegrift to announce, "The Negro Marines are no longer on trial. They are Marines, period."[22] General James F. Amos said:

> Every Marine from private to general will know the history of those men who crossed the threshold to fight not only the enemy they were soon to know overseas, but the enemy of racism and segregation in their own country. My promise to you is that your story will not be forgotten. It will take its rightful place and will be forever anchored in the rich history of the United States Marine Corps.[23]

As ironic as the twists and turns were, these great giants of New River, North Carolina, have fully emerged and will forever live in Marine Corps history and in our lives and hearts as well. These are the Montford Point Marines.

Likewise, during this period of time there were many achievements that were recognized and noticed with regard to the Montford Pointers. These achievements showed that not only were these Black Marines capable of handling the tasks of being outstanding Marines, and that when given the opportunity to demonstrate their capabilities without overt negative criticism, they, the NCOs, and other officers of these companies could work together with these Black Marines as an outstanding team. Furthermore, it also indicated that both Blacks and Whites, all Marines, could work together for the common cause of the United States. Furthermore, it showed that these men would be rewarded and not be allowed to continuously go unnoticed for their actions on the battlefield.

Around this time, Dad, like so many others, was beginning to have trouble with his feet. The location and work at the ammo dumps were harsh. The ground was usually unstable. Cramped in boots after the feet were swollen and damp and always working overtime moving boxes and crates and pallets to meet the demands of the fighting men were not advantageous to one's feet, as many military men can attest to. Dad was transferred back to Camp Catlin base to have them checked out. He said that on Camp Catlin the barracks had originally been built for the White soldiers, but that they had moved out, and these were the facilities that the Black Marines were to use as their facilities. They were wooden and dark green in color and suitable.

While there, he requested a transfer to the clerical typist department. He began to serve his remaining time there along with two other men from his outfit and to keep records of his company men as well as other duties. He typed and recorded what is known as the Muster Roll for his company, and he knew who the men were, or of them, stationed at his location and elsewhere, in what capacity they were serving, along with other classified information. His tour in Hawaii lasted twenty-two or twenty-three months, until the latter part of March 1946, at which time he sailed back to the United States, and as dad worded it, "under the Golden Gate Bridge on April 1, 1946."[24]

CHAPTER 19

Home Sweet Home

Although it was fortunate that Dad's time was served in and around the Hawaiian Islands at the ammunition sites, of course this was not to be the case with the thousands of the other Montford Pointers. Most of the Montford Point Marines were anxious to see combat, and although many were disappointed, having to serve in auxiliary units and cleanup details after the Pacific Islands were secured by White Marines, many were not. Men in ammunition companies and depot companies saw combat on the beaches of Iwo Jima, Saipan, Peleliu, and Okinawa, just to name a few. Despite the general notion that Blacks were not ready for combat, they were integrated into combat experiences, which earned the respect of their White counterparts. What the White Marines saw was how these Montford Point Marines excelled in forced battle while at the same time continued supplying the White assault Marines who were on the front lines with ammo and other supplies, and then still had to carry the wounded and killed away from the front lines and other areas.

Yes, this group of Montford Point Marines was there. When the flag was raised by the White Marines, which many Americans have seen in the legendary photo on the mountain known as Mount Suribachi on Iwo Jima, these brave Montford Point Men were the ones supplying those front line Marines with the ammunition and support needed to take that location.

What some people did not know was that these other men of Montford Point, such as Al Banker, Joseph Ginyard, Harris Ginyard, Theodore Peters, and Randolph Harrell were men like Thomas Mosley. These men came from homes like my father's. Many came from families that called on the Lord both day and night, in good times and in bad. Do you think the Lord would let their calls go unnoticed? The Lord heard the cries of these men and their families. The Lord has now revealed these gallant men from Montford Point and raised them to the very top of society.

Who do people think they are that they can take a mother's child away, philosophically speaking, send them into hell and hellholes, send them into battle and take their lives, innocence, and youth, and not compensate their mother or sisters or brothers for that? Not compensate their children, their nieces and nephews, and grandchildren for that! Or to pretend that their lives are not as important as someone whose skin color is different. Dad always stressed the importance of being patient and always said that things would work out because God sees everything. "Don't be so quick-tempered," he'd say. One of his favorite clichés is still, "The proof is in the pudding."[1]

With that being said, let's now look at the reward that the Creator has bestowed on these sons and fathers that were Montford Pointers for having the ultimate patience and remaining calm even after sixty years. They have received the highest award that any human being can receive in this country. They have officially received the Congressional Gold Medal. This Congressional Gold Medal also allows family members, friends, and comrades to share in the dignity and to hold their heads up even higher than we were able to do before. We are all a part of this master plan.

Another segment and irony to this unfolding plan is that I received a phone call sometime in mid-June 2012. It was from a longtime friend of my family named Pearl Garner of Timmonsville, South Carolina. Pearl's mother and my mom were best friends while growing up in Timmonsville. Pearl and I talk from time to time as well as Pearl and my oldest sister, Helen. It is always refreshing to talk to Pearl as she tells me stories about my mom, who is now deceased, and relates things to me that I did not know. She has always revered my family and held us in high esteem, and so I have a tremendous amount of respect and love for her.

Since I was not able to receive Pearl's call at the time of her call, she left a voice message for me indicating that someone she knew from Timmonsville, a very prominent person and a lifelong acquaintance of her family, had also received a Congressional Gold Medal, and that my dad may know this gentleman. Since I was extremely busy, I was not able to call her back right away, but later I finally did. With more detail this time, she related information to me of Mr. Randolph Harrell, a native of Timmonsville. I took some time, went online, and saw a newspaper article that Pearl said had been written about Mr. Harrell in the *Florence Morning Times*.

I called Mr. Harrell, and we began exchanging pleasantries and talking about the people he knew growing up in Timmonsville. Before you know it, he was telling me about members he knew and grew up with from Pearl's family. I later started talking about my family members, and he told me that my mother's first cousin, Johnny Lee Young, whom I also knew when I was a child, but of course was much older, and he were best friends as kids. It turns out they went to the same schools, both played intermural sports together, and they were close friends. Not only did he know Johnny Lee but also some of the other siblings. That would not last long, though, because just four days after high school, Randolph was headed to New York City.[2]

While heading to New York, Mr. Harrell ended up landing a job working at the Navy Yard in Norfolk, Virginia. He wanted to be where his sister was in New York but somehow meandered his way to Norfolk. "I didn't know that as long as I worked at the yard that I would not be drafted. I then decided to do some other things and left the yard to become a traveling salesman for a while. The money seemed like it could be better. But the moment I left the yard, I received my draft card. I did not realize that while I was at the Navy Yard, I was on deferment by working for the U.S. government."[3] His two choices at that time were the Navy or the Marines. The Marine Corps uniform looked good, and the next thing you know, he's in the Marine Corps. That uniform stood out in his mind, and in fact, he said, "I didn't want to be stuck on a ship."[4] This was in 1945.

Mr. Harrell spent his time at Montford Point Camp along with the other Marine recruits experiencing the same type of workload and experiences that other recruits were receiving. One thing that sticks out in Mr. Harrell's mind, he indicated, is that there was very little time wasted after boot camp, and then it was onto the train that carried him and others in his platoon to California. However, while at Montford Point there were some very noticeable things that stood out to Randolph Harrell. He says he did not notice any Black officers, and although he was puzzled about it, he did not allow it to bother him. Mr. Harrell says "I always had a positive mind because my family did not teach prejudice."[5]

That, coupled with the fact that when he was a kid his family worked for a White family in Timmonsville, and Randolph had gotten a surprise from the father of this family. I don't remember if he told me the name. As he recalled, he began the story. This man had been out shopping and happened to notice a shoe-shine kit that he decided to purchase for Randolph, along with some polish. When Randolph saw him again, this man called out to Randolph with the nickname he called him by.

"Hey, Ran," he said, "C'mere, I got something for you."

Randolph went to the man. "Whatchu got for me?" Randolph said.

"I got you a shoe-shine kit, and I'm going to show you how to make some money. I'm going to show you how to shine shoes. But every Sunday before you go up to the post office where I want you to go, you have to come by my house and shine my shoes first, OK?"[6]

Mr. Harrell began to shine those shoes and began making money as well. He said he made a nickel with each shine, but that this man also gave him a whopping twenty-five cents with every shine Randolph imparted to him. Mr. Randolph was one of thirteen children, and this was in the mid-1930s. Mr. Harrell never forgot this story. He says he was "earning some dough."[7]

Time moved forward, and now Randolph Harrell was in the Marine Corps, in a company called the 2nd Colored Replacement Company.[8] He says it was a company that was specific to guard duty. It certainly held true because right after boot camp they were on the train headed to California. With no long layover once off the train, their immediate destination was on board a ship headed to Pearl Harbor. After a short stint there, his next destination was Guam, which was also a short layover, then onto the main destination—Saipan, where he would spend the next nine months of his life.

Mr. Harrell said there was one large prison camp on Saipan.[9] Within that camp there were all Japanese men. He describes it as a large camp with hundreds of Japanese, and he and the other guards did their guarding primarily from guard towers interspersed every so often along the perimeter. One thing he remembered with surprise is when I asked him how he communicated with the Japanese. "They understood English, and many of them spoke English,"[10] he said. Mr. Harrell got a chance to go around the island of Saipan and observe with "wonder and amazement, the memories of the fierce fighting that had taken place on this island."

Since finding out about the colored replacement battalions

or the colored replacement draft, I have heard other mentions of these or similar outfits from Montford Point Camp. It seems these outfits were begun in the mid-to-late 1940s because the mentions come from Marines that were enlisted or drafted around the latter part of the war. One indication came from a Marine who was at Montford Point named Charles O. Foreman. I was not able to glean much information from the passage that I saw his information in, but nevertheless he was in the 1st Colored Replacement Battalion, and he says there were about a hundred men in the group. Most replacement groups, it seems, were bound for Saipan as prison guards at the camps there for the Japanese. I will continue to research these companies.

More detailed information was extracted about Montford Pointers from interviews in a series of transcripts by the Montford Point Marine Association, from an interview done with another Montford Pointer named Corporal Averet Corley, who was born in Indianapolis, entered the Corps in 1945 and was recalled for a tour of duty during the Korean War, but initially served at Montford Point. Corley started his military life in the Army Air Corps. No sooner had he completed his preflight training than they found out his age; he was just sixteen, and he was honorably discharged. Totally dissatisfied with civilian life, he decided to join the Marine Corps on July 21, 1945. He says the Marine Corps did not spare anything on his outfits training and equipment because these recruits were being shipped out just as soon as they had enough information and training to do the jobs at hand that were required of them.[11]

Mr. Corley's specialty was communication and as a telephone lineman. He was in the 6th Replacement Draft Company, which was being sent to Saipan, and he was sent to Saipan as a replacement unit for the 52nd Defense Battalion. These again were the heavy antiaircraft artillery Montford Pointers. It was now time for some of these men to be relieved, and the 6th Replacement had to get to Saipan expeditiously to man the heavy equipment that was now unmanned there.[12]

Mr. Corley says by the time he arrived on Saipan, his duty became guarding the two thousand or so Japanese prisoners that were taken captive on the island until they could be repatriated to Japan. While there, he would also be a part of the crew that would replace the electrical lines and telephone systems that had been destroyed. The next venture that happened as rapidly as this deployment was that Mr. Corley was sent to Guam within another outfit. There he would be a part of the 49th Depot Company.[13]

Mr. Corley left the Corps in 1951, completed a bachelor's degree in agriculture at Purdue University and a master's in education at Indiana University, and went on to a successful career as an educator. He last resided in Indianapolis as of 2004.[14]

Another part of this story shows how things go full circle in life, and to show how many times things are meant to be, not just happenstance. While we were in Washington, D.C., my wife and I decided to go to meet some of the Montford Pointers who were staying at the Hampton Inn Hotel, which is also where my dad was staying. Adjoining the Hampton Inn was the Radisson, where additional Montford pointers were being lodged. Being the first night of the Montford Pointers in town, some traveling from as far away as California, arrangements had been made by the Marine Corps, including Dr. James T. Averhart and others, for an evening of meet-and-greet, an icebreaker for these travelers.[15]

Driving onto the semicircular driveway in front of the Hotel, I spotted and exclaimed to my wife that there is Past National President Master Gunnery Sergeant Joseph Geeter of the Montford Point Marine Association. Sergeant Geeter served as the 16th National President of the association, from 2005 to 2009. During the 2010 National Convention held in Fredericksburg, Virginia, Mr. Geeter was inducted into the Hall of Fame for the Montford Point Marine Association. As of 2021 his current position with the association is the National Legislative Officer, and he also serves as the National Public Relations Officer. Mr. Geeter is an awesome individual. He is really down-to-earth and treats you with warmth and sincerity.[16]

After reading his history one day, long before I met him, I thought to myself, "This man could easily be in almost any capacity he seeks in any public office." However, when one catches one's thoughts properly and you see just what he was able to accomplish for these Montford Pointers and the achievement of obtaining these Congressional Gold Medals for these men from President Barack Obama and Congress, you realize what the significance of his background means, and also that he was in the capacity he needed to be in, in order to help secure this level of honor for these men, their families, and the country. One day in 2007, Master Gunnery Sergeant Geeter received a phone call from a Marine, a World War II veteran named James "Rudy" Carter, who at the time was ninety years old. Mr. Carter had just finished reading an article about the renowned Tuskegee Airmen. No doubt there was a little "spice" in his voice after the article he read indicated that the Tuskegee Airmen had recently received Congressional Gold Medals for their service in World War II, while the Montford Point Marines, who braved some of the harshest treatment as new inductees in the Marine Corps at that time and also while overseas in battle, were hardly recognized at all. All these years later!

Mr. Carter had one major question. At the time Master Gunnery Sergeant Geeter was the National Montford Point Marine Association President of the first Black Marines. Mr. Carter had no doubt that the Tuskegee Airmen deserved this esteemed medal, but also knew his crew, the Montford Point Marines, who served in the swamps, the death traps, and the mosquito-laden jungles of Southeast Asia while fighting the Japanese Empire, also deserved to be rewarded the highest of honors as well. So he asked Master Gunnery Sergeant Geeter his question: What was he planning to do about it?[17]

The weight of this question was unmistakable. There was no backing up or sidestepping it, and the only answer came to Master Gunnery Sergeant Geeter's mind. He replied: "Well, Rudy, it looks like I'm going to get the Congressional Gold Medal for the Montford Point Marines."[18] These words reverberated in his mind, although he had no concrete idea of how to proceed. The one thing he did know was that the Congressional Gold Medal came from Congress as a result of a bill passed, and the halls of Congress would be his new stomping grounds. He eventually met Florida State Senator Anthony "Tony" Hill (D), who introduced him to others, including U.S. Representative Corrine Brown (D-Fla.) as well as members of the Congressional Black Caucus of U.S. legislators and others.

At one point, they almost had to completely start over, and the bill had to be reintroduced into the House of Representatives in July 2011. Senator Kay Hagan (D-N.C.) did all that she could do as well to lobby her fellow senators, and she was a staunch supporter of the Montford Pointers receiving this prestigious award.

There were still lots of roads through Congress to navigate and with the help of Representative Corrine Brown, who agreed to cosponsor the legislation, and Master Gunnery Sergeant Geeter having to learn to write a flawless bill to present, but eventually the bill came out perfectly. On November 23, 2011, President Barack Obama signed the bill into law, bestowing the highest honor to the Montford Point Marines. In the end Master Gunnery Sergeant Joe Geeter kept his word and could report back to James

"Rudy" Carter and the other Montford Point Marines that his mission was complete.[19]

He knew that he had to seek the highest recognition for these men and that anything short of a Congressional Gold Medal would not be good enough. He set about that task, and after years of hardship and toil, he was able to hit the mark. As he related to me during one of our conversations, he had tried and tried again, and just when he thought he was almost there, he lost some of his supporters in Congress, and then later, after the hardship of gaining new supporters, was told he needed a bill to be put on the floor of Congress. He then had to learn to write a bill to be presented by his lobbyists. On and on this process went, one step at a time, until some years later, in 2011, gold was finally struck.[20]

This was a great opportunity to finally meet such a distinguished person. We pulled the car up next to Sergeant Geeter, who was standing at the entrance to the hotel. I rolled the window down and spoke to him by calling out his name, "Sergeant Joseph Geeter!" thinking he might recognize my voice after having spoken with him at some length by telephone seven or eight times. He said hello, and I told him who I was, but it didn't seem to ring a bell. He said what I typically knew was his favorite line, "Why don't you refresh my memory?" I did, and then introduced my wife. I told him I'm going to park the car, and he walked over to where we parked. After an engaging conversation, I decided to show him the manuscript that I was working on at the time, titled *Footprints of the Montford Point Marines,* which was in the trunk of my car. He began to look at it by the light of the trunk while sitting on the edge of the car. It was now dark outside, but the sergeant continued to read. I was completely intrigued by him.[21]

After maybe ten or fifteen minutes passed, two other Marines walked by, and he said to one of them, "Colonel Willie, did you bring a copy of your book with you?"

"No, I didn't," he said. Master Gunnery Sergeant Geeter introduced my family to him, including my wife, Soonai, sister Sandra, and of course my dad. Colonel Willie and Master Gunnery Sergeant Geeter both spoke to my dad for quite some time while many other people were jostling for conversations with them. When there was a break for Colonel Willie, I inquired about the book that Sergeant Geeter had mentioned. He told me the title of the book was *African American Voices from Iwo Jima,* and also his full name, Lieutenant Colonel Clarence E. Willie (USMC-Ret.). Colonel Willie began to describe some of the details of his book to bring my wife and I up to speed regarding Iwo Jima and the Montford Point Marines.[22]

Master Gunnery Sergeant Geeter revealed to Colonel Willie that I was currently working on a draft of a book in its early stages. With enthusiasm, Colonel Willie began asking me about my book. I decided to show him a copy of my manuscript by holding it up against my chest so that he could look at the title at eye level. He was surprised and elated and later gave my wife and me some very positive feedback. Master Gunnery Sergeant Geeter, seemingly captivated, told Colonel Willie, while holding another draft of my book, "This is all a labor of love for Gene, Colonel," indicating that I undertook this task to further the story of the Montford Point Marines. Master Gunnery Sergeant Geeter then said, "Gene, make sure I get a copy of this when it is complete."

I was seriously euphoric and excited about this turn of events and said, "I absolutely will."[23]

Now back home in New Jersey, while researching more of the stories of the colored replacement battalions, I read a story of another Marine named Sergeant Alvin Banker. Mr. Banker was from New Orleans and volunteered for the draft on July 16, 1942. After arriving at Montford Point Camp, he became part of what was known as the Special Duty Platoon, which consisted of cooks, butchers, bakers, and barbers. Since Montford Point Camp was just beginning to be established for the new inductees at the time, these were some of the occupational specialties that were needed at the camp. He went on to describe that there were 124 fiberboard huts for their barracks, and in his platoon, there were twenty-five men. He was actually a part of the 51st Battery Composite Defense Battalion and in Headquarters Platoon.[24]

Sergeant Banker was trained to be a cook, Marine Corps–style, while in the Marines. Prior to this he had no training in cooking, he says, except to maybe cook himself an egg or two from time to time, "and I might have messed that up."[25]

During an interview by the University of North Carolina Wilmington's William M. Randall Library and the Cape Fear Museum, a joint venture called *World War II: Through the Eyes of the Cape Fear,* Mr. Banker describes the 51st Battalion as an "all-volunteer group that went into the Corps" before things got hot over in the Pacific and they started drafting through the Selective Service. Sergeant Banker says that around August or September

1943, the 51st was broken up and reorganized into several other units, as the draft was bringing in large amounts of recruits. As Sergeant Banker describes:

> They reorganized the 52nd Defense Battalion, recruit training battalion, a storage branch battalion, which is something the Corps never had prior to Blacks going into the Corps, and as the recruits trained from recruit training battalion, they were sent to the other battalions to bring them up to strength. After that, when the 51st came up to strength, they sent them overseas.[26]

Sergeant Banker describes his orders prior to being transferred overseas for the first time since the war began. On September 20, 1946, First Sergeant Max Russo and Banker, then a Master Technical Sergeant, were transferred to the 6th Colored Replacement Draft Marines of Montford Point. One of his overseas stops was on Saipan in the Mariana Islands.

> In Saipan, we had our own camp there. We had several White staff NCOs in our group and the Marine Corps began to get integrated more gradually ... to clean up, mop up, because when we went to Saipan, we were going out at night on patrols routing out Japanese because right across from our camp was a POW camp and some of the Japanese were still hiding out in the hills after the war ended. We rounded them up and gradually repatriated them back to Japan.[27]

As I was so fascinated to learn of another outfit from Montford Point called the Colored Replacements, of which so little had been written or spoken about, I decided to try to contact Sergeant Banker. Unfortunately, Sergeant Alvin Banker had passed away some time ago, but Mrs. Banker, who was so extremely kind and forthright, engaged me in conversation for as long as I had questions or inquiries. She gave me an enlightening history of her family, including her children.[28]

Of course, I had to mention to her that I was working on a book with all the questions I was presenting to her, and how I had read the story of her husband and of his unique background. By this time, we were wrapping the conversation up, and she told me that it was not a problem that I had called and asked of her time because she does receive calls on a regular basis from people inquiring of her husband or her husband's friends reaching out to say hello from all over the country. "As a matter of fact, there were a couple of people I personally knew who had written books. One of those persons," she said, "lived right behind my development, and his name is Willie."

Right then I stopped her and asked, "Wait a minute—are you talking about Lieutenant Colonel Clarence E. Willie?"

"Yes," she replied. "He lives right behind me. As a matter of fact, I have to call him as soon as I get off the phone with you to respond to an invitation that he needs a reply on."[29]

What a small world it can be sometimes, I thought. I was just with Colonel Willie less than a month ago, if that long, and now he was coming up in conversation again. So, with that, I bid Mrs. Banker farewell and later spoke with Colonel Willie that evening. Needless to say, he was as shocked as I was. We talked at length about Sergeant Alvin Banker. Colonel Willie shared many stories about Sergeant Banker, as they were extremely close friends.

Sergeant Banker had a distinguished career in the Marine Corps. He served for twenty-four years and saw such places as Saipan, Tokyo, South Camp Fuji, Guam, and Europe, and served in the Korean War. He is also one of the founding members of the Montford Point Marine Association and was voted into the Montford Point Marine Association Hall of Fame in 1998.[30]

When I was a child, my father used to take my mom and my siblings to South Carolina for vacation during the summer months, and also so that my mother could renew her bonds with friends and relatives there while he embarked to North Carolina on TDY to work at the Air Force Base at Goldsboro. One summer we got lucky, and Dad was able to rent our family a house for the summer so that we would be able to have extra rooms and not have to share already tight quarters. Seven children sometimes make a tight squeeze. This way we all stayed under one big roof as opposed to a couple of us staying with other relatives here and there.

During this time, we made a lot of friends, as young kids do. This particular summer was about the year 1962. One of these playmates my brother and I had lived directly across the street from our house. I remember going across the street on many occasions to play in front of his house and was fascinated by his father's sawmill and lumber business, which sat behind the main house. His family had a type of shrubbery in front of the house that this kid and I would jump over while we played. The following year I remember that that shrubbery had grown so large that it was too large for us to jump over. That always fascinated me. As the years went by, I often thought about that kid and the sawmill business.

While describing the location of this house that we rented to Mr. Harrell, who grew up in Timmonsville all of his life, and hoping that he would know what I was talking about and hoping he would pick up on what I thought was some type of lumber yard across the street from the house we were at, I got a huge surprise.

Ironically, after talking with Mr. Harrell, I found out some specific details regarding the ownership of the house we rented, about the business, and also about the kid, my playmate, across the street. Mr. Harrell gave me more information than I had bargained for. As it turns out, the woman that was kind enough to rent us the house was named Modena Bird-Thomas, and as unbelievable as it sounds, the kid turned out to be Mr. Harrell's nephew, named Moses Harrell Jr.; Moses's father is Mr. Harrell's brother. Wow![31]

Mr. Harrell seemed mighty proud of receiving a Congressional Gold Medal and to have served his country. He was one of thirteen children and knew that he had fared well in his life. He spent many years in higher education, earning an associate degree in science at Virginia State University with a minor in sociology. He then spent two more years studying insurance and working his way into becoming an insurance broker. Not quite where he wanted to be, he continued pursuing education and completed his business education at Smith Madden Business College in Richmond, Virginia.[32]

With all the honors being bestowed upon him and the other Montford Pointers, his only wish was that more young people would take an interest in what was happening with it all.

I said to Mr. Harrell, "My hopes and goals are to be able to go into schools with the youngsters, and also upper-level students, and be able to impart this information to them on a regular basis around the country."

Mr. Harrell said, "Maybe you can take me along with you."

I responded, "I'd love to."[33]

Mr. Randolph Harrell continues to reside in Timmonsville and has a granddaughter who works for Congresswoman Corrine Brown. To his wish of younger people taking more of an interest in these affairs, I'd say his dream has come true.[34]

CHAPTER 20

What Is the Congressional Gold Medal?

Since the American Revolution, Congress has commissioned gold medals as its highest expression of national appreciation for distinguished achievements and contributions. Each medal honors a particular individual, institution, or event. Although the first recipients included citizens who participated in the American Revolution, the War of 1812, and the Mexican-American War, Congress broadened the scope of the medal to include actors, authors, entertainers, musicians, pioneers in aeronautics and space, explorers, lifesavers, notables in science and medicine, athletes, humanitarians, and public servants. The medal was first awarded in 1776 by the 2nd Continental Congress to General George Washington.[1]

Corporal Thomas Mosley, recipient of the Congressional Gold Medal, at the Marine Barracks in Washington, D.C., June 28, 2012.

The Gold Medal and the Presidential Medal of Freedom are generally considered to carry the same level of prestige (though significantly fewer Gold Medals have been awarded). The chief difference between the two is that the Freedom Medal is personally awarded by the President of the United States (executive branch), and Congressional Gold Medals are awarded by acts of the Congress (legislative branch).[2]

A Congressional Gold Medal is the highest civilian award that can be given. It is the highest expression of national appreciation for distinguished achievements and contributions given by the United States government. It also can't just be given because someone thinks it is appropriate to give—it must be awarded. "Per committee rules, legislation bestowing a Congressional Gold Medal upon a recipient must be cosponsored by a certain number of members of both the House of Representatives and the Senate before their respective committees will consider it."[3]

In the House, the legislation must be cosponsored "by at least

Thomas Mosley (right) waiting with the crowd. You can only imagine the thoughts in their minds that morning.

two-thirds of the members of the House," while in the Senate, the Banking, Housing, and Urban Affairs Committee in the example of "the 116th Congress requires that at least sixty-seven Senators cosponsor any Congressional Gold Medal before being considered by the committee."[4]

Congresswoman Corrine Brown, who represented the 3rd District in Florida, introduced the bill to grant a Congressional Gold Medal to the Montford Point Marines. She is a key member of the Congressional Black Caucus and the House Committee on Veterans Affairs. The bill she introduced was HR 2447. This she introduced to the House.[5] A related Bill, S 1527, was introduced in the Senate by Senator Kay Hagan, who was a Democrat representing the State of North Carolina.[6]

With this was the idea—to expound upon the process that goes into the sponsoring of legislation. Keep in mind that the people such as Master Gunnery Sergeant Joe Geeter and others also had many other Senators and members of the House of Representatives working with them and lobbying on their behalf as these bills were being introduced. There is a tremendous amount of work that goes into granting any type of legislation. Hopefully, this information will give a better understanding of the awarding of this Gold Medal and the significance of it as well. Prior to the Tuskegee Airmen and the Buffalo Soldiers, less than three hundred had ever been awarded to any person or group of people since George Washington.

The patient look of these men, who had traveled from all parts of the country, says it all.

The bill was passed in the House with 422 votes and not one dissent. It was also overwhelmingly passed in the Senate as well. Then it went before President Barack Obama on November 23, 2011, and today, the Montford Point Marines have raced to the gold.

One thing is for certain: it is a "huge golden spoon."

This Congressional Gold Medal is not a common award. This award raises the men of Montford Point to a lofty station in life. These men, from whatever station in life they derived from, have now been accepted onto a level that few Americans are at or will ever be. These Montford Pointers, or better yet, as some general officers and other officers have referred to them as, "the chosen few," have now become the men that the Marine Corps wants to make every officer and every other Marine emulate.

This is what is being taught this very day by the Marine Corps. These Montford Pointers have now become the gold standard of the United States Marine Corps. These are the men that all officers must now teach every recruit and every enlisted man and woman in the Marine Corps about. They must also learn themselves about these great men. What I have written here in these brief pages is but a drop in the bucket of their history. To use an analogy: if the bucket is five gallons of water, then these other Marines, no matter who they are, from generals to privates to new recruits, must learn that history until they learn and absorb all the information that there is to know about them.[7]

Theodore Peters of Chicago, June 2012. Peters served in the 51st Defense Battalion, A Battery, from 1943 to 1946.

Robert D. Lewis, chapter president of the Montford Point Marine Association No. 12, San Diego, California, on the medal ceremony day, June 28, 2012.

The Marine Corps has broken down the many facets of life that these Montford Pointers had to endure and are recreating them so that all Marines not only understand how multitalented these men were but also must go through some of the rigorous training that these Montford Pointers had to endure. No doubt it was a serious hardship for most at that time. The Marine Corps has set up all types of training facilities, obstacle courses, and educational facilities that reflect the training of Montford Point Camp during World War II. It is with this in mind that that new recruits must now go through, and it is all designed to show how high the standards have been raised because of men like Sergeant Gilbert "Hashmark" Johnson, Master Gunnery Sergeant Huff, Corporal Thomas Mosley, Sergeant Joseph Ginyard, Gunnery Sergeant Carrol Reavis, Fred Ash, Joseph Carpenter, Leroy Clifton Grayson, and David Dinkins, just to name a few.

Corporal Clifford Primus of Windsor, Connecticut. Primus was in the 51st Defense Battalion, D Battery, one of the antiaircraft artillery groups of the Montford Point Marines.

Former New York City mayor David Dinkins was in the ranks of Montford Point, and with the others awaited his Congressional Gold Medal, June 28, 2012.

An unidentified Montford Pointer.

Stanley Costley, from Plainfield, New Jersey.

From left: Sandra Walker, the author's sister; the author, Eugene S. Mosley; Thomas Mosley.

The formal ceremony of presenting the Congressional Gold Medal to the Montford Point Marines, June 28, 2012. Almost 400 World War II veterans from Montford Point Camp were awarded.

Thomas Mosley (with red tie and no glasses), awaiting the start of the Congressional Gold Medal ceremony at the Marine Barracks in Washington, D.C., June 28, 2012.

Congressional Gold Medal awarded to a Montford Pointer, June 28, 2012.

Congressional Gold Medal awarded to a Montford Pointer, June 28, 2012.

A Montford Point Marine receives the Congressional Gold Medal from a three-star general, June 28, 2012.

A Montford Point Marine receives the Congressional Gold Medal.

Corporal Thomas Mosley receives the Congressional Gold Medal from Lieutenant General Robert E. Milstead Jr., deputy commandant for Manpower and Reserve Affairs.

Thomas Mosley, moments after receiving the Congressional Gold Medal.

CHAPTER 21

No Longer Just an Ordinary Man

Everyone in our family and friends who read this report must recognize the true importance of what this history of the Montford Point Marines is all about. If the entire Marine Corps is obligated to learn it, shouldn't that teach us the importance of this information? Should this information not tell us the true type of makeup that is in our being? Is this not a perfect script to teach our children about and for them to teach their children? I know a person this day whose ancestor was in the Revolutionary War, and she is in an organization called *Daughters of the Revolutionary War.* They celebrate as if the Revolutionary War was fought and won only fifty years ago. They have never let their history fade.

We should not either. We know that throughout our family history, and history generally, there have been some great people. Many of them we have never known. Many of them have faded in history. Some of them have achieved great things in modern times and no doubt will go down in history themselves with their great achievements. However, this Montford Point story, with our own Thomas Mosley, gives us a perfect example to show that we should and must cherish our rich history and appreciate each other more.

This story is about Great Montford Point Marines in general, so that we may know this history, but it was also a part of my journey in helping to teach my family members and associates about who Mr. Thomas Mosley was in this world. Thomas Mosley will forever be inscribed in history. He and those brave 19,167 other men who served in the Marine Corps at Montford Point showed the Marine Corps what a true Marine is all about. They were kept hidden for over seventy years from all but a few because many officials and other soldiers in the Corps knew that they were shown up by these men they initially had no faith in.

Remember General Holcomb before the Navy Board, for example. These were not West Pointers; they were not from the academies or other higher military institutions that taught *The Art of War* and other outstanding military tactics. These men had the worst training facilities. Originally, some went into the Marine Corps just because they thought the uniforms looked good, not knowing what they were about to embark on. There were many that had educational and professional training and careers, but it was not recognized. They had the worst investments by the Corps. At times they were told to leave the base and go back home because nobody there cared. However, they used what they had, even though many of them themselves did not think whatever they had was good enough, because they were told it wasn't good enough, at least for a long period of time.

Thomas Mosley (center) in a more casual moment with his daughter-in-law Soonai (left), daughter Annette, and daughter Sandra.

These Montford Pointers provided the link that was an absolute must for sustaining the war effort. Without these men providing the link that was missing in the South Pacific chain of islands, the war was unsustainable in many areas. How must it have been for some of the Marines on the front lines, after fighting for days and weeks on end, to have to return to the rear and try to secure food, clothing, ammunition, and medical supplies for many of the thousands of troops that were still engaged? It was a monumental task to begin with, let alone having to sort through thousands of crates and boxes, and then to separate the good from the tarnished or rusted or even rotten, then to find the troops that needed these urgent supplies, and then distribute them.

Of course, once this was done, these men had to pick up where they left off, which no doubt was back to the front. As described, it was a huge undertaking. One cannot forget also that as these men were fighting, they were progressively moving most times in a forward or lateral movement, which meant that after days and weeks on end of fighting, these supplies were just that much farther behind. Instead of hundreds or thousands of yards, now these same supplies were miles behind. This included ammunition, and I'm sure that others would agree that even though these other articles of supplies were deadly important, the ammunition was the most important of all. When we speak of ammunition, we are

Thomas Mosley (left) with Sergeant Joseph Ginyard of Philadelphia at the celebration held at Philadelphia's Kroc Center, July 2012, hosted by Pastor Ginyard, Sergeant Joe Geeter, and the Montford Point Marine Association's Philadelphia chapter.

not just speaking of sidearm ammo. This ammunition also consisted of rifle ammo, machine-gun ammo, antiaircraft ammo, grenades, and other items related to arms. Many times the ammunition ran out under intense battle.

Once the Montford Pointers came on board, the operation began to smooth itself out. The frontline Marines could feel the impact immediately. Items that were critical began to reach those in need in an expeditious manner. Not only did the supplies reach those frontline Marines in a timely fashion, but also men that were wounded could be removed by the Montford Pointers, and taken to safety, and evacuated in a timely fashion. Just as importantly, those that had made the ultimate sacrifice could be removed from the front as well.

Most importantly, and too many times and too often, we as a people of African American descent have been left out of the history of America. In the book titled *History of World War II, Armed Services Memorial Edition,* by Francis Trevelyan Miller, a book of 967 pages and copyrighted in 1945, I was only able to find four photographs and less than one hundred words to describe African

Phillip Ginyard (right), son of Dr. Joseph Ginyard, directs Montford Pointers, including Thomas Mosley (second from left), and Sergeant Ben Bynum (in white), as they are introduced at the Philadelphia celebration, July 2012.

American soldiers in World War II. I intentionally scoured this book without finding the insertions of what our African American men were truly doing in this war. I was pretty thorough in reading and scouring the book in research for *Footprints of the Montford Point Marines.* Not only in the chapters of the book did I not find this information, but also in the "Chronology of the War," at the end of the book, I was not able to find insertions. However, I will continue to look for this information. It is an exceptional book that covers the additional aspects of World War

II in a most excellent manner. The possibility exists that the information about the Montford Pointers was not there for them to insert. That is not for me to discern.

My greatest point in this matter is not to criticize unduly or unjustly what has been written, but to impart information that is now vital to the descendants of those men who sacrificed their lives, and their families that shared in those sacrifices as well. These men who partook in the war effort as well as their families have to know that their lives and efforts were not in vain. To that end, this story must be told. Why should we continue to think that someone else's life is more important than ours are? These are cold facts, but the truth can no longer be hidden. These African American men played a vital and a major role in every major battle in the South Pacific, and they must receive credit for the jobs that they did, just as everyone else who took part in the war has received. I am sure that the men who were on the front lines and waiting, as recipients of what these men were ferrying to them, such as medical supplies, food, ammunition, would agree.

Thomas Strickland Turner of the Montford Point Marine Association's Philadelphia chapter at the Philadelphia celebration, July 2012.

Philadelphia councilman David Oh (left) with the author at the Philadelphia celebration, July 2012.

Nevertheless, these are more of the heroes of the Marine Corps. Not that there aren't others, but these are more people that we can truly look up to. These are people that some of us may know and most, of course, we do not know. My father has always been humble and has always had such a strong belief in God and country. I truly thank the Creator that Dad witnessed the monumental event of him and the other Montford Pointers receiving the Congressional Gold Medal.

The author, Eugene Mosley (left), with his wife, Soonai Mosley, and Dr. James T. Averhart Jr. at a reception in Washington, D.C., June 2012.

Eugene Mosley (left) with Dr. James T. Averhart Jr.

On Tuesday, December 14, 2011, which was before the confirmation of the Congressional Gold Medal, I asked Dad a question. "Dad," I began, "can you imagine how your mom and dad must be smiling while looking down on you right now?"

He replied, "I always tried to do my best and I thank Mom and Dad for all that they have done to instill a love of the Lord in me. Not only them, but Uncle Will Boone and my Grand Mom Adeline." He also said that he thought about his brother Andrew quite a bit, who was in the Korean War. Uncle Andy, as he was known, "suffered while in the service, and also afterward, because of shrapnel sustained on the battlefield in Korea. The Korean War was another devastating war that took lots of lives and created many injuries. Much of the shrapnel had never been able to be removed from Andy." He finalized the conversation by saying that "Whatever it is that is happening now with the adulations surrounding me and the Congressional Gold Medal is the Lord's doing, but I am thankful for it all."[1]

As I think about my father's words, "thankful for it all," I can't help but think about how long this has taken to come together, and of all the people that it took to make it happen. It is imperative also to think about how this information was not put out publicly for over seventy years and how it must have been shrouded to continue to be hidden. As strange as it seems, though, I am not surprised. We must learn to take responsibility to reach out for our valued history. Look at the richness of this story. Look at the significance of this history. Look at the shining example that these men set not only for us African Americans as a people but for the entire Marine Corps. Think of this: These 19,168 men are shining examples and models of the U.S. Marine Corps. There can be no higher stage. They are a part of the new bar.

Hopefully, America will now begin to use these examples of the effort that was given by these men as a catalyst to embrace the African American family as a whole. As described in earlier chapters, African Americans have always used the opportunity, when called upon, to gain freedom in battle. The question has always been, Will this be the time we will be looked upon as equal human beings in these United States of America? Not only in the Marine Corps, in the Army, in the Navy, in the Air Force, and other branches of service has the African American soldier shouldered their load, but they have given their lives as well. Is this the time for true brotherhood and equality? Another question is what else could be asked for from these soldiers, both men and women? Is it still not enough?

It reminds me of one line that I always think about coming from my brother Thomas when we would talk about the champions of boxing matches of which we happened to be good fans of. Many times, as we spoke and were analyzing some particular matchup, our enthusiasm would get more and more profound when we talked about how a win was achieved by the underdog boxer over another. Then Thomas really emphasized the words

Left to right: General James F. Amos, USMC, 35th Commandant of the U.S. Marine Corps; Sandra Walker, the author's sister; and the author, Eugene S. Mosley, at the Montford Point Marine Association's 51st National Convention in Jacksonville, North Carolina, in 2016, commemorating the Montford Point Marines and the sacrifices they made. This ceremony was held at Marston Pavilion on Camp Lejeune, where the Black Marines were not allowed during World War II.

aloud when the winner was about to be announced. he said, *"and new,"* to indicate the newest champ, and the underdog getting the championship belt, and how the crowd would go wild. With that in mind, there is a new champion in the Marine Corps that we have to cheer about. We, as a race of people, have been fighting all of our lives, and we must continue to fight and to cheer for victory, and without question this is a great victory.

As of this writing, time seems to have flown, and the confirmation hearings have taken place, both in the Senate and in the House of Representatives. The Congressional Gold Medal ceremony has taken place. There is nothing in my world that I have done that has dazzled me to the degree that this process and ceremony has, and I have had some exciting moments too that I should share to explain the exhilaration that I felt and still feel.

Back in the early seventies, for example, I used to be on security for Muhammad Ali when he was in or around Philadelphia, preceding him giving speeches at various locales. Along with that, my duties, given by one Da'ood Nasir, an expert in security, in conjunction with some other people I knew, and some I had trained in the art of security, were to sweep whatever building Ali may have been getting ready to do his speech in, as well as protect Ali when he arrived at the site. *Sweep* means to check every nook and cranny, under all the seats, rooms, closets, or other places that may be hidden. It was a big job because some of these buildings were massive. You had to check rooms and areas that nobody ever used, or that would never cross the general public's mind to ever think about even going into. I had a lot of leeway in setting up my part of this operation after being given instructions on my area of operation. This included putting people in various locations for opening doors, or having people surround Ali in the front, sides, or rear as we went to our destination within the building. I would always put my two brothers whenever possible into significant positions so they too could be around "The Champ."

This was a major role also. Although there were other people that played a significant part as well, I always seemed to get that direct but playful snarl from Ali because I was always up front or nearby to greet him and open the car door as his limousine pulled up. Once he was out of his car and he spotted me, on a few occasions, he would curl his lip up and put those fast-as-lightening fists of his up at me as if he were getting ready to battle in the ring with me—imagine that feeling—and maybe bob around a bit. There was never any question about who it was directed at. The other guys would snicker or laugh out loud while these antics were going on. You knew he was joking, though, but he did it in such a way that I always had to say, "go 'head, Ali, you the champ," several times. Then he would back off and shake my hand. Oftentimes he had his brother, Rahman (pronounced rock-mahn) Ali—who also fought as a heavyweight fighter—with him. He too was likewise a wonderful guy.

I don't think there is a person in the United States, or in many parts of this world, for that matter, who cannot imagine these scenarios being played out with, at the time, the biggest name in the sports arena. It was so thrilling to be a part of this. It was exciting, and it was colossal. Whether people liked him or not, he was still gigantic and mystical to be around. There were hundreds of people trying to get around him, just to be up close or to shake his hand. One can just imagine this excitement and thrill. I thought about all of this and more while being a part of the Congressional Gold Medal ceremony.

Being an avid musician as well, I've thought about the times that my good friend and fellow musician, Warren, a great Philadelphia bass player, composer, arranger, and concert organizer, would always hire me as the stage manager for some of the major acts at the main stage that was part of the West Oak Lane Jazz and Arts Festival. This was a yearly event in Philadelphia. It lasted almost ten years and would have continued longer, I'm sure, if not for the tumbling economy at the time. My friend is a great organizer and a superb guy. I've known him for many years, and anytime we describe our relationship to anyone else, we say, "We go all the way back!" I'm not using his name as he is a humble person and asked for that.

The author, Eugene S. Mosley (left), and CWO5 Dr. James T. Averhart Jr., National President of the Montford Point Marine Association, at the 51st National Convention in 2016, where a moment of silence was held and a bell was rung in commemoration of the sacrifices of the Montford Point Marines during World War II.

From the advent of these concerts, and me being the stage manager of the main stage, and there were four huge stages at every concert, I've gotten to meet, be around, and spend time with so many great musicians and other people. Let me also add that when I say I was around, it wasn't like just "around." From the moment some of these accomplished musicians came into the enclosed private areas behind the stage, this is when my time with them began. I've met musicians that could headline a stage anywhere, such as Chaka Khan, War, Roy Ayers, Al Jarreau, Mandrill (the Wilson Brothers), Billy Paul, Esperanza Spalding, Pieces of a Dream, Arpeggio Jazz Ensemble, and members of their bands, Jeffrey Osborne, and Christian McBride. Some I've met five, six, or seven times over the years. I've also talked to some of these musicians for hours at a time. People like Umar Rahim, who plays all three saxes, Billy Thorpe, who plays baritone sax, tenor sax, flute, and other instruments and who personally is just a great spiritualist. There is Greg "Juju" Jones, one of the most dynamite drummers I've ever met. Mark Adams, a great key-boardiest and member of Roy Ayers band for around twenty years, and world entertainer whose own band members include Lonnie Liston Smith and Mark Jackson, is another, and Ray Gaskins, who masterfully plays saxophones and keyboards. How exciting is all of this? It is so exciting that it is like a dream come true. It is like you are somewhat in a fog the first couple times it happens, and even more stunning when someone like Roy Ayers gets off his bus or out of a van and calls you by name.

Thomas Mosley (left) at home in Macon, Georgia, with Master Gunnery Sergeant Mel Ragin, president of MPMA chapter 35, Warner Robins/ Macon, Georgia, February 2012.

Even with all of this—and it was enormous to me, and I loved it—but with all due respect of the highest order, to me, it did not compare to the ceremonies of watching Dad, Sergeant Ginyard, and these other men, after seventy-plus years, receive their just dues in receiving the Congressional Gold Medal for the bravery they displayed under intense enemy fire, the injuries they sustained and the lives lost, and for the love they demonstrated for the Corps and the country. The Congressional Gold Medal ceremony took first place overall. There is no way to describe the days that led to or the days following the ceremony. Not just the days, but the months prior to the event. We were moving on pure adrenaline as we witnessed history in the making. It was a totally different vibration than I had ever experienced, and it lasted a long time. As the months continued to pass, the excitement calmed on the outside, but the undercurrent was very much deep inside. It was euphoric.

Why must we continue to forge ahead and fight? If you look at the length of time for this worthy honor to manifest itself, it is indicative why we must continue to fight. As Colonel Willie and I recently were talking about the time frame of African Americans being allowed into the service, there were some serious points and issues that were brought out. One of Colonel Willie's major points is that even with the Selective Training and Service Act, which was signed into law on September 16, 1940, it did not desegregate the military; it just assured that men between the ages of twenty-one and thirty-six had to register for the draft.[2]

The Corps did not open its doors to African Americans until 1942, and they served in all-Black units. Other races were accepted

From left, the author, Eugene Mosley; Thomas Mosley; and Mel Ragin, president of MPMA chapter 35, Warner Robins/Macon, Georgia, February 2012.

somewhat more easily and were in White Marine units. Even after World War II was over, the Corps wanted to end the time of Blacks in its units completely, but it was not to be. Colonel Willie brought up the fact that after the war was over, many Blacks suffered, as all other races had suffered with this war. There were deaths, injuries, as well as PTSD in Black communities, but very little if any types of benefits for these soldiers, which was totally unfair in light of what these men had done to assist and accelerate those services that were needed for the frontline soldiers and others who were a part of the huge war machine of World War II.[3]

Once again, let us not forget the courage from a man called A. Philip Randolph. He organized and led the Brotherhood of

Sleeping Car Porters, which was the first predominantly Black labor union. During the early part of the civil rights movement, Randolph led the March on the Washington Movement, which convinced President Franklin D. Roosevelt to issue Executive Order 8802 in 1941, banning discrimination in the defense industries during World War II. After the war, Randolph pressured President Harry S. Truman to issue Executive Order 9981 in 1948, ending segregation in the armed services. I suggest further study on Mr. A. Philip Randolph, who was an extremely remarkable and brilliant man. He really is a must-study for any wise individual. I regret not being able to give more space and time here, but my space is too limited to cover such a scholar. My last comment regarding desegregation and the military is to say that although Executive Order 9981 required integration of all races into the military, it was not until 1954 that the last all-Black unit was disbanded.[4]

The author, Eugene Mosley, with the Thomas Mosley display at the Tubman Museum in Macon, Georgia.

Below is the Copy of Executive Order 9981:

Executive Order 9981

Establishing the President's Committee on Equality of Treatment and Opportunity in the Armed Forces.

WHEREAS it is essential that there be maintained in the armed services of the United States the highest standards of democracy, with equality of treatment and opportunity for all those who serve in our country's defense:

NOW THEREFORE, by virtue of the authority vested in me as President of the United States, by the Constitution and the statutes of the United States, and as Commander in Chief of the armed services, it is hereby ordered as follows:

1. It is hereby declared to be the policy of the President that there shall be equality of treatment and opportunity for all persons in the armed services without regard to race, color, religion, or national origin. This policy shall be put into effect as rapidly as possible, having due regard to the time required to effectuate any necessary changes without impairing efficiency or morale.
2. There shall be created in the National Military Establishment

an advisory committee to be known as the President's Committee on Equality of Treatment and Opportunity in the Armed Services, which shall be composed of seven members to be designated by the President.

3. The Committee is authorized on behalf of the President to examine into the rules, procedures, and practices of the Armed Services in order to determine in what respect such rules, procedures and practices may be altered or improved with a view to carrying out the policy of this order. The Committee shall confer and advise the Secretary of Defense, the Secretary of the Army, the Secretary of the Navy, and the Secretary of the Air Force, and shall make such recommendations to the President and to said Secretaries as in the judgment of the Committee will effectuate the policy hereof.
4. All executive departments and agencies of the Federal Government are authorized and directed to cooperate with the Committee in its work, and to furnish the Committee such information or the services of such persons as the Committee may require in the performance of its duties.
5. When requested by the Committee to do so, persons in the armed services or in any of the executive departments and agencies of the Federal Government shall testify before the Committee and shall make available for use of the Committee such documents and other information as the Committee may require.
6. The Committee shall continue to exist until such time as the President shall terminate its existence by Executive order.

Harry Truman
The White House
July 26, 1948[5]

The Congressional Gold Medal.

CHAPTER 22

Quotes

The Commandant of the Marine Corps, **General James F. Amos,** who was a strong advocate for passage of the bill that granted the Congressional Gold Medal, stated:

> "Every Marine ... from private to general ... will know the history of those men who crossed the threshold to fight not only the enemy they were soon to know overseas, but to the enemy of racism and segregation in their own country. My promise to you this evening is that your story will not be forgotten... It will take its rightful place and will be forever anchored in the rich history of our Corps."[1]

Here are some of the first words spoken to me by the National President of the Montford Point Marines, **Dr. James T. Averhart Jr.,** CWO5, U.S. Marine Corps. This was the first of many conversations, beginning in 2011.

> We've all heard of the Tuskegee Airmen and the Buffalo Soldiers, but we never heard of the Montford Point Marines because they kept them from us. They used to tell them "We don't want you. Leave quietly and go home. Nobody will miss you or come looking for you. It's dark now. Be gone by morning. You are not cut out to be Marines." Look at where the Montford Point Marines are now. Eugene, your father is a hero, man. Wait till you see how I treat these men. You haven't seen anything yet.

Through my first phone conversation with Dr. Averhart, the impact of this message on me was so strong that I literally cried on the phone while listening to him articulate to me that my dad was a hero. It is a powerful message.[2]

Camp Gilbert H. Johnson

On April 19, 1974, Montford Point Camp was renamed Camp Gilbert H. Johnson in honor of this outstanding man. the *H* stands for "Hashmark," or the many stripes that he earned and wore on his sleeves. Sergeant Gilbert "Hashmark" Johnson served two three-year terms in the Army, then ten years in the Navy, and finally seventeen years in the Marine Corps. He wore more service stripes, or "hashmarks," than rank stripes for a time.[3]

Below are the words spoken by **General Leonard F. Chapman Jr.**, late Commandant of the Marine Corps:

> The footprints of the Montford Point Marines were left on the beaches of Roi-Namur, Saipan, Guam, Peleliu, Iwo Jima, and Okinawa. Tides and winds have long ago washed them into the seas of history, but "the chosen few" in field shoes and canvas leggings also left their mark in the firm concrete of Marine Corps history. And as new generations of Marines learn to march in those footprints, their cadence assumes the proud stride of the men from Montford Point.

The words are inscribed at Arlington National Cemetery, Section 23.[4]

Master Gunnery Sergeant Joseph Geeter (left), former National President of the Montford Point Marine Association, with the then-president, CWO5 Dr. James T. Averhart Jr. Sergeant Geeter is the person who started the process of lobbying for the Congressional Gold Medal, and Dr. Averhart worked tirelessly with him.

CHAPTER 23

Granting the Congressional Gold Medal

Words of President Barack Obama

"Despite being denied many basic rights, the Montford Point Marines committed to serve our country with selfless patriotism," President Obama wrote. "Embodying the Marine Corps motto of *Semper Fidelis,* Always Faithful, these heroes paved the way for future generations of warriors, regardless of background, to serve in the finest military the world has ever known."

Some of Thomas Mosley's Medals from World War II

U.S. Armed Forces Retired ribbon and medal

U.S. Marine Corps Service ribbon and medal

Marine Corps Good Conduct ribbon and medal

Criteria: Awarded to any enlisted member of the Marine Corps completing three consecutive years of "honorable and faithful service."

Asiatic Pacific Victory World War II ribbon and medal

American Defense Service ribbon and medal

World War II Victory ribbon and medal

American Campaign ribbon and medal

World War II Victory ribbon and medal

Overseas Service ribbon and medal

U.S. Marine Corps Honorable Discharge ribbon and medal

U.S. Marine Corps Weapons Qualification: Rifle Sharpshooter
Earned on January 27, 1944.

Fleet Marine Force ribbon

Navy and Marine Corps Overseas ribbon

I'd also like to thank the members of New Hope Missionary Baptist Church in Macon, Georgia, under the leadership of the pastor, Reverend Christopher Cabiness. Thank you, your wife, Lady Katina, and all of the wonderful members there that created such a wonderful atmosphere for our dad for over fifty years. I do not have all the names of the proud members that I would like to thank, but a few do come to mind. Sister Lucille Clark, Thelma Glover, Joan Burney, and an exceptional human being, Elaine Miller. Please forgive me as I do not know many of the members' names. Cynthia Warren Ross: thank you very much.

CHAPTER 24

Shout-Outs: Words from the Children of Thomas Mosley

Daughter Annette

Our Dad ... before he was a father, before he was a husband, before he really knew what life was all about, had respect and honor and dignity toward others and wanted to share it. One way in which he did this was by enrolling in the service; wanting to give to his country. Unfortunately, what he wanted to give was not received properly or appreciated ... at that time. But despite all his trials, he still gave his best. Turns out it was The Best!

Usually in this world, when a person is unjustly treated, they may tend to retaliate and be bitter towards the world and others, but not our dad. He was *always* kind; sometimes too kind for his own good [smile].

Thanks to the author's insight, research, and persistence, his work has helped me to see a large percentage of what has really shaped my father's personality and understand him better as to what makes him who he is and why he raised us the way he did, and I am glad and proud that he is my dad. So, although he received medals and ribbons, may he never, for a moment, think that because he has received those things that it has made me love him or respect him any more than I always have.

I have always compared him to other men and fathers in this world, through the years, and I will say he was and is one of the best. I talked about him so much through the years; my friends have always wanted to meet him.

Although I believe, as humans, we should not think more of ourselves than is necessary to think, it saddens me a little that he missed out on the recognition and accolades that should have been his through many decades. So, I am happy that finally he was given his just due and honor.

Daughter Sandra

I'm so grateful that my dad was still here to experience and accept this much deserved award and all of the things that happened for him after. It's just so sad to me that most of these brave Black men are gone, never getting any kind of recognition or thanks for their courageous service, never knowing the impact of their service. Can you imagine? They were despised and treated worse than animals just because of the color of their skin, but, oh, look what they achieved in spite of it all. it's remarkable, really.

The Montford Point Marines, with my dad being part of it all, changed the rules of the United States Marine Corps, and will be forever remembered in history, and rightfully so. My dad and I once spoke about the word *fortitude,* and whether he knew it or not, *he* was the very definition of the word. So bless you, Dad, and thank you for always standing strong and "staying the course." And to the author of this book, my brother Eugene, take a bow.

Son James

As a teenager I thought I had all the answers. I had also received what were words of advice from some others, mainly relatives, but after actualizing that advice over the forthcoming years, I found that it was truly far off the mark and only served to let me know that one must be careful of what information is accepted, no matter where that advice comes from. Not only that, but it can cause many wasted years. My dad, Tommy, had already given me the best of information, and as I've gotten older, I realize how I had emulated him in so many ways nevertheless. I see the wonderful value of the discipline that he has imparted to me, and I am forever grateful to my wonderful, sweet father. My only regret is that I did not carefully follow his advice much sooner, because it was all there. Thomas Mosley was an extraordinary human being and was one of the greatest dads that anyone could ever have.

He was so exceptional and played such an invaluable role in the weaving of the fabric of the United States of America, including World War II, that he truly deserved these honors. It was my greatest honor to see them bestowed upon him and in the memory of my mother, Rebecca.

Daughter Karen

Greatness deserves recognition. When I think of my father, those are the words that best describe him. He was not just a great dad but a great man in no uncertain terms. He strived for excellence and instilled that in his children. Every week of our growing up years, he would gather us all in the living room and would talk to us. Sometimes it would be about the struggles of life of what we'd have to face as we grew into adults. Sometimes he would retrieve his Sunday school books to teach us about God. As a kid I resented those talks, but as an adult I was very thankful for them. Those talks were the tools that saved me through some tough times in my life—my daddy's teachings—something that that didn't stop because we grew up. I look back on those things with great pride. Even without the Gold Medal and all the numerous accolades he received, I was just glad and prideful that Mr. Thomas Mosley was my daddy. Not a day goes by that I don't think of him, that I don't miss him. I love you very much, Daddy.

Son, Thomas Edward

As a kid I knew my father had a tough life growing up because he talked with us many times as his children. He told us of the struggles of his parents and others in the family. However, I did not know about the trials and tribulations he went through in Montford Point Camp and overseas as an ammunition handler in World War II.

I recognize now the impact that the war had on him as well as the other Marines that went through Montford Point Camp during those disparaging and judgmental times. I also know about the blood, sweat, and tears these men went through to obtain the accomplishments that they achieved in the worse environment ever. Even though they were made to feel that they had only accomplished a trivial amount, they had a major impact on their families, their communities, and also the world. In fact, how they overcame the odds to achieve the greatness that they did, not only for themselves, but for the United States of America, is beyond the pale.

I have to say that no matter what he himself went through, which I know was unfathomable, he was always there for us as his family, and we had no idea what he had been through. He was always there as a father, along with our mother, to give us those things we needed so that we could have harmony as a family. He was a true hero.

Son Eugene, the Author

One special note I leave. I'm hopeful that this reading sheds some additional light on these courageous men from Montford Point to the American public and to the world. My wish, and also the wish from those who followed behind these men in the United States Marine Corps and others who are now aware, is that more people will see the significance of these men as they played vital roles in the weaving of the fabric of this great nation. After all, how can one really miss seeing giants? In all of our finest dress, Montford Point Marines, we salute you all.

And to Dad, thank you so much for being the ordinary father you thought you were, you giant!

At ease, soldier.

The End

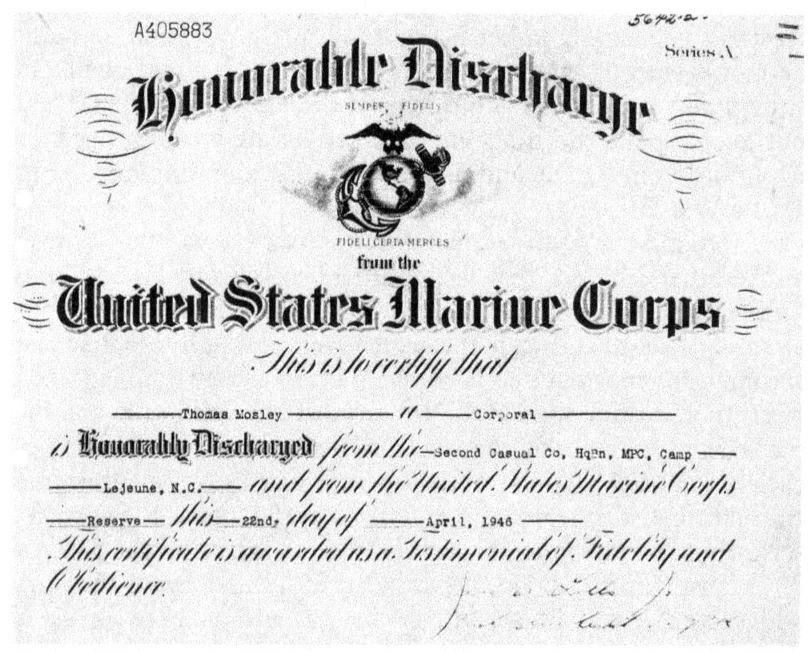
A405883

Series A

Honorable Discharge

SEMPER FIDELIS

FIDELI CERTA MERCES

from the

United States Marine Corps

This is to certify that

Thomas Mosley — a — Corporal

is Honorably Discharged from the Second Casual Co, HqBn, MPC, Camp Lejeune, N.C. and from the United States Marine Corps Reserve this 22nd day of April, 1946

This certificate is awarded as a Testimonial of Fidelity and Obedience.

Corporal Thomas Mosley's honorable discharge.

Appendixes

APPENDIX I

Montford Point Marines Resolution Awarded by Congress

SRES 587 ATS

111th CONGRESS
2d Session
S. RES. 587
Designating August 26, 2010, as "Montford Point Marines Day".
IN THE SENATE OF THE UNITED STATES
July 20, 2010

Mr. BURR (for himself and Mr. BURRIS) submitted the following resolution: which was referred to the Committee on the Judiciary
July 22, 2010
Committee discharged; considered and agreed to

RESOLUTION

Designating August 26, 2010, as 'Montford Point Marines Day'.

Whereas, on June 25, 1941, President Franklin D. Roosevelt issued Executive Order 8802, which established the fair employment practices that began to erase discrimination in the Armed Forces.

Whereas in 1942, President Franklin D. Roosevelt issued a Presidential Directive that integrated the United States Marine Corps.

Whereas approximately 20,000 African-American Marines received basic training at Montford Point in the State of North Carolina between 1942 and 1949.

Whereas the African-American Marines trained at Montford Point became known as the Montford Point Marines.

Whereas the African-American volunteers who enlisted in the United States Marine Corps during World War II—

(1) joined the United States Marine Corps to demonstrate their

commitment to the United States, despite the practice of segregation.
(2) served the United States in a most honorable fashion.
(3) defied unwarranted stereotypes; and
(4) achieved distinction through brave and honorable service.

Whereas, during World War II, African-American Marine Corps units fought and served in the Pacific theater, participating in the liberation of the Ellice Islands, the Eniwetok Atoll, the Marshall Islands, the Kwajalein Atoll, Iwo Jima, Peleliu, the Marianas Islands, Saipan, Tinian, Guam, and Okinawa.

Whereas Robert Sherrod, a correspondent for *Time* magazine in the central Pacific during World War II, wrote that the African-American Marines that entered combat for the first time in Saipan were worthy of a 4.0 combat performance rating, the highest performance rating given by the Navy.

Whereas the heroism, commitment, and valor demonstrated by the Montford Point Marines—

(1) changed the negative attitudes of the military leadership toward African-Americans; and
(2) inspired the untiring service of future generations of African-Americans in the United States Marine Corps.

Whereas in July 1948, President Harry S. Truman issued Executive Order 9981, which ended segregation in the military.

Whereas in September 1949, the Montford Marine Camp was deactivated, ending 7 years of segregation in the Marine Corps.

Whereas in September 1965, over 400 former and active duty Marines met in Philadelphia, Pennsylvania at a reunion to honor the Montford Point Marines, leading to the establishment of the Montford Point Marine Association.

Whereas 2010 marks the 45th anniversary of the establishment of the Montford Point Marine Association; and

Whereas the sacrifices, dedication to country, and perseverance of the African-American Marines trained at Montford Point Camp are duly honored and should never be forgotten: Now, therefore be it

Resolved, That the Senate—

(1) designates August 26, 2010, as 'Montford Point Marines Day'.
(2) honors the 68th anniversary of the first day African-American recruits began training at Montford Point.
(3) recognizes the work of the members of the Montford Point Marine Association—
    (A) in honoring the legacy and history of the United States Marine Corps; and
    (B) in ensuring that the sense of duty shared by the Montford Point Marines is passed along to future generations.
(4) recognizes that—

(A) the example set by the Montford Point Marines who served during World War II helped to shape the United States Marine Corps; and

(B) the United States Marine Corps provides an excellent opportunity for the advancement for persons of all races; and

(5) expresses the gratitude of the Senate to the Montford Point Marines for fighting for the freedom of the United States and the liberation of people of the Pacific, despite the practices of segregation and discrimination.[1]

APPENDIX 2

Montford Point History Now Part of OCS

By Gina Cavallaro, Staff writer, *Marine Corps Times*, Marinecorpstimes.com

Posted Wednesday Dec 7, 2011, 9:04 EST
The history of the Montford Point Marines, the Corps' first black enlistees, is now being taught in class at officer Candidates School at Marine Corps Base Quantico, Va. It is part of an ongoing effort by Commandant General Jim Amos to secure the legacy of the Montford Point Marines and to promote one of his top priorities: to create greater diversity in the Corps.

The Montford Point Marines were named after the patch of land on the edge of Camp Lejeune, North Carolina, where from 1942 to 1949 they were trained in a segregated boot camp. They were recently recognized by Congress for their service in World War II with approval of the Congressional Gold Medal.

That effort was spearheaded by Amos, who also approved the addition of a history lesson on the Montford Marines tied to an event during *The Crucible* at boot camp. On Dec. 9, the Montford Point Marines will be recognized by the student body at OCS, with a four-mile challenge race.

In the Montford Point Challenge, teams comprising candidates from all the OCS companies will negotiate a four-mile course while carrying ammo cans and simulated casualties. Each phase of the race will honor the courage and sacrifice of the Montford Point Marines, who supported frontline units in the Pacific during the war. Following the race, the candidates will participate in a guided discussion about the benefits of diversity in the Marine Corps and the sacrifices black troops have made throughout the Corps' history.[2]

APPENDIX 3

First Black Marines' Story to Be Taught During Basic Training

The Marine Corps wants the nation to honor the first black Marines; a story to be taught in basic training

By The Associated Press

OCEANSIDE, Calif. (AP) The story of the first black Marines is a part of history few Americans, and even few Marines, have learned, but the Marine Corps' new commandant intends to change that.

Commandant Gen. James Amos is lobbying to get the Montford Point Marines the Congressional Gold Medal, the nation's highest civilian award. Congress will vote on that Tuesday.

The Corps also next year will teach all Marines the story of Montford Point, the base set up for black Marines in 1942 in North Carolina to keep them separate from white Marines.[3]

APPENDIX 4

Gold Medal Approved by President Barack Obama

Lindell Kay, *Daily News* Staff

December 7, 2011, 5:48 PM
The first Blacks to serve in the Marines Corps will receive the nation's highest civilian honor for distinguished achievement.

With the recent signature of President Barack Obama, the Bill to award the Congressional Gold Medal to the Montford Point Marines has become law.

From 1942–1949, black men from across the country came to the Montford Point Camp in Jacksonville seeking the American Dream of inclusion and the opportunity to defend our country as a U.S. Marine, said General James F. Amos, commandant of the Marine Corps. "Like the wider society at large that was socially and culturally divided by race, the Marine Corps trained these men separately, denying them their rightful place in the Corps and in its rich tradition of service," Amos said. "These men served in battle, provided critical supplies to those on the front lines and evacuated the wounded to safety."

Retired Marine Sergeant Major Nathaniel James, past president of the national Montford Point Marine Association and current president of the local chapter No. 10 stated, "History books and Hollywood accounts are chock full of stories highlighting the accomplishments of the first black soldier and aviators of the highly lauded Buffalo Soldiers and Tuskegee Airmen. Now the Congressional Gold Medal will help people realize that the contributions of the Montford Point Marines were just as important. There are big plans underway to celebrate the 70th anniversary of the beginning of the program next year: a reunion is in the works for the original Montford Pointers; the organization's national conference will meet in Jacksonville; the state has designated August 26 as Montford Point Marine Day; and the first phase of a monument to honor the first black Marines is expected to be complete by summertime. The announcement that the Marines will be receiving the medal coincides with a greater effort within the Corps to teach recruits about the sacrifices and achievements of the Montford Point Marines."

"The Montford Point Marines acted with professionalism and proved their courage in epic battles of the Pacific like Saipan, Iwo Jima, and Okinawa," Amos said. "Because of the perseverance of the Montford Point Marines, the Corps underwent a social awakening laying the foundation for greater equality and opportunity. Many Montford Point Marines carried their exceptional strength of character to their lives outside the Marine Corps, becoming leaders in their communities as mayors, ambassadors, educators, lawyers, ministers, and doctors. Some went on to integrate the shipyards of America, weaving equality of opportunity into the fabric of our society. Their story is one of triumph over adversity. Their legacy of courage and perseverance is an inspiration to all Marines."[4]

APPENDIX 5

Pelosi Speech Supports Congressional Gold Medal

To Honor Montford Point Marines

Nadeam Elshami

October 25, 2011
Washington, D.C.—Democratic Leader Nancy Pelosi spoke on the House floor today on HR 2447, which grants the Congressional Gold Medal to the Montford Point Marines. Below are the Leader's remarks:

"I thank the gentleman for yielding and thank you, Mr. Speaker, for recognition. And I'm pleased to join my colleagues: Congresswoman Corrine Brown, who has been relentless in calling for this day, our colleague from Missouri, Mr. Clay, thank you for your leadership on all of this as well. To our colleagues on the other side, the Ranking Member on the Banking Committee and then Mr. Pearce as well who spoke about this. We come together in a bipartisan way for a very patriotic occasion for our country.

What a thrill it will be when we can tell our constituents we were there to vote for this important resolution, which will, as we all know, call for the striking of a gold coin, directing the Treasury Secretary to strike a single gold medal of appropriate design in honor of the Montford Point Marines. How exciting!

I know that many of those Marines or their families are here on Capitol Hill today. We look forward to welcoming them to a ceremony where these medals will be bestowed. I only wish that all of the Marines who ever served, sacrificed, that were willing to sacrifice their lives for our country—some of them did, some of them have left us, have passed since then, all of them are the subject of the respect and honor that we pay.

It's just another example of some of the inequality that has existed in our country earlier on. Long overdue time for us to address some of that, we've had occasion in the rotunda over the last few years to recognize the work of President Truman when he called for the desegregation of the military. General, Secretary, National Security Advisor—he has many titles—Powell was here with us that day.

We've had occasion to honor our Tuskegee Airmen on another occasion, so it is long overdue to, again, take this other step to recognize the important work that all Americans have played in that most important responsibility to protect and defend.

I will say this to all the Marines who approached me about this legislation outside the Congress, that every time they did, I said 'Corrine Brown has already gotten to us. Lacy Clay has already gotten to us.' Corrine was absolutely relentless on this, and we are all here because of her leadership and all of the work the members of our Congressional Black Caucus and the bipartisan support that we have and, of course, we wouldn't be on the floor without the leadership of our speaker who enabled this bill to come to the floor. But it's a proud day for the Congress. We'll look forward to an even prouder day when these medals will be bestowed. With that, Mr. Speaker, I yield back."[5]

APPENDIX 6

Text From Congress Granting the Congressional Gold Medal

Bill Text Versions

112th Congress (2011-2012)

HR 2447

HR 2447—To grant the Congressional Gold Medal to the Montford Point Marines. (Enrolled Bill [Final as Passed Both House and Senate]—ENR)

HR 2447

One Hundred Twelfth Congress

of the

United States of America

AT THE FIRST SESSION

Begun and held at the City of Washington on Wednesday, the fifth day of January, two thousand and eleven

An Act

To grant the Congressional Gold Medal to the Montford Point Marines.

Be it enacted by the Senate and House of Representatives of the United States of America in Congress assembled,

SECTION 1. FINDINGS.

Congress makes the following findings:

(1) On June 25, 1941, President Franklin D. Roosevelt issued Executive Order No. 8802 establishing the Fair Employment Practices Commission and opening the doors for the very first African-Americans to enlist in the United States Marine Corps.

(2) The first Black Marine recruits were trained at Camp

Montford Point, near the New River in Jacksonville, North Carolina.

(3) On August 26, 1942, Howard P. Perry of Charlotte, North Carolina, was the first Black private to set foot on Montford Point.

(4) During April 1943, the first African-American Marine Drill Instructors took over as the senior Drill Instructors of the eight platoons then in training: the 16th Platoon (Edgar R. Huff), 17th (Thomas Brokaw), 18th (Charles E. Allen), 19th (Gilbert H. Johnson), 20th (Arnold R. Bostic), 21st (Mortimer A. Cox), 22nd (Edgar R. Davis, Jr.), and 23rd (George A. Jackson).

(5) Black Marines of the 8th Ammunition Company and the 36th Depot Company landed on the island of Iwo Jima on D-Day, February 19, 1945.

(6) The largest number of Black Marines to serve in combat during World War II took part in the seizure of Okinawa in the Ryuku Islands with some 2,000 Black Marines seeing action during the campaign.

(7) On November 10, 1945, the first African-American Marine, Frederick C. Branch, was commissioned as a second lieutenant at the Marine Corps Base in Quantico, Virginia.

(8) Overall, 19,168 Blacks served in the Marine Corps in World War II.

(9) An enterprising group of men, including original Montford Pointer Master Sergeant Brooks E. Gray, planned a reunion of the Men of Montford Point, and on September 15, 1965, approximately 400 Montford Point Marines gathered at the Adelphi Hotel in Philadelphia, Pennsylvania, to lay the foundation for the Montford Point Marine Association Inc., 16 years after the closure of Montford Point as a training facility for Black recruits.

(10) Organized as a nonmilitary, nonprofit entity, the Montford Point Marine Association's main mission is to preserve the legacy of the first Black Marines.

(11) Today the Montford Point Marine Association has 36 chapters throughout the United States.

(12) Many of these first Black Marines stayed in the Marine Corps like Sergeant Major Edgar R. Huff.

(13) Sergeant Major Huff was one of the very first recruits

aboard Montford Point.

(14) Sergeant Major Huff was also the first African-American Sergeant Major and the first African-American Marine to retire with 30 years of service which included combat in three major wars, World War II, the Korean War, and the Vietnam War.

(15) During the Tet Offensive, Sergeant Major Huff was awarded the Bronze Star Medal with combat 'V' for valor for saving the life of his radio operator.

(16) Another original Montford Pointer who saw extensive combat action in both the Korean War and the Vietnam War was Sergeant Major Louis Roundtree.

(17) Sergeant Major Roundtree was awarded the Silver Star Medal, four Bronze Star Medals, three Purple Hearts, and numerous other personal and unit awards for his service during these conflicts.

(18) On April 19, 1974, Montford Point was renamed Camp Johnson after legendary Montford Pointer Sergeant Major Gilbert 'Hashmark' Johnson.

(19) The Montford Point Marine Association has several memorials in place to perpetuate the memory of the first African American Marines and their accomplishments, including-

(A) the Montford Point Marine Association Edgar R. Huff Memorial Scholarship which is offered annually through the Marine Corps Scholarship Foundation.

(B) the Montford Point Museum located aboard Camp Johnson (Montford Point) in Jacksonville, North Carolina.

(C) the Brooks Elbert Gray, Jr. Consolidated Academic Instruction Facility named in honor of original Montford Pointer and the Montford Point Marine Corps Association Founder Master Gunnery Sergeant Gray. This facility was dedicated on 15 April 2005 aboard Camp Johnson, North Carolina; and

(D) during July of 1997 Branch Hall, a building within the Officers Candidate School in Quantico, Virginia, was named in honor of Captain Frederick Branch.

SEC. 2. CONGRESSIONAL GOLD MEDAL.

(a) Award Authorized—The Speaker of the House of Representatives and the President pro tempore of the Senate shall make appropriate arrangements for the award, on behalf of the Congress, of a single gold medal of appropriate design in honor of the Montford Point Marines, collectively, in recognition of their personal sacrifice and service to their country.

(b) Design and Striking—For the purposes of the award referred to in subsection (a), the Secretary of the Treasury (hereafter in this Act referred to as the 'Secretary') shall strike the gold medal with suitable emblems, devices, and inscriptions, to be determined by the Secretary.

SEC. 3. DUPLICATE MEDALS.

Under such regulations as the Secretary may prescribe, the Secretary may strike and sell duplicates in bronze of the gold medal struck under section 2, at a price sufficient to cover the costs of the medals, including labor, materials, dies, use of machinery, and overhead expenses.

SEC. 4. NATIONAL MEDALS.

Medals struck pursuant to this Act are National medals for purposes of chapter 51 of title 31, United States Code.

SEC. 5. AUTHORIZATION OF APPROPRIATIONS; PROCEEDS OF SALE.

(a) Authorization of Appropriations—There is authorized to be charged against the United States Mint Public Enterprise Fund, an amount not to exceed $30,000 to pay for the cost of the medals authorized under section 2.

(b) Proceeds of Sale—Amounts received from the sale of duplicate bronze medals under section 3 shall be deposited in the United States Mint Public Enterprise Fund.

Speaker of the House of Representatives.

Vice President of the United States and
President of the Senate.[6]

APPENDIX 7

Others Who Received the Congressional Gold Medal

Below are some people who have been awarded the Congressional Gold Medal:

George Washington: 1776

John Fox Slater, United States philanthropist known for assisting in the education of emancipated slaves: 1883

Charles Lindbergh: May 4, 1928

Thomas Edison: May 29, 1928

Major Walter Reed: February 28, 1929

Robert Frost: September 13, 1960

Bob Hope: June 8, 1962

Douglas MacArthur: October 9, 1962

Walt Disney: May 24, 1968

Winston Churchill: May 7, 1969

Marian Anderson: March 8, 1977

Robert Kennedy: November 1, 1978

Joe Louis: August 26, 1982

Harry Truman: May 8, 1984

Roy Wilkins: April 23, 1991

Jesse Owens: September 20, 1988

General Colin Powell: April 3, 1991

General H. Norman Schwarzkopf: April 23, 1991

Nelson Mandela: July 29, 1998

The Little Rock Nine: October 21, 1998

Rosa Parks: May 4, 1999

Jackie Robinson: October 29, 2003

Dr. Dorothy Height: December 6, 2003

Dr. and Mrs. Martin Luther King: October 25, 2004

Tuskegee Airmen: April 11, 2006

Neil Armstrong, Edwin "Buzz" Armstrong, Michael Collins, John Glenn: August 7, 2009

Montford Point Marines: November 23, 2011

including

Corporal Thomas Mosley

5th Marine Division, 5th Ammunition Company, 365th Platoon

A Montford Point Marine

Notes

Acknowledgments

1. Dr. Pastor "Sergeant" Joseph Ginyard, an original Montford Point Marine and Congressional Gold Medal recipient, in the eulogy for the author's mother-in-law, Mrs. Tae-im Johnson, Philadelphia, September 2012.
2. Biography of Dr. James T. Averhart Jr., CWO5, https://jamesaverhart.com/wp-content/uploads/2019/08/James-Averhart-Bio-Full.pdf.
3. Joe Geeter, III, quoted in "The History Makers: African American Video Oral History Collection," www.loc.gov/folklife/civilrights/survey/view_collection.php?coll_id=951.
4. Ibid.
5. Sergeant Mel Ragin, in conversation with Thomas Mosley and the author at a Montford Point Marine Association meeting in Macon, Georgia, February, 2012.

1. It All Starts at Home

1. Thomas Mosley, in discussion with the author, May 21, 2011.
2. Story of Grandmom and Mary, Thursday, November 27, 1986.
3. Thomas Mosley, in discussion with the author, May 21, 2011.

2. Life One Step at a Time

1. Thomas Mosley, in discussion with the author, personal interview, May 23, 2011.
2. Ken Burns and Lynn Novick, "The War: At Home, War Production," WETA and American Lives II Film Project, 2007. www.pbs.org/kenburns/the-war/war-production/.

3. Ibid.
4. Ibid.
5. Doris Kearns Goodwin, "The Way We Won: America's Economic Breakthrough During World War II," *The American Prospect,* Fall 1992. Accessed September 12, 2012. https://prospect.org/health/way-won-america-s-economic-breakthrough-world-war-ii/; Executive Order 8802: Prohibition of Discrimination in the Defense Industry (1941), U.S. National Archives & Records Administration. www.ourdocuments.gov/doc.php?doc=72.
6. Ibid.
7. Doris Kearns Goodwin, *No Ordinary Time: Franklin, and Eleanor Roosevelt: The Home Front in World War II* (New York: Simon and Shuster, 1994), p. 624.
8. Andrew E. Kersten, *A. Philip Randolph: A Life in the Vanguard* (Lanham, MD: Roman Littlefield, 2007), pp. 50–53.
9. Goodwin, *No Ordinary Time,* pp. 163–73, 246–50.
10. Morris J. MacGregor and Bernard C Nalty, *Blacks in the United States Armed Forces: Basic Documents, Volume VI* (Wilmington, DE: Scholarly Resources, 1977), Doc. 5, Letter, Congressman W. R. Poage to Secretary Frank Knox, December 10, 1941, p. 12.
11. MacGregor and Nalty, *Blacks in the United States Armed Forces,* Poage letter, p. 12.
12. Ibid.
13. MacGregor and Nalty, *Blacks in the United States Armed Forces,* Doc. 6, Letter, Secretary Frank Knox to Gifford Pinchot, January 19, 1942, p. 13.
14. Ibid.
15. MacGregor and Nalty, *Blacks in the United States Armed Forces,* Doc. 21, memorandum, Commandant of the Marine Corps to the Chairman General Board, February 27, 1942, Subject: Enlistment of men of the colored race in other than messman branch, p. 75.
16. Rice University, "Franklin Roosevelt and the New Deal, 1932–1941," OER Commons, www.oercommons.org/courseware/module/15533/overview.
17. Bethune-Cookman University, "The Historical Roots of Bethune-Cookman University," www.cookman.edu/history/.
18. Ibid.
19. Thomas Mosley, discussion with the author, August 25, 2014.
20. Audrey McCluskey and Elaine M. Smith, eds., *Mary Mcleod*

Bethune: Building a Better World, Essays and Selected Documents by Mary McLeod Bethune (Bloomington, IN: Indiana University Press, 1999).

21. MacGregor and Nalty, *Blacks in the United States Armed Forces,* Item 3, letter, A. Philip Randolph, Director of Negro March-on-Washington Committee, to Secretary Knox, June 4, 1941, p. 8.
22. Ibid.
23. Ibid., p. 9.
24. Ibid.
25. Ibid.
26. Kersten, *A. Philip Randolph,* p. 54.
27. Herbert G. Ruffin II, "William Monroe Trotter," Black Past, January 23, 2007, https://blackpast.org/aah/trotter-william-monroe-1872-1934.
28. Kersten, *A. Philip Randolph,* pp. 50–54.
29. Ibid., p. 54.
30. John Simkin, "March on Washington in 1941," Spartacus Educational, September 1997, https://spartacus-educational.com/USAmarchW.htm.
31. Ibid.
32. Joseph B. Robinson, "The New Fair Employment Law," *Ohio State Law Journal* 20:4 (August 1959), https://kb.osu.edu/handle/1811/68185.
33. Christopher A. Browning, "Segregation versus Integration: The Racial Policy of the Marine Corps from 1942–1962," (master's thesis, Marine Corps Command and Staff College, 2013), p. 4. https://apps.dtic.mil/sti/citations/ADA601677.
34. Robinson, "New Fair Employment Law."
35. Ibid.

3. Orders from Franklin D. Roosevelt

1. Executive Order 8802, p. 39. Transcription courtesy of the United States Equal Employment Opportunity Commission.
2. Thomas Mosley, in discussion with the author, June 2011.

4. Chosen, Accepted, but Unwanted Marines

1. Edward Ayres, "African Americans and the American Revolution," Jamestown Settlement and American Revolution Museum at Yorktown, n.d., https://tinyurl.com/27ev9fdm.
2. Ibid.

3. Ibid.
4. Gary B. Nash, *Red, White, and Black: The Peoples of Early America* (Englewood Cliffs, NJ: Prentice Hall, 1974), p. 285.
5. Ibid., p. 43.
6. Ibid.
7. Ibid.
8. MacGregor and Nalty, *Blacks in the United States Armed Forces,* "Hearings Before the General Board of the Navy, 1942," Transcript of the discussion before the General Board concerning the possible enlistment of Negroes. Also includes written comments of the Commandants of the Marine Corps and Coast Guard, p. 48.
9. Ibid.
10. Ibid., p. 49.
11. Morris J. MacGregor Jr., *Integration of the Armed Forces, 1940–1965* (Washington, DC: Center of Military History, U.S. Army, 1985), p. 103.
12. Ibid., p. 100.
13. MacGregor and Nalty, *Blacks in the United States Armed Forces,* Doc. 21, memorandum, p. 75.
14. MacGregor, *Integration of the Armed Forces,* p. 101.
15. Ibid., p. 104.
16. MacGregor and Nalty, *Blacks in the United States Armed Forces,* Item 105, memorandum, Division of Plans and Policies to Director, Division of Plans and Policies, December 26, 1942, subject: Colored personnel, plans for the procurement and assignment of 1,000 Negroes per month in such a manner as to preclude, insofar as possible, integration, p. 420.
17. Ibid.
18. Ibid.
19. Interview with Sgt. Joseph Geeter, Past National President of the Montford Point Marine Association (MPMA) and current President of the Philadelphia Chapter 1 MPMA, January 19, 2019.

5. All Might Needed Against Hideki Tojo

1. Herbert Aptheker, *To Be Free* (New York: Carol Publishing, 1948), pp. 75–80.
2. San Diego Buffalo Soldiers, "Buffalo Soldier History, San Diego, California 9th & 10th (Horse) Cavalry Association," n.d., http://sandiegobuffalosoldiers.org/history.html.
3. Ibid.

4. C. Peter Chen, "C. Peter Chen," World War II Database, March 15, 2012, https://ww2db.com/person_bio.php?person_id=179.
5. C. Peter Chen, "Hideki Tojo," World War II Database, n.d., https://ww2db.com/person_bio.php?person_id=65.
6. Herbert P. Bix, *Hirohito and the Making of Modern Japan* (New York: HarperCollins, 2000), pp. 418–19.
7. Ibid., pp. 317–20.
8. Encyclopedia Britannica, s.v. "Nanjing Massacre: Chinese History or Second Sino-Japanese War 1937–1945," www.britannica.com/event/Second-Sino-Japanese-War.
9. Ibid.
10. C. P. Fitzgerald, *A Concise History of East Asia* (New York: Praeger, 1970), pp. 190–95.
11. Ibid., p. 193.
12. Bix, *Hirohito,* p. 416.
13. Ibid., p. 417.
14. Ibid., p. 419.
15. Louis Morton, "Strategy and Command: The First Two Years," *United States Army in World War II: The War in the Pacific* (Washington, DC: Office of the Chief of Military History, Dept. of the Army, 1953), www.ibiblio.org/hyperwar/USA/USA-P-Strategy/Strategy-6.html.
16. "Japanese Operations in the Southwest Pacific Area, Volume II—Pre-War Japanese Military Preparations 1941," *Reports of General MacArthur* (Washington, DC: Dept. of the Army, repr. 1994). p. 2, https://history.army.mil/books/wwii/MacArthur%20Reports/MacArthur%20V2%20P1/macarthurv2.htm.
17. Fitzgerald, *Concise History of East Asia,* p. 192.
18. Ibid., pp. 192–93.

6. Last Stop: Montford Where?

1. Henry I. Shaw Jr. and Ralph W. Donnelly, *Blacks in the Marine Corps* (Washington, DC: History and Museum Division Headquarters, U.S. Marine Corps, 2002), p. 5.
2. Discussion with Thomas Mosley.
3. Shaw and Donnelly, *Blacks in The Marine Corps,* p. 8.
4. Nyeesa Aziz, "Congress Considers Honor for First Black Marines," BET, October 24, 2011, www.bet.com/news/national/2011/10/24/congress-considers-honor-for-first-black-marines.html.

5. Bennie McRae Jr., "Gunnery Sergeant Elijah Abram, (USMC-Ret.) Vice President, Montford Point Marine Association 1998 speech, 'The History of the Chosen Few, The Men of Montford Point,'" Lest We Forget: African American Military, http://lestweforget.hamptonu.edu/page.cfm?uuid=9FEC4420-A96D-AABD35FFCAEB46A2C81D.
6. Shaw and Donnelly, *Blacks in The Marine Corps*, p. 5.
7. Ibid.
8. Ibid.
9. Benis M. Frank and Henry I. Shaw, *Victory and Occupation: History of U.S. Marine Corps Operations in World War II*, Volume V (Washington, DC: Historical Branch, G-3 Division, Headquarters, U.S. Marine Corps, 1968), pp. 679–81, www.ibiblio.org/hyperwar/USMC/V/USMC-V-VI-2.html. See also Kenneth W. Condit, Gerald Diamond, and Edwin T. Turnbladh, *Marine Corps Ground Training in World War II* (Washington, DC: Headquarters Branch, G-3, Headquarters, U.S. Marine Corps, 1956), https://archive.org/details/MarineCorpsGroundTrainingInWWII-nsia.
10. Ibid.
11. Lee Douglas Jr., "Montford Point Marines Transcripts," University of North Carolina Wilmington, Randall Library, 2006, interview by Dr. Clarence E. Willie, Lieutenant Colonel, Retired, United States Marine Corps, and Dr. Melton McLaurin, https://library.uncw.edu/web/montford/contact.html.
12. Ibid.
13. Ibid.
14. Isaac David Frasier, "Montford Point Marines Transcripts," University of North Carolina Wilmington, Randall Library, 2006.
15. Truman Boone, telephone interview with the author, March 20, 2012.
16. Ibid.

7. Why Me, Oh, Lord?

1. Thomas Mosley, discussion with the author, May 28, 2011.
2. MacGregor and Nalty, *Blacks in the United States Armed Forces*, Document 104, memorandum, Director, Division of Plans and Policies, to Commandant, October 29, 1942, subject: Enlistment of colored personnel in the Marine Corps Reserve. Reports on number of Negroes recruited and outlines plans for training of black specialists.

3. Shaw and Donnelly, *Blacks in The Marine Corps,* p. 2.
4. Ibid.
5. Thomas Mosley, interview with the author, May 28, 2011.
6. Shaw and Donnelly, *Blacks in The Marine Corps,* p. 12.
7. Sergeant Major Gilbert H. Johnson, USMC, "Home of the Original Montford Point Marines," National Montford Point Marine Association, www.montfordpointmarines.org/history.
8. Ibid.
9. Gail Buckley, American Patriots, *The Story of Blacks in the Military from the Revolution to Desert Storm* (New York: Random House, 2001) p. 314.
10. Thomas Mosley, discussion with the author, May 2011.
11. Ibid.
12. Ibid.
13. Ibid.
14. Interview with Sergeant Major Edgar Richard Huff, Library of the Marine Corps Portal, Catalog no. 14045. Archives and Special Collections Branch, Alfred M. Gray Marine Corps Research Center, http://guides.grc.usmcu.edu/content.php?pid=283343&sid=2335057.
15. Ibid.
16. Ibid.
17. Thomas Mosley, discussion with the author, May 28, 2011.
18. Ibid.
19. Ibid.
20. Ibid.
21. Ibid.
22. Ibid.
23. Truman Boone, phone interview, May 24, 2012.
24. Macgregor and Nalty, *Blacks in the United States Armed Forces,* Doc. 106, memorandum, Commandant, U.S. Marine Corps, to Distribution List, March 20, 1943, Subject: Colored Personnel, pp. 423–25; Bernard C. Nalty, *The Right to Fight: African American Marines in World War II* (Washington, DC: History and Museums Division, Headquarters, U.S. Marine Corps, 1995), p. 6.
25. Truman Boone, phone interview, May 24, 2012.
26. Sergeant Joseph Ginyard, interview with the author and my wife's childhood mentor and pastor, February 14, 2013.
27. Ibid.
28. Shaw and Donnelly, *Blacks in the Marine Corps,* p. 12.
29. Ibid.

30. Huff interview, Marine Corps Research Center, http://guides.grc.usmcu.edu/montford.

8. Camp Lejeune: Part Training, Part Resort

1. Gertrude S. Carraway, *Camp Lejeune Leathernecks* (New Bern, NC: Owen G. Dunn, 1946).
2. Ibid.
3. U.S. Marine Corps, "Marine Corps Base Camp Lejeune," n.d., www.lejeune.Marines.mil/visitors/history.aspx.
4. Carraway, *Camp Lejeune Leathernecks,* p. 18.
5. Ibid., p. 100.
6. Ibid.
7. Ibid.
8. Ibid.
9. Ibid., p. 35.
10. Ibid., p. 54.
11. Ibid., p. 27.
12. Ibid.

9. The USS Lamar Heading to the Pacific Islands

1. Gary P. Priolo, "USS *Lamar* (APA-47) ex USS *Lamar* (AP-92) (1943–1944)," NavSource Online: Amphibious Photo Archive, 1996, www.navsource.org/archives/10/03/03047.htm.
2. History Central, "*Lamar* APL-47," n.d., www.historycentral.com/navy/MISC/lamar.html.
3. Truman Boone, phone interview, March 15, 2012.
4. Ibid.
5. History Central, *Lamar.*
6. Priolo, "USS *Lamar.*"
7. Ibid.
8. History Central, *Lamar.*
9. Ibid.
10. Ibid.
11. George W. Garand and Truman R. Strowbridge, *Western Pacific Operations: History of the Marine Corps Operations in World War II* (Washington, DC: Historical Branch, G-3 Division, Headquarters, US Marine Corps, 1971), "Part III, The Palaus: Gateway to the Philippines," p. 64, www.ibiblio.org/hyperwar/USMC/IV/USMC-IV-III-1.html.
12. Ibid.

13. Bix, *Hirohito,* p. 45.
14. Alfred Thayer Mahan, *The Influence of Sea Power Upon History, 1660–1783* (1890; repr. London: Methuen, 1965), ch. 2.
15. Gary P. Priolo, USS *Lamar.*
16. Ibid.
17. Ibid.

10. The Military and Tales of "Black Tails" on Hawaii

1. Jane L. Scheiber and Harry N. Scheiber, "Martial Law in Hawaii," Densho Encyclopedia, July 22, 2020, https://encyclopedia.densho.org/Martial_law_in_Hawaii.
2. Beth Bailey and David Farber, "The Double-V Campaign in World War II Hawaii: African American Americans, Racial Ideology, and Federal Power," *Journal of Social History* 26:4 (Summer 1993), p. 818, doi:10.1353/jsh/26.4.817. See also Beth Bailey and David Farber, *The First Strange Place: Race and Sex in World War II Hawaii* (Baltimore: Free Press/Macmillan, 1992), p. 133.
3. Bailey and Farber, *First Strange Place,* p. 139.
4. Ibid.
5. Ibid.
6. Bailey and Farber, "Double-V Campaign," pp. 819–20.
7. Ibid.
8. Ibid., p. 821.
9. Bailey and Farber, *First Strange Place,* p. 141.
10. Emmett J. Scott, *Scott's Official History of the American Negro in the World War* (1919; repr. London: FB & Co., 2017), p. 259.
11. Ibid.
12. Gail Buckley, *American Patriots: The Story of Blacks in the Military from the Revolution to Desert Storm* (New York: Random House, 2001), pp. 164, 194–96.
13. Eric Durr, "'Rainbow Division' That Represented the United States Formed in New York in August 1917," U.S. Army, July 24, 2017, https://tinyurl.com/adktd84k.
14. Ibid.
15. Bailey and Farber, *First Strange Place,* p. 148.
16. Jeff Livingston, "Who Built the OR&L?" *Akahele I Ke Ka'aahi* 40:6 (Nov.–Dec. 2010), www.hawaiianrailway.org/historian/Articles/WhoBuiltTheORL.html.
17. Bailey and Farber, *First Strange Place,* pp. 149–56.
18. Thomas Mosley, interview with the author, May 16, 2012.
19. Truman Boone, interview with the author, April 20, 2012.

20. Benjamin A. Patterson, "Interview by Dr. Clarence E. Willie, Lieutenant Colonel, Retired, United States Marine Corps, and Dr. Melton McLaurin," Montford Point Marines, August 11, 2005, http://library.uncw.edu/web/montford/collection.html.
21. Nalty, *Right to Fight,* p. 12.
22. Eiichiro Azuma, "Brief Historical Overview of Japanese Emigration, 1868–1998," International Nikkei Research Project, Japanese American National Museum, February 28, 2014, www.discovernikkei.org/en/journal/2014/2/28/historical-overview/.
23. Jean Pfaelzer, *Driven Out: The Forgotten War Against Chinese Americans* (New York: Random House, 2007), pp. 167–68.
24. Jerome A. Hart, *In Our Second Century* (San Francisco: Pioneer Press, 1931), pp. 52–53.
25. Pfaelzer, *Driven Out,* pp. 33–4.
26. Ibid., pp. 65–6.
27. Ronald Takaki, *Strangers from a Different Shore: A History of Asian Americans* (Boston: Little, Brown and Co., 1989), pp. 14, 29, 40, 65, 91, 110–112.
28. Ibid., p. 28.
29. Chinese Exclusion Act (1882), National Archives, www.ourdocuments.gov/doc.php?doc=47.
30. Office of the Historian, "Repeal of the Chinese Exclusion Act, 1943," U.S. Department of State, n.d., https://history.state.gov/milestones/1937-1945/chinese-exclusion-act-repeal.
31. Ibid.
32. Laurie Mercier, "Japanese Americans in the Columbia Basin," Washington State University, n.d., https://content.libraries.wsu.edu/digital/collection/cchm/custom/ja-overview.
33. Eiichiro Azuma, "The Issei Arrive in Oregon," Discover Nikkei, October 23, 2017, www.discovernikkei.org/en/journal/2017/10/23/oregon-1.
34. "Gentlemen's Agreement," History.com, October 9, 2009, www.history.com/topics/immigration/gentlemens-agreement.
35. Takaki, *Strangers from a Different Shore,* pp. 201, 272, 296, 297, 298.
36. Ibid., p. 200.
37. Ibid.
38. Ibid., pp. 27, 46, 50, 65, 203, 337, 491.
39. Ibid., pp. 201–3.
40. Mercier, "Japanese Americans in the Columbia Basin."
41. Ibid.

11. The Depot and Ammo Companies

1. Nalty, *Right to Fight,* p. 18.
2. Ibid.
3. "World War II," History.com, n.d., www.history.com/topics/world-war-ii.
4. "The Battlefield of Iwo: An Ugly Island Becomes a Memorial to American Valor," *Life* magazine, April 9, 1945, https://tinyurl.com/j7ra9x8s.
5. Eric Hammel, *Iwo Jima: Portrait of a Battle: United States Marines at War in the Pacific* (St. Paul, MN: MBI Publishing, 2006), p. 59.
6. Andy J. Hurt, "Legends: Corps Celebrates 59th Anniversary of Landing at Iwo Jima," Marine Corps Logistics Base Barstow, February 26, 2004, https://tinyurl.com/33aytj3d.
7. Hammel, *Iwo Jima,* p. 235.
8. Steven E. Anders, "Quartermaster Supply in the Pacific During World War II," *Quartermaster Professional Bulletin,* Spring 1999, www.quartermasterfoundation.org/article/quartermaster-supply-in-the-pacific-during-world-war-ii/.
9. Ibid.
10. Nalty, *Right to Fight,* p. 18.
11. MacGregor and Nalty, *Blacks in the United States Armed Forces,* Doc. 102, memorandum, Commandant, U.S. Marine Corps, to District Commanders, All Reserve Districts except 10th, 14th, 15th, 16th, May 25, 1942, subject: Enlistment of colored personnel in the Marine Corps. Explains plan for recruitment and assignment of black Marines to begin on June 1, 1942, p. 416.
12. MacGregor and Nalty, *Blacks in the United States Armed Forces,* Doc. 103, memorandum, Commandant, U.S. Marine Corps, for Secretary of the Navy, 23 June 1942, subject: Enlistment of Negroes. Blames failure of enlist the number of black Marines agreed upon to lack of physically and mentally qualified applicants. Expects considerable acceleration of program in future, p. 417.
13. MacGregor and Nalty, *Blacks in the United States Armed Forces,* Doc. 104, memorandum, p. 418.
14. Ibid.
15. Thomas Mosley, interview with the author, Feb 1, 2012.

12. The 5th at Work: The Spearhead

1. Thomas Mosley, interview with the author, Feb 5, 2012.
2. Eric Bergerud, *Touched with Fire: The Land War in the South Pacific* (New York: Penguin, 1996), pp. 90–92.
3. Ibid.
4. Ibid.
5. Garand and Strowbridge, *Western Pacific Operations: Iwo Jima,* ch. 3, "The Preliminaries," section 482, www.ibiblio.org/hyperwar/USMC/IV/USMC-IV-VI-3.html.
6. Joseph H. Alexander, *Closing In: Marines in the Seizure of Iwo Jima* (Washington, DC: History and Museums Division, Headquarters, U.S. Marine Corps, 1994), www.ibiblio.org/hyperwar/USMC/USMC-C-Iwo/.
7. Ibid.
8. Ibid., sections 4–6.
9. Bix, *Hirohito,* p. 484.
10. Steve Rabson, "American Literature on the Battle of Okinawa and the Continuing U.S. Military Presence," *Asia-Pacific Journal, Japan Focus* 15:20 (October 15, 2017), https://apjjf.org/2017/20/Rabson.html, quoting Jo Nobuko Martin, *A Princess Lily of the Ryukyus* (Tokyo: Shin Nippon Kyoiku Tosho, 1984).
11. Garand and Strowbridge, *Western Pacific Operations,* ch. 3, "The Preliminaries."
12. Nalty, *Right to Fight,* p. 23.
13. J. David Rogers, "Iwo Jima: The Costliest Battle in American History," n.d., https://web.mst.edu/~rogersda/american&military_history/BATTLE-OF-IWO-JIMA.pdf.
14. The National World War II Museum, New Orleans, "The Battle for Iwo Jima," n.d., www.nationalww2museum.org/sites/default/files/2017-07/iwo-jima-fact-sheet.pdf.
15. Jim Rundles, quoted in "The Montford Point Marines Worked and Fought on Iwo Jima," *The Jackson Advocate,* Jackson, MS, February 23–March 1, 1995. Permission granted from Ms. Alice Tisdale, associate publisher. Retrieved from Jim Rundles, "The Montford Point Marines Worked and Fought on Iwo Jima," 1995, Lest We Forget: African American Military, http://lestweforget.hamptonu.edu/page.cfm?uuid=9FEC4392-E2BA-3AA6-7E992F09F2CAB48E.
16. Hammel, *Iwo Jima,* p. 23.
17. Ibid., p. 69.

18. Ibid., p. 71.
19. Rundles, "Montford Point Marines."
20. Ibid.
21. "Archibald Mosley," Montford Point Marines, University of North Carolina Wilmington, December 17, 2004, https://library.uncw.edu/web/montford/transcripts/Mosely_Archibald.html.
22. Ibid.
23. Nalty, *Right to Fight,* p. 24.
24. Ibid.
25. "Archibald Mosley," Montford Point Marines.
26. Ibid.
27. Ibid.
28. Shaw and Donnelly, *Blacks in the Marine Corps,* p. 39.
29. Franco Ordonez, "70 Years Gone, Montford Point Marines Get Their Due," McClatchy Newspapers, June 27, 2012, www.mcclatchydc.com/news/politics-government/article24731887.html.
30. Ibid.
31. Hammel, *Iwo Jima,* p. 235.
32. Ibid.

13. Montford Point Ammunition Specialists

1. Morris J. MacGregor Jr., *Integration of the Armed Forces 1940–1965* (Washington, DC: Center of Military History, U.S. Army, 1981), p. 109.
2. Major Giesel, telephone conversation with the author.
3. MacGregor, *Integration of the Armed Forces,* p. 106.
4. Mark Flowers, "M1 Service Rifle," WW2 Gyrene, February 2013.
5. Mark Flowers, "M1903," WW2 Gyrene, February 2013.
6. Mark Flowers, "M1918 Browning Automatic Rifle," WW2 Gyrene, February 2013.
7. Mark Flowers, "U.S. Carbine, 30 Caliber, M1," WW2 Gyrene, February 2013.
8. Mark Flowers, "Thompson Machine Gun," WW2 Gyrene, February 2013.
9. Mark Flowers, "Rifle Grenade Launcher, M7," WW2 Gyrene, February 2013.
10. Thomas Mosley, phone conversation, August 2012.
11. Theodore Peters, personal conversation, interview with the author, June 27, 2012.

12. Mark Flowers, "Light Machine Gun M1919A4," WW2 Gyrene, February 2013.
13. Ibid.
14. Ibid.
15. Mark Flowers, "Pack Howitzer 75-mm," WW2 Gyrene, February 2013.
16. Richard L. DeNoyer, "Proceedings of the 113th National Convention of the Veterans of Foreign Wars of the United States," Veterans of Foreign Wars of the United States, July 21–25, 2012, www.govinfo.gov/content/pkg/CDOC-113hdoc35/pdf/CDOC-113hdoc35.pdf.
17. Lee Hattabaugh, "M1A1 90mm Anti-Aircraft Gun," Historical Marker Database, April 14, 2011, www.hmdb.org/marker.asp?marker=41683.
18. Bix, *Hirohito,* pp. 481, 485.
19. Ibid., p. 475.
20. Ibid.
21. Nalty, *Right to Fight,* p. 1.
22. Carroll Reavis, interview by Dr. Clarence E. Willie, Lieutenant Colonel, Retired, United States Marine Corps, and Dr. Melton McLaurin, Montford Point Marine Transcripts and UNCW, July 23, 2004, https://library.uncw.edu/web/montford/transcripts.html.
23. Ibid.
24. Charles R. Smith, "Securing the Surrender: Marines in the Occupation of Japan," United States Marine Corps History and Museums Division, 1997, www.nps.gov/parkhistory/online_books/wapa/extContent/usmc/pcn-190-003143-00/sec2.htm.

14. The Fleet Marine Force

1. Garand and Strowbridge, *Western Pacific Operations,* section 13.
2. Ibid., section 14.
3. Ibid., section 16.
4. Alfred Dunlop Bailey, "Alligators, Buffaloes, and Bushmasters: The History of the Development of the LVT through World War II," (Washington, DC: History and Museums Division Headquarters, U.S. Marine Corps, 1986), p. 21, https://tinyurl.com/k5pjbt5y.
5. Garand and Strowbridge, *Western Pacific Operations,* section 14.

6. Ibid., section 16.
7. Ibid., section 17.
8. Ibid.
9. Ibid.
10. Ibid., sections 21–22.

15. The Fleet Was Massive

1. Garand and Strowbridge, *Western Pacific Operations,* sections 26–28.
2. Thomas Mosley, personal discussions, June 12, 2014.
3. Nalty, *Right to Fight,* p. 20.
4. Ibid.
5. Ibid.
6. Ibid.
7. Ibid., p. 21.
8. Ibid.
9. Ibid.
10. Ibid., p. 22.
11. Ibid.
12. Shaw and Donnelly, *Blacks in the Marine Corps,* pp. 36–37.
13. Nalty, *Right to Fight,* p. 22.
14. George M. Watson, "Bernard C. Nalty: (1931–2015)," *Air Power History* 62:4 (Winter 2015), p. 66.
15. Nalty, *Right to Fight,* p. 22.
16. MacGregor and Nalty, *Blacks in the United States Armed Forces,* item 110, memorandum, Commanding Officer, Fourth Marine Ammunition Company, Fifth Field Depot, Supply Service, Fleet Marine Force, Pacific, to Commandant, November 8, 1944, subject: Colored personnel, report of. A detailed and negative report on the training and activities of a black ammunition company in the Pacific, pp. 433–35.
17. Ibid.
18. Ibid.
19. Ibid.
20. Shaw and Donnelly, *Blacks in the Marine Corps,* p. 37.
21. Ibid.
22. Ibid.
23. Ibid.
24. Nalty, *Right to Fight,* p. 24.
25. Ibid.
26. "Turner G. Blount," interview by Dr. Clarence E. Willie, Lieutenant Colonel, Retired, United States Marine Corps, and

Dr. Melton McLaurin, Montford Point Marine Transcripts and UNCW, https://library.uncw.edu/web/montford/transcripts/Blount_Turner.html.
27. Francis Trevelyan Miller, *History of World War II* (Philadelphia: Universal Book and Bible House, 1945), p. 649.
28. Ibid., p. 649.
29. Brian Blodgett, "The Invasion of Saipan," Blodgett's Historical Consulting, March 7, 2003, https://sites.google.com/site/blodgetthistoricalconsulting/the-invasion-of-saipan.
30. Philip A. Crowl, *United States Army in World War II: The War in the Pacific, Campaign in the Marianas* (Washington, DC: Center of Military History, United States Army,1993), pp. 53–55, https://history.army.mil/html/books/005/5-7-1/CMH_Pub_5-7-1.pdf.
31. Ibid., p. 57.
32. Ibid., pp. 57–60.
33. Ibid., p. 59.
34. Ibid.
35. Miller, *History of World War II,* p. 650.
36. Ibid.
37. Nalty, *Right to Fight,* p. 20.
38. Alan Schom, *The Eagle and the Rising Sun: The Japanese-American War, 1941–1943* (New York: W. W. Norton & Co., 2004), 117.
39. Crowl, *United States Army in World War II,* p. 257.
40. Bix, *Hirohito,* pp. 475–76.
41. Turner Blount interview by Clarence E. Willie.

16. The Kamikaze Pilots

1. Bix, *Hirohito,* p. 451.
2. Ibid.
3. Kingsley Perry, "The Royal Australian Navy at Leyte Gulf October 1944," Naval Historical Society of Australia, September 23, 2017, www.navyhistory.org.au/ranships/hmas-arunta-i/.
4. Bix, *Hirohito,* p. 451.
5. Jaime Erickson, "Honor in Death: Kamikaze Pilots of World War II," Marquette University History Department, n.d., https://academic.mu.edu/meissnerd/erickson.html#Abstract.
6. Yutaka Yokota and Joseph D. Harrington, *The Kaiten Weapon* (New York: Ballantine, 1962) p. 32, www.worldhistory.biz/download567/TheKaitenWeapon_worldhistory.biz.pdf.

7. Ibid., p. 34.
8. Ibid., pp. 24–25, 31.
9. Ibid., p. 31.
10. Ibid., pp. 31–32.
11. Yuki Tanaka, "Japan's Kamikaze Pilots and Contemporary Suicide Bombers: War and Terror," *Asia-Pacific Journal, Japan Focus* 3:7 (July 6, 2005).
12. Ibid.
13. Ibid.
14. Nambu World, "Senninbari, Thousand Stitch Belts," n.d., www.nambuworld.com/senninbari.htm.
15. Ibid.
16. Ibid.
17. War History Online, "Kamikaze Pilots: The Final Ceremony Included a Drink of Spiritual Concoction That'd Ensure Success in the Mission," February 13, 2018, www.warhistoryonline.com/instant-articles/kamikaze-pilots-the-final-ceremony.html.
18. U.S. History, "Kamikaze," n.d., www.u-s-history.com/pages/h1740.html.
19. Ibid.
20. Ibid.
21. Ibid.

17. Another Dazzling Chess Move: Navajo Code Talkers

1. Adam Jevec, "Semper Fidelis, Code Talkers," *Prologue* magazine 33:4 (Winter 2001), www.archives.gov/publications/prologue/2001/winter/navajo-code-talkers.html.
2. Chester Nez and Judith Schiess Avila, *Code Talker* (New York: Berkley Caliber, 2012), p. 91.
3. Jevec, "Code Talkers."
4. Nez and Avila, *Code Talker*, p. 91.
5. Ibid., p. 93.
6. "The Code Talkers," Children of the Sun: Native Culture, n.d.
7. Jevec, "Code Talkers."
8. Naval History and Heritage Command, "Navajo Code Talkers: World War II Fact Sheet," April 16, 2020, www.history.navy.mil/research/library/online-reading-room/title-list-alphabetically/n/code-talkers.html.
9. Ibid.
10. Ibid.
11. Ibid.
12. Ibid.

18. The End of the War

1. U.S. Department of Energy, "Japan Surrenders, Bringing an End to World War II (August 10–15, 1945)," The Manhattan Project: An Interactive History, n.d., www.osti.gov/opennet/manhattan-project-history/Events/1945/surrender.htm.
2. Robert W. Coakley, *American Military History: World War II: The War Against Japan* (Washington, DC: Center of Military History, 1989), section 523–24, https://history.army.mil/books/AMH/amh-toc.htm.
3. Ibid., pp. 524–25.
4. Nalty, *Right to Fight,* pp. 21–22.
5. Ibid.
6. Ibid.
7. Ibid., p. 22.
8. James Taylor, *The Army Air Forces in World War II, Volume 5: Preparation for Combat, The Pacific: Matterhorn to Nagasaki, June 1944 to August 1945* (Washington, DC: Air Force Historical Advisory Committee, 1983), ch. 17, www.ibiblio.org/hyperwar/AAF/V/AAF-V-17.html.
9. Daniel L. Haulman, *Hitting Home: The Air Offensive Against Japan* (Washington, DC: Airforce History and Museums Program, 1999), p. 22. https://media.defense.gov/2010/Sep/27/2001330168/-1/-1/0/AFD-100927-081.pdf.
10. Ibid., pp. 19–20.
11. Ibid., p. 22.
12. Ibid., p. 23.
13. Ibid.
14. Ibid. p. 25.
15. Mark Selden, "American Fire Bombing and Atomic Bombing of Japan in History and Memory," *Asia Pacific Journal, Japan Focus* 14:23 (December 1, 2016).
16. Ibid.
17. Bix, *Hirohito,* p. 496.
18. Nalty, *Right to Fight,* pp. 22–23.
19. Ibid.
20. Ibid.
21. Ibid.
22. Ibid.
23. Coral Anika Theill, "World War II Montford Point Marines Receive Congressional Gold Medal," *Salem News,* Jun. 19, 2012. www.salem-news.com/articles/june192012/coral-1.php.

24. Thomas Mosley, in discussion with the author, March 12, 2012.

19. Home Sweet Home

1. Thomas Mosley. Discussions over time, life lessons.
2. Randolph Harrell, March 2, 2013.
3. Ibid.
4. Ibid.
5. Ibid.
6. Ibid.
7. Ibid.
8. Ibid.
9. Ibid.
10. Ibid.
11. Averet Corley, "Montford Point Marines Transcripts," University of North Carolina Wilmington, Dr. Melton McLaurin, Randall Library, https://library.uncw.edu/web/montford.
12. Ibid.
13. Ibid.
14. Ibid.
15. Dr. James T. Averhart.
16. Master Gunnery Sergeant Joseph Geeter.
17. James "Rudy" Carter, quoted in "Conquering Congress: Park Alumnus and Newly Appointed Trustee Pursues the Halls of Congress to Bestow the Country's Highest Honor on Unsung Marine Heroes," *Park University Magazine* 4:1 (Spring 2012), 14–17. https://issuu.com/parkalumni/docs/parkmagazine.spring2012/16.
18. Master Gunnery Sergeant Joe Geeter, quoted in "Conquering Congress."
19. Ibid.
20. Master Gunnery Sergeant Joseph Geeter.
21. Ibid.
22. Ibid.
23. Ibid.
24. Master Sergeant Alvin Banker, "World War II: Through the Eyes of the Cape Fear," University of North Carolina Wilmington's William M. Randall Library and the Cape Fear Museum, Remembering World War II, Transcript No. 046, interviewer Steven Hefner, World War II Veterans Oral

History Preservation Project, December 20, 2000, https://library.uncw.edu/capefearww2/voices/046bio.html; Alvin J. Banker biography, July 14, 1992.
25. Ibid.
26. Ibid.
27. Ibid.
28. Mrs. Alvin J. Banker, July 25, 2012, phone interview by the author.
29. Colonel Willie, telephone interview by the author, July 25, 2012.
30. Ibid.
31. Randolph Harrell, telephone discussion with the author, March 2, 2013.
32. Ibid.
33. Ibid.
34. Ibid.

20. What Is the Congressional Gold Medal?

1. United States House of Representatives, "Congressional Gold Medal Recipients," n.d., https://history.house.gov/Institution/Gold-Medal/Gold-Medal-Recipients/.
2. *New World Encyclopedia,* s.v. "Congressional Gold Medal."
3. Ibid.
4. Jacob R. Straus, "Congressional Gold Medals: Background, Legislative Process, and Issues for Congress," Congressional Research Service, March 18, 2019, www.senate.gov/CRSpubs/b95bd703-f5bb-46af-b44b-4bd9831ee99e.pdf.
5. Congresswoman Corrine Brown, "HR 2447: "Congressional Gold Medal to the Montford Point Marines," *Congressional Record* 157:161, October 25, 2011, www.congress.gov/congressional-record/2011/10/25/house-section/article/H7024-3.
6. Senator Kay Hagan, "S. 1527 (112th): A bill to authorize the award of a Congressional Gold Medal to the Montford Point Marines of World War II," 112th Congress, 1st Session, September 8, 2011, www.govtrack.us/congress/members/kay_hagan/412324.
7. Julie Watson, "Marine Corps to Teach Story of First Black Marines," *Philadelphia Tribune,* October 24, 2011, https://tinyurl.com/dwfn92vr.

21. No Longer Just an Ordinary Man

1. Thomas Mosley, discussion with the author, December 11, 2011.
2. Colonel Clarence E. Willie, interview with the author, October 3, 2012.
3. Ibid.
4. Executive Order 9981: Desegregation of the Armed Forces (1948), www.ourdocuments.gov/doc.php?doc=84.
5. Ibid.

22. Quotes

1. General James F. Amos, Commandant of the Marine Corps, "Prepared Remarks for the Montford Point Marine Association 46th Annual National Convention and Banquet," Office of the Commandant of the Marine Corps, July 30, 2011, www.hqmc.Marines.mil/Portals/142/Docs/110730%20MPMA%20Remarks(CMC%20FINAL).pdf.
2. CWO5 Dr. James T. Averhart, phone discussion with the author, December 3, 2011.
3. "Montford Point Marine Memorial," City of Jacksonville, NC, www.jacksonvillenc.gov.
4. Commandant Leonard F. Chapman, "Montford Point Marines, The First Black Marines, 1942–1949," Historical Marker Database, September 14, 2008, www.hmdb.org/marker.asp?marker=11472.

Appendixes

1. Senator Richard Burr, R-NC, S.Res.587: "A resolution designating August 26, 2010, as 'Montford Point Marines Day,'" www.congress.gov/bill/111th-congress/senate-resolution/587.
2. Gina Cavallaro, "Montford Point History Now Part of OCS," *Marine Corps Times*, n.d.
3. Associated Press, "Marine Corps Wants Nation to Honor First Black Marines; Story to be Taught in Basic Training," Fox News, October 4, 2011, www.foxnews.com/us/Marine-corps-to-teach-story-of-first-black-Marines.
4. Lindell Kay, "Gold Medal Approved by President Barack Obama," *Jacksonville Daily News*, December 7, 2011.
5. Nadeam Elshami and Drew Hammill, "Pelosi Floor Speech Supporting Congressional Gold Medal to Honor Montford Point Marines," October 25, 2011, www.speaker.gov/newsroom/

pelosi-floor-speech-supporting-congressional-gold-medal-honor-montford-point-Marines.

6. "HR 2447—To grant the Congressional Gold Medal to the Montford Point Marines, 112th Congress (2011–2012)," U.S. House of Representatives, November 23, 2011, www.congress.gov/bill/112th-congress/house-bill/2447/text.

Bibliography

Alexander, Joseph H. *Closing In: Marines in the Seizure of Iwo Jima.* Washington, DC: History and Museums Division, Headquarters, U.S. Marine Corps, 1994.

Allen, Louis. *Japan: The Years of Triumph: From Feudal Isolation to Pacific Empire.* New York: American Heritage Press, 1971.

Anders, Steven E. "Quartermaster Supply in the Pacific During World War II." *Quartermaster Professional Bulletin.* Spring 1999. www.quartermasterfoundation.org/article/quartermaster-supply-in-the-pacific-during-world-war-ii/.

Aptheker, Herbert. *Afro American History: The Modern Era.* Secaucus, NJ: Citadel Press, 1971.

Aptheker, Herbert. *To Be Free.* New York: Carol Publishing, 1948.

Astor, Gerald. *The Right to Fight: A History of African Americans in the Military.* Novato, CA: Presidio Press, 1988.

Ayres, Edward. "African Americans and the American Revolution." Jamestown Settlement and American Revolution Museum at Yorktown. n.d. https://tinyurl.com/27ev9fdm.

Aziz, Nyeesa. "Congress Considers Honor for First Black Marines." BET. October 24, 2011. www.bet.com/news/national/2011/10/24/congress-considers-honor-for-first-black-marines.html.

Azuma, Eiichiro. "Brief Historical Overview of Japanese Emigration, 1868–1998." International Nikkei Research Project, Japanese American National Museum. February 28, 2014. www.discovernikkei.org/en/journal/2014/2/28/historical-overview/.

Azuma, Eiichiro. "The Issei Arrive in Oregon." Discover Nikkei. October 23, 2017. www.discovernikkei.org/en/journal/2017/10/23/oregon-1.

Bailey, Beth, and David Farber. *The First Strange Place: Race and Sex in World War II Hawaii.* Baltimore: Free Press/Macmillan, 1992.

Bailey, Ronald H. *The Home Front U.S.A.* Alexandria, VA: Time-Life, 1978.

Bergerud, Eric. *Touched with Fire: The Land War in the South Pacific.* New York: Penguin, 1996.

Bethune-Cookman University. "The Historical Roots of Bethune-Cookman University." www.cookman.edu/history.

Bix, Herbert P. *Hirohito and the Making of Modern Japan.* New York: HarperCollins, 2000.

Blodgett, Brian. "The Invasion of Saipan." Blodgett's Historical Consulting. March 7, 2003. https://sites.google.com/site/blodgetthistoricalconsulting/the-invasion-of-saipan.

Browning, Christopher A. "Segregation versus Integration: The Racial Policy of the Marine Corps from 1942–1962." Master's thesis, Marine Corps Command and Staff College, 2013. https://apps.dtic.mil/sti/citations/ADA601677.

Buckley, Gail. *American Patriots: The Story of Blacks in the Military from the Revolution to Desert Storm.* New York: Random House, 2001.

Burns, Ken, and Lynn Novick. "The War: At Home, War Production." WETA and American Lives II Film Project, 2007. www.pbs.org/kenburns/the-war/war-production/.

Carraway, Gertrude S. *Camp Lejeune Leathernecks.* New Bern, NC: Owen G. Dunn, 1946.

Coakley, Robert W. *American Military History: World War II: The War Against Japan.* Washington, DC: Center of Military History, 1989.

Condit, Kenneth W., Gerald Diamond, and Edwin T. Turnbladh. *Marine Corps Ground Training in World War II.* Washington, DC: Headquarters Branch, G-3, Headquarters, U.S. Marine Corps, 1956. https://archive.org/details/MarineCorpsGroundTrainingInWWII-nsia.

Crowl, Philip A. *United States Army in World War II: The War in the Pacific, Campaign in the Marianas.* Washington, DC: Center of Military History, United States Army,1993. https://history.army.mil/html/books/005/5-7-1/CMH_Pub_5-7-1.pdf.

DeNoyer, Richard L. "Proceedings of the 113th National Convention of the Veterans of Foreign Wars of the United States." Veterans of Foreign Wars of the United States. July 21–25, 2012. www.govinfo.gov/content/pkg/CDOC-113hdoc35/pdf/CDOC-113hdoc35.pdf.

Douglas, Lee Jr. "Montford Point Marines Transcripts." University of North Carolina Wilmington, Randall Library. 2006.

Durr, Eric. "'Rainbow Division' That Represented the United States Formed in New York in August 1917." U.S. Army. July 24, 2017. https://tinyurl.com/adktd84k.

Erickson, Jaime. "Honor in Death: Kamikaze Pilots of World War II." Marquette University History Department. n.d. https://academic.mu.edu/meissnerd/erickson.html#Abstract.

Fitzgerald, C. P. *A Concise History of East Asia.* New York: Praeger, 1970.

Fleet Marine Force. "Marine Corps History." May 3, 2013. www.globalsecurity.org/military/agency/usmc/history.htm.

Frank, Benis M., and Henry I. Shaw. *Victory and Occupation: History of U.S. Marine Corps Operations in World War II.* Volume V. Washington, DC: Historical Branch, G-3 Division, Headquarters, U.S. Marine Corps, 1968). www.ibiblio.org/hyperwar/USMC/V/USMC-V-VI-2.html.

Frasier, Isaac David. "Montford Point Marines Transcripts." University of North Carolina Wilmington, Randall Library. 2006.

Garand, George W., and Truman R. Strowbridge. *Western Pacific Operations: History of the Marine Corps Operations in World War II.* Washington, DC: Historical Branch, G-3 Division, Headquarters, US Marine Corps, 1971.

Goodwin, Doris Kearns. *No Ordinary Time: Franklin, and Eleanor Roosevelt: The Home Front in World War II.* New York: Simon and Shuster, 1994.

Hammel, Eric. *Iwo Jima: Portrait of a Battle: United States Marines at War in the Pacific.* St. Paul, MN: MBI Publishing, 2006.

Hart, Jerome A. *In Our Second Century.* San Francisco: Pioneer Press, 1931.

Hattabaugh, Lee. "M1A1 90mm Anti-Aircraft Gun," Historical Marker Database. April 14, 2011. www.hmdb.org/marker.asp?marker=41683.

Haulman, Daniel L. *Hitting Home: The Air Offensive Against Japan.* Washington, DC: Airforce History and Museums Program, 1999. https://media.defense.gov/2010/Sep/27/2001330168/-1/-1/0/AFD-100927-081.pdf.

History Central. "*Lamar* APL-47." n.d. www.historycentral.com/navy/MISC/lamar.html.

Hogg, Ian V. *The Encyclopedia of Infantry Weapons of World War II.* New York: Military Press, 1977.

Hough, Frank O., Verle E. Ludwig, and Henry I. Shaw. "U.S.

Marine Corps in World War II." HyperWar. www.ibiblio.org/hyperwar/USMC.

"Interview of Alvin J. Banker." World War II: Through the Eyes of Cape Fear. Interview by Steve Hefner at the Barbee Branch Library in Oak Island, NC. University of North Carolina Wilmington, December 20, 2000. http://library.uncw.edu/capefearww2/voices/banker046.html.

"Interview Transcript of Montford Point Marines: Averet Corley. Interview by Dr. Clarence E. Willie, Lieutenant Colonel, Retired. University of North Carolina Wilmington, William M. Randall Library. July 23, 2004. http://library.uncw.edu/web/montford/collection.html.

Japanese American Citizen League. *An Unnoticed Struggle: A Concise History of Asian American Civil Rights Issues.* San Francisco: JACL, 2008.

Jevec, Adam. "Semper Fidelis, Code Talkers." *Prologue* magazine 33:4 (Winter 2001). www.archives.gov/publications/prologue/2001/winter/navajo-code-talkers.html.

Kersten, Andrew E. *A. Philip Randolph: A Life in the Vanguard.* Lanham, MD: Roman Littlefield, 2007.

Lee, Ulysses. *The Employment of Negro Troops*. Washington, DC: Center of Military History United States Army, 1965.

Little, Arthur W. *From Harlem to the Rhine: The Story of New York's Colored Volunteers*. New York: Covici Friede, 1936.

Livingston, Jeff. "Who Built the OR&L?" *Akahele I Ke Ka'aahi* 40:6 (Nov.–Dec. 2010). www.hawaiianrailway.org/historian/Articles/WhoBuiltTheORL.html.

MacGregor, Morris J. Jr. *Integration of the Armed Forces 1940–1965.* Washington, DC: Center of Military History, U.S. Army, 1981.

MacGregor, Morris J., and Bernard C Nalty. *Blacks in the United States Armed Forces: Basic Documents, Volume VI.* Wilmington, DE: Scholarly Resources, 1977.

Mahan, Alfred Thayer. *The Influence of Sea Power Upon History, 1660–1783.* First published 1890. Reprinted London: Methuen, 1965.

Manhattan Engineer District. *The Atomic Bombings of Hiroshima and Nagasaki.* June 29, 1946. www.abomb1.org/hiroshim/hiro_med.html.

Marine Corps Association. "MCA Ammo Tech Awards Dinner." May 24, 2011.

Martin, Jo Nobuko. *A Princess Lily of the Ryukyus.* Tokyo: Shin Nippon Kyoiku Tosho, 1984.

McCluskey, Audrey, and Elaine M. Smith, eds. *Mary Mcleod Bethune: Building a Better World, Essays and Selected Documents by Mary McLeod Bethune.* Bloomington, IN: Indiana University Press, 1999.

Melson, Major Charles D. *Condition Red: Marine Defense Battalions in World War II.* Washington, DC: Marine Corps Historical Center, 1996.

Mercier, Laurie. "Japanese Americans in the Columbia Basin." Washington State University. n.d. https://content.libraries.wsu.edu/digital/collection/cchm/custom/ja-overview.

Miller, Francis Trevelyan. *History of World War II.* Philadelphia: Universal Book and Bible House, 1945.

Morton, Louis. "Strategy and Command: The First Two Years." *United States Army in World War II: The War in the Pacific.* Washington, DC: Office of the Chief of Military History, Dept. of the Army, 1953. www.ibiblio.org/hyperwar/USA/USA-P-Strategy/Strategy-6.html.

Nalty, Bernard C. *Strength for the Fight: A History of Black Americans in the Military.* New York: Free Press/MacMillan, 1986.

Nash, Gary B. *Red, White, and Black: The Peoples of Early America.* Englewood Cliffs, NJ: Prentice Hall, 1974.

Nez, Chester, and Judith Schiess Avila. *Code Talker.* New York: Berkley Caliber, 2012.

Ordonez, Franco. "70 Years Gone, Montford Point Marines Get Their Due." McClatchy Newspapers. June 27, 2012. www.mcclatchydc.com/news/politics-government/article24731887.html.

Perry, Kingsley. "The Royal Australian Navy at Leyte Gulf October 1944." Naval Historical Society of Australia. September 23, 2017. www.navyhistory.org.au/ranships/hmas-arunta-i/.

Pfaelzer, Jean. *Driven Out: The Forgotten War Against Chinese Americans.* New York: Random House, 2007.

Pforzheimer, Carl. H. *Immigration to the United States 1789–1930.* Harvard University Library, 2002. https://library.harvard.edu/collections/immigration-united-states-1789-1930.

Priolo, Gary P. "USS *Lamar* (APA-47) ex USS *Lamar* (AP-92) (1943–1944)." NavSource Online: Amphibious Photo Archive. 1996. www.navsource.org/archives/10/03/03047.htm.

Rabson, Steve. "American Literature on the Battle of Okinawa and the Continuing U.S. Military Presence." *Asia-Pacific Journal* 15:20 (October 15, 2017). https://apjjf.org/2017/20/Rabson.html.

Rice University. "Franklin Roosevelt and the New Deal, 1932–1941." OER Commons. www.oercommons.org/courseware/module/15533/overview.

Robinson, Joseph B. "The New Fair Employment Law." *Ohio State Law Journal* 20:4 (August 1959). https://kb.osu.edu/handle/1811/68185.

Rogers, David. "Iwo Jima: The Costliest Battle in American History." n.d. https://web.mst.edu/~rogersda/american&military_history/BATTLE-OF-IWO-JIMA.pdf.

Ruffin, Herbert G. II. "William Monroe Trotter." Black Past. January 23, 2007. https://blackpast.org/aah/trotter-william-monroe-1872-1934.

Rundles, Jim. "The Montford Point Marines Worked and Fought on Iwo Jima." 1995. Lest We Forget: African American Military. http://lestweforget.hamptonu.edu/page.cfm?uuid=9FEC4392-E2BA-3AA6-7E992F09F2CAB48E.

Scheiber, Jane L., and Harry N. Scheiber. "Martial Law in Hawaii." Densho Encyclopedia. July 22, 2020. https://encyclopedia.densho.org/Martial_law_in_Hawaii.

Schom, Alan. *The Eagle and the Rising Sun: The Japanese-American War, 1941–1943.* New York: W. W. Norton & Co., 2004.

Scott, Emmett J. *Scott's Official History of the American Negro in the World War.* First published 1919. Reprinted London: FB & Co., 2017.

Selden, Mark. "American Fire Bombing and Atomic Bombing of Japan in History and Memory." *Asia Pacific Journal, Japan Focus* 14:23 (December 1, 2016).

"Sergeant Major Gilbert 'Hashmark' Johnson." United States Marine Corps History. n.d.

Shaw, Henry I. Jr., and Ralph W. Donnelly. *Blacks in the Marine Corps.* Washington, DC: History and Museum Division Headquarters, U.S. Marine Corps, 2002.

Simkin, John. "March on Washington in 1941." Spartacus Educational. September 1997. https://spartacus-educational.com/USAmarchW.htm.

Takaki, Ronald. *Strangers from a Different Shore: A History of Asian Americans.* Boston: Little, Brown and Co., 1989.

Tanaka, Yuki. "Japan's Kamikaze Pilots and Contemporary Suicide Bombers: War and Terror." *Asia-Pacific Journal, Japan Focus* 3:7 (July 6, 2005).

Taylor, James. *The Army Air Forces in World War II, Volume 5: Preparation for Combat, The Pacific: Matterhorn to Nagasaki, June*

1944 to August 1945. Washington, DC: Air Force Historical Advisory Committee, 1983. www.ibiblio.org/hyperwar/AAF/V/AAF-V-17.html.

U.S. Marine Corps. "Marine Corps Base Camp Lejeune." n.d. www.lejeune.Marines.mil/visitors/history.aspx.

Ulbrich, David J. *Preparing for Victory: Thomas Holcomb and the Making of the Modern Marine Corps,1936–1943.* Annapolis, MD: Naval Institute Press, 2011.

Watson, George M. "Bernard C. Nalty: (1931–2015)." *Air Power History* 62:4 (Winter 2015).

Winkler, Allan M. *Home Front U.S.A.: America during World II.* Wheeling, IL: Harlan Davidson, 1986.

Yokota, Yutaka, and Joseph D. Harrington. *The Kaiten Weapon.* New York: Ballantine, 1962. www.worldhistory.biz/download567/TheKaitenWeapon_worldhistory.biz.pdf.

Photography Credits

Cover image and pages 41, 43, 50, 51, 54, 56, 57, 58, 61, 62, 65, 68, 79, 86, 121 courtesy of the University of North Carolina Wilmington, Randall Library.

Page 218: Matthew Odom.

Other images:

United States National Archives
Montford Point Marine Association
Photo Collection of Thomas Mosley
Photo Collection of Sandra Mosley Walker
Photo collection of Eugene S. Mosley

Index

H

I

J

K

L

M

R

S

Printed in the USA
CPSIA information can be obtained
at www.ICGtesting.com
LVHW012306241023
761958LV00015B/583/J